Imperial Vanities

IMPERIAL VANITIES

The Adventures
of the Baker Brothers and
Gordon of Khartoum

BRIAN THOMPSON

HarperCollins*Publishers*

HEAD AND TAILPIECES: Natives of Lira and
Madiin, the camp at Shooa. *Drawing by Samuel
Baker © Royal Geographical Society*
ENDPAPER: Burnaby by Tissot © *By courtesy of the
National Portrait Gallery, London*

HarperCollins*Publishers*
77–85 Fulham Palace Road,
Hammersmith, London w6 8jb

www.**fire**and**water**.com

Published by HarperCollins*Publishers* 2002
1 3 5 7 9 8 6 4 2

Copyright © Brian Thompson 2001

The Author asserts the moral right to
be identified as the author of this work

A catalogue record for this book
is available from the British Library

ISBN 0 00 257188 9

Set in Postscript Linotype Baskerville by
Rowland Phototypesetting Ltd,
Bury St Edmunds, Suffolk

Printed and bound in Great Britain by
Clays Ltd, St Ives plc

To Elizabeth

List of Illustrations

The *Black Watch* cheering Lord Wolseley on the Nile, 1884 © *The Illustrated London News Picture Library.*

Anti-slavery demonstration at Exeter Hall © *Illustrated London News Picture Library.*

Valentine Baker as a young man. *Courtesy of Mrs Erica Graham. Reproduced from* Baker, A. *A Question of Honour,* 1996.

Valentine Baker in the army © *Hulton Archive.*

Samuel Baker as a hunter in Ceylon © *Hulton Archive.*

Samuel Baker © *Mary Evans Picture Library.*

Charles Gordon © *Hulton Archive.*

David Livingstone, 1870 © *Public Record Office Image Library.*

Laurence Oliphant, 1854. *(Mr Godfrey Oliphant) from* Taylor, A. *Laurence Oliphant,* 1982.

Florence Baker © *Royal Geographical Society.*

Queen Victoria with Indian servant. *The Royal Archives/HM Queen Elizabeth II/Hills and Saunders.*

The Prince of Wales © *Mary Evans Picture Library.*

Fredrick Burnaby, 1885 © *Public Record Office Image Library.*

Maharajah Duleep Singh. *Painting by Franz Xavier Winterhalter* © *AKG London/Erich Lessing.*

HRH George, Duke of Cambridge © *Mary Evans Picture Library.*

Baker Pasha by Ape. *Vanity Fair,* 1878.

Slave Market, Zanzibar, 1860. *Photograph by Colonel J.A. Grant* © *Royal Geographical Society.*

Sam and Florence Baker in Cyprus © *Royal Geographical Society.*

List of Illustrations in Text

Preface

This book is the interweaving of three remarkably self-willed lives. The careers of the two Baker brothers and Charles Gordon crossed and recrossed, very seldom in England itself, more usually at the eastern end of the Mediterranean (on occasions even further afield) coming at last to a tragic denouement in Egypt and the Sudan. They were Victorians with a taste for the heroic who made their friends and enemies from among the same restless kind. So, in these pages, we find also the enigmatic traveller, Laurence Oliphant; the explorers James Hanning Speke and Richard Francis Burton; the missionary David Livingstone; and soldiers as wildly unlike as Major-General Sir Garnet Wolseley and the irrepressible Captain Fred Burnaby.

There is a common connection, in that all these men were servants of Empire. Even Burton, such an inventively bitter critic of his own country and enemy to most of what we usually label Victorianism, put on his KCMG decoration for the first and last time in June, 1887, and celebrated Victoria's Golden Jubilee in the grounds of the consulate in Trieste with these ringing words: 'May God's choicest blessings crown her good works!'

That particular weekend, toasts like this were uttered in every British embassy and consulate across the globe, as well as all the Queen's dominions. As the sick and world-weary Burton himself put it, in a sudden and late flowering of imperial sentiment 'May the loving confidence between her Majesty and all English-speaking-peoples, throughout the world, ever strengthen and endure to all time.'

The God that was invoked was held without question to be an Englishman. God the Englishman had subjugated half the world, bringing the blessings of civilization to heathens considered in desperate need of it. This is the background theme to much of what you are about to read. There could hardly be a greater vanity. Joseph Conrad was enough of a genius to look into its psychological first cause:

'It is better for mankind to be impressionable than reflective. Nothing humanely great-great, I mean, as affecting a whole mass of lives – has come from reflection. On the other hand you cannot fail to see the power of mere words: such words as Glory, for instance, or Pity . . . Shouted with perseverance, with ardour, with conviction, these two by their sound alone have set whole nations in motion and upheaved the dry, hard ground on which rests our whole social fabric. There's "virtue" for you if you like!'

These words, which were written to preface Conrad's own experimental autobiography, *A Personal Record*, published in 1908, put the case admirably for the present book. Under only slightly different circumstances, a different throw of the dice, he might have applied them to the revolutionary politics of his father, Appollonius Korzeniowski. But in 1886, Conrad became a naturalised British citizen and at the time of the Jubilee and all its imperial celebration he was sailing about the Malay Archipelago, his eyes wide open to what brought white men to the ends of the earth – and kept them there.

My main intention has been to tease out the connections between three men, their lives and times. But there is also a desire to replicate what was itself a minor Victorian addition to the art of the book, one that has given pleasure right down to the present day.

As the story opens out, little by little a seemingly solid picture arises, in which elements that have no clear immediate purpose bend and unfold until, when the covers are finally laid flat, a man in uniform stands at the steps to a Governor's palace. One hand is drawn across his chest in a gesture of fidelity to God and in the other a revolver dangles. Many intricate pleats and folds of coloured paper have brought him to life. By the strange compulsion we have to know about these things, the moment that is illustrated is also the moment of his death.

Nothing can make the little cardboard figure turn away, any more than the rush of all those turbanned men can be halted. The death of General Gordon had, for Victorians, all the elements of terror and pity evoked for us in a later age by the assassination of John F. Kennedy. Among Gordon's contemporaries, for months, then years, the flux of history seemed, as it were, to shudder in its course. And then, inevitably, the story dwindled, along with the vanities that brought it into being. The two Baker brothers and Charles Gordon, who they were to each other and what constituted their life achievements, the joy they had of the world and its sorrows, fell like stones into the waters of the Nile.

I should like to thank Yvonne and Anthony Hands for many hours of genial encouragement in the writing of this book; John Crouch and Thomas Howard for some helpful pieces of research; an exemplary literary agent, David Miller, and not least Arabella Pike, an editor whose zestful enthusiasm for a good human interest story never sleeps. Finally, the work is dedicated, not without an element of apprehension, to a writer I have greatly admired for more than thirty years, whose good opinion is always worth having.

Prologue

In 1815 a specially severe hurricane hit the island of Jamaica, tearing hundreds of houses and shanties from their foundations and dumping them in the sea. Over a thousand people were drowned or simply disappeared from the face of the earth. When the news was carried back to England, the only anxiety raised was what consequences there might be for the sugar plantations, for the Bristol and Liverpool merchants who controlled the trade realised at once that the victims of the hurricane were for the most part black. Jamaica was a slave island – the most ruthless and successful of them all – and the death of so many people was counted simply as additional loss of property. There was a verb much used whenever disaster of this magnitude occurred among the black population: the agents of the great plantations talked calmly about the need to 'restock'.

To be British in Jamaica at that time was to live at the edge of things, almost but not quite beyond the reach of Europe's civilising virtues. Whatever law that was enacted at Westminster touching the island's affairs arrived in the Caribbean like ship's biscuit, in a weevilly condition. For example, when it was seen that Parliament intended, after unrelenting effort by William Wilberforce and his parliamentary supporters, to bring about the abolition of slavery, one response of the planters was to encourage their women slaves to marry and end the common practice of abortion. They were looking ahead. If they could not at some time in the future import slaves, they would need to factory farm them on site.

After the Act of 1807 it was a crime for a Briton to buy a slave or transport one on a ship bearing the British flag. Nothing much changed locally. Beautiful though the islands might be, seen as a landfall after a wearisome Atlantic crossing, a miasma of ignorance and stupidity hung over them all. The Society for the Propagation of the Gospel had already provided the most telling example of how difficult it was to think straight in the West Indies. In slavery's heyday it was quite usual to brand newly acquired human animals as one would cattle and the SPG asserted its ownership and high purpose at one and the same time. Its slaves were seared across the chest with a white-hot iron bearing the word SOCIETY, without causing the slightest intellectual or moral embarrassment to anyone. For many years those who defended the institution of slavery held to the opinion that its victims were happier and better looked after than the poor of Europe. This point of view was one readily adopted by visitors to the islands, who confined their acquaintance-ship to house slaves, whose servitude was – at any rate on the surface – uncomplaining.

The irrepressible memoirist William Hickey made a false start on Jamaica when he was a young man. Sent out by his father in 1775 and speedily frustrated in his attempt to be admitted to the Jamaica Bar, he whiled away his time at parties and drinking sessions, making visits to plantations and reporting what he saw with an uncritical eye. On arriving at a Mr Richards's estate he was greeted by 500 slaves in an apparent ecstasy of happiness. 'They all looked fat and sleek, seeming as contented a set of mortals as could be,' he commented. This was something his host ascribed to a particular style of management. 'He was convinced by his own experience that more was to be effected by moderation and gentleness than ever was accomplished by the whip or punishments of any sort.' Hickey was easily persuaded but agreed to go with Richards next day to a neighbouring estate nine miles distant. There they found a girl of sixteen tied to a post being whipped half to death by a young manager. She had refused his sexual advances. Mr Richards's indignation was great. Such brutality was bad for business and it showed in the ledgers.

'The annual produce until the last five years was five hundred hogsheads of the very best sugar and four hundred puncheons of rum [he explained to Hickey], whereas now it yields not one third of either and is every year becoming worse, the mortality among the slaves being unparalleled, and all this owing to a system of the most dreadful tyranny and severity practised by a scoundrel overseer.'

Though the two unexpected visitors intervened before the girl could be killed and the story ended with the arrest and death of her tormentor (he was shot trying to escape from his soldier escort while on his way to Kingston), it did not occur to Hickey to question, then or ever, whether slavery under any guise, benign or not, was acceptable. This sprang not from ignorance but a socially conditioned indifference. Hickey was no stranger to foreign parts. He had already sailed as a cadet in the East India Company army to Madras, found he did not like it, and came home again via Canton and Macao. Nothing he saw of other countries and peoples made a mark on him. His patriotism was of the hearty, negligent sort common to the age – he was most at his ease with his own kind, which he found in the guise of ships' captains, bleak old soldiers and the better sort of commercial agent. As for the rest of the world, it was no more than a passingly interesting puppet show; in the end a tedious exhibition of local colour. Here, racketing round Jamaica, the ownership of one human being by another was as unremarkable and obvious as the weather. Only the most incendiary sort of crank would draw attention to it.

Very few Europeans had ever seen or could picture a free African. The ones who escaped their bondage on Jamaica and ran away into the mountains were not free, but criminal. Up there the dreaded Maroons held sway, their lives a reversion to their previous existence in Africa – simple and, when necessary, invisible. They lived in lean-to shacks deep in the forest, the sites indicated only by the smoke from their fires rising above the tree canopy and – from time to time – the eerie sound of signal drums. The white planters hired these Maroons to hunt down escaped slaves. When the most persistent of these were caught and executed, it was customary to display the severed heads on pikes set in some prominent place, to discourage crime and reassure the more nervous of the white population. It was just another part of the landscape.

There was an echo on the island of better things. Many plantations taught their more biddable house servants music and ate to the wailing of string quartets, or danced to the accompaniment of a black band got up in velvet livery, wearing powdered wigs. Several times a year the great houses would be a blaze of light, with patriotic bonfires and the discharge of fireworks to honour some royal birthday or distant feat of arms. The planters liked to celebrate and raise hell in this way for the same reason they might whistle crossing a graveyard. Death was very near. A major player in the affairs of the islands was yellow fever. In the three-year campaign that began in 1794 to capture Martinique, St Lucia and Guadeloupe, 16,000 European soldiers died of the fever and were buried in the rags of their uniforms.

Yellow Jack knew no boundaries. It was swift and remorseless. Seized with a chill, in three days a man would be blowing bloody bubbles from his mouth and nose, unable any longer to speak or sign. The fever had no friends and attacked rich and poor alike. To be posted to the Jamaica garrison was a sentence of death for many a ploughboy who had taken the king's shilling. The hated Baptist missionaries who stirred up such agitation on the island in the name of love of their fellow man had a life expectancy of three years.

The obvious comparison was with the way the East India Company managed its trade. This was a different model of colonialism altogether. Again, William Hickey is a useful witness. Two years after his abortive trip to Jamaica he set sail for India again, this time to Calcutta and the Bengal presidency, armed with a bulging portfolio of introductory letters provided for him by his father's distinguished London cronies. Though the administration was in temporary financial crisis, Hickey found his place. He was appointed Solicitor, Attorney and Proctor of the Supreme Court and began his new life as he meant to go on, by commissioning a £1000 refurbishment of a house he selected as appropriate to his station. He purchased a new phaeton to drive about in, laid up the best wines in his cellar, gave extravagant parties – and started to shake the pagoda-tree. Though the glorious profits of the East India Company were tainted by slavery in all but name and the company was hardly there to exercise philanthropy, this was a far nobler occupation than the Atlantic trade could ever be. Hickey scrupulously names all his influential friends, being sure to indicate, wherever appropriate, the aristocratic titles they later inherited. India pleased him. There was honour to be had there, as well as wealth. Who could say that of the Caribbean, for ever tainted by its shameful African connections?

To all of which the sugar merchants had a single answer. The value of exports from the Caribbean colonies exceeded by far those from India and all other British possessions put together. By 1815 the West Indies exercised a virtual world monopoly on sugar. As for Africa, over which the abolitionists exercised their bleeding hearts as the true home of the black man, what was it but a trackless desert, without history, unlit by civilisation, contrary and pestilential? Even on the slave coasts, nobody had been more than a few miles inland, gliding along greasy brown rivers into an overwhelming aboriginal silence. Africa was an aside, an irrelevance. People wanted sugar. How it came to the table did not much concern them. Though the storm signals were flying for the Atlantic trade at home and abroad, it took an exceptionally far-sighted man to act on them.

In practice, every plantation was a petty kingdom where violence and terror was the norm and compassion as rare as window-glass. To whom did the governor report the abuses of the plantation system and with what consequence? For generations of ministries, Colonies had been bundled up with War – the one a consequence of the other. The loss of the American colonies made the humanitarian argument for an end to slavery very difficult for Britain to endorse. As the home country was forced to admit, in tolerating its calamities in the Caribbean it was also hanging on grimly to – and in the wars against the French doing all it could to increase – what was left of what it once had.

Soldiers and sea-captains had given Britain the original imperial

advantage. So assiduous was Captain Cook in exploring the South
Seas, for example, that the Whig wit Sydney Smith once estimated
ruefully that if there was a rock anywhere in the world large enough
for a cormorant to perch on, someone would think to make it
British. It was a witty exaggeration of a not uncommon point of
view, for the chief concern of home government was not the glory
of overseas possessions, or the honour of their discovery, but how
much it cost to garrison them. A common statistic of the early
nineteenth century was that simply having a seaborne empire
employed 250,000 men and tied up 250,000 tons of shipping. For
many years the expenditure Britain was put to in its geopolitical
adventures far exceeded revenue.

In this picture, Jamaica was strikingly different, a piratical trea-
sure chest with the lid thrown back. Figures provided to the House
of Commons in 1815 showed a value in exports of £11,169,661.
Such public works as existed were maintained by a nugatory tax
income of £1200. This was the plantation system at its apogee.

Everything that was so spectacular and fantastical about
Jamaica's wealth derived from the island's dependence upon slavery. The standard agricultural implement was not the spade or the
hoe but the cutlass. The standard punishment for an absconding
slave was to lop off both ears. Nobody thought it of any great
account. Visitors to Jamaica, who knew very well that fortunes were
being made and fine country houses raised by the sugar merchants
at home in England, were amazed by the coarseness and vulgarity
of the planter society put in place to garner the profits of these
great men. Most striking of all, the English men and women who
lived on Jamaica and ran it for their absentee landlords affected
to need nearly a third of a million slaves to sustain their position.
Wellington had commanded an allied force of half that number
to make himself master of all Europe.

This is how the story begins, on an island remote from Europe
by 3000 miles. The word old-fashioned sits well with the Jamaican
colonists. At the end of the war with Napoleon Britain controlled
almost every Caribbean island – and who had won these great
victories if not table-thumping, punch-drinking patriots cut from

the old cloth, men William Hickey would be honoured to call his friends? Jamaica in 1815 was in triumphalist mood. It did not need capital – its wealth was in its labour force. It did not need fine gentlemen and, as it was making clear in its own surly and combative way, it did not need evangelical ministrations either. Put simply, Jamaica did not need improvement.

This shortsightedness was to be its undoing. Fifteen years later the value of sugar fell from £70 a ton to £25. In 1833, a law enacting the complete emancipation of the slaves changed the nature of the trade irrevocably. The unimaginable came to pass. The old planter society, which seemed as permanent and reliable as sunrise, was soon enough nothing but a romantic ruin. The factor in play here was much more important than the price of sugar. The reforming zealotry of a new age turned its mind to overseas possessions and found them wanting. The haphazard collection of islands and factories, plantations and anchorages was, within a generation, transformed. The Empire, which before had hardly merited its capital letter, became a single thing, an idea: in the hearts and minds of this new age, a crusade.

The people whose lives make up this book were not law-makers; neither were they in any sense radicals. They were Victorians of a particular stamp – adventurous, at times maddeningly complacent and, as far as feelings for their country were concerned, sentimental to a fault. None of them went to university – two of them were soldiers – and it could be argued that what we see in their experience is merely the exchange of one form of naivety for another. Certainly their patriotism was unquestioning enough to jar a modern sensibility. 'Hurrah for old England!' one of them cried as the scarecrow figures of Speke and Grant tottered into Gondokoro on the Nile, after walking from one hemisphere to the other. This is a shout whose echo has died completely, except perhaps on foreign football terraces, where the Union flag is more likely to be worn as a pair of shorts than a banner snatched up in the heat of battle.

What distinguishes these men is something new to the history of the nation. To their undoubted bravery was added the utter

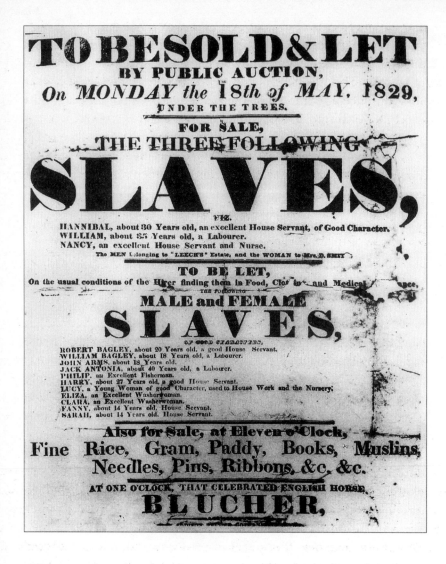

conviction of being chosen for a purpose even a child could understand. Throughout the nineteenth century there existed the belief
that a Briton was the summit of God's creation and the instrument
of His will. This was never so clearly demonstrated as when he was
abroad. Once a more or less random collection of properties – in
which, for example, it could be contemplated that to exchange the
whole of Canada for the strategic anchorage of St Lucia was a
sensible trade with France – the Empire became the expression of
a divine purpose. Nor was dominion over other people simply for
economic advantage.

> Let us endeavour to strike our roots into their soil, by the
> gradual introduction and establishment of our own principles
> and opinions; of our laws, institutions and manners; above all,
> as the source of every other improvement, of our religion and
> consequently of our morals.

This is Wilberforce, writing about India. The great evangelical
Christian is indicating how not just India but the whole world
was to be set free – by imposing upon it, however sympathetically
expressed, a superior way of being. If in the end breechloading
rifles and gunboats were the swifter teachers of this great lesson,
it had deeper and, to such as Wilberforce, nobler origins. It started
with the determination that nothing should be left undone to
help the peoples of the world understand that their own histories,
their own cultures and religious beliefs were mere shadows. The
men whose story this is were evangelicals like Wilberforce only in
this one sense: they took the missionary zealotry implicit in evangel-
ism and expressed it in what seemed to their age heroic action.
They were that new thing that animated Britain for a hundred
years: they were imperialist romantics. Their virtue was in their
character.

A young man called Samuel Baker visited Jamaica in the year
of the great hurricane to inspect his family estates. They had come
down to him through his father, the redoubtable Captain Valentine
Baker. Thirty years earlier, while commanding a mere sloop, Captain Baker had engaged a French frigate, forced it to strike its

colours and then brought it into Portsmouth in triumph. (The unfortunate French captain, when he realised how small a vessel had overwhelmed him, went below to his cabin and cut his throat.) A French-built frigate was considered the acme of naval architecture and when the news was carried across country to Bristol, the merchants there made haste to present Baker with a handsome silver vase as a mark of their appreciation. The gesture was not entirely patriotic. At the time of this stirring engagement Captain Baker was sailing under letter of marque. A less polite way of describing his activities was to call him a privateer. Baker rose in the estimation of his employers and 1804 found him master of the *Fame,* as large an armed vessel as ever left Bristol under private commission. With his share of the profits he bought land – Jamaica land, tilled by black slaves.

His son Samuel had good reason to thank his father, for had the good captain stayed in the Royal Navy he might have bequeathed the family a modest house in Hampshire, a few medals and the esteem of the service. As a privateer he had done very much better. When Mauritius – in another ocean altogether – was captured from the French in 1810, family money had been swiftly invested in plantations there too. Just as thirty years earlier Captain Baker had seized the chance to invest in sugar and shipping, now his son was positioning himself to exploit that initial advantage. Eighteen fifteen was an excellent year for Samuel to contemplate such good fortune because no sooner had the war with Napoleon ended than the Navy Estimates were ruthlessly pruned and many a captain was cast up on the beach with thirteen shillings a day, never to be employed again. The banks of white sail that indicated the naval squadrons and their enemies disappeared from the Jamaican horizon like snow in May. Now there was no greater redundancy to be had anywhere on earth than to be a military officer marooned in some ruined West Indies fort, looking out on to an empty ocean. The lizards ran across the rusting cannon and a deep, almost druggy somnolence blurred the passage of one day into another. Lucky the man who had a return passage.

The youthfully cocky Samuel Baker was just such a person. He was not on Jamaica to settle but to inspect. Rum, sunshine and a superfluity of servants made his Christmas agreeable but when the talk turned to how badly the planters were being treated, he had nothing much to say. His hosts were exactly what they said they were – social pariahs. For all the hearty eating and loyal toasts, the embarrassingly vulgar balls and calamitous routs, Jamaican society always had something about it that was skulking and ill-tempered. It came out over the Christmas churchgoing. Church attendance was encouraged for the 'good' blacks – the house servants and the superstitious elderly, anyone who did not walk habitually with a cutlass dangling from one hand. They and their beaux dressed in a mockery of their masters' clothes and paid each other elaborate address at the lych gate – 'Howd'di do, Missy?' 'Am fine, jes' fine, tankah, Massa' – all under the noses of their lobster-red owners. Each set of worshippers thought the other incurably stupid.

Baker kept a lock and key on his tongue. His Jamaican hosts saw with approval that he accepted what he found without comment and certainly without any mumping wringing of hands. He was an agreeable young man with a calm mind and a penchant for outdoor activities. He rode well and drank hard. They learned that he had been sent out 'to improve his health' and this they easily and cheerfully rephrased. He was there to learn some discipline and discover where his money came from. A secondary reason was undoubtedly to check the accounts – proprietors were commonly robbed blind by their agents. Here too Baker was a quick study. He was polite and non-committal but showed a liking for ledgers. Like his father before him, he had his feet set firmly on the ground. When one day he inherited and became master of the land over which he now rode, things would go on much as before, though perhaps with greater attention to accurate book-keeping. As for his slaves, his attitude to them was hearty and dismissive. Much given to singing, they had recently been taught words to celebrate a distant victory:

> Ay! Heyday! Waterloo!
> Waterloo! Ho! Ho! Ho!

Only a few months earlier Samuel Baker was a genial and unquestioning young man riding about Bristol with nothing more on his mind than the cut of a boot or a pair of breeches. Now, he was startled to find himself at the rim of civilisation, staring into the dark. He was not in the slightest bit reflective by temperament. All the same, what he was witnessing was life lived at the edge, the junction between everything that was familiar and recoverable; and fathomless ignorance. It was exhilarating to peer into this chasm. When they were in the fields and out of sight of the main house, young Mr Baker's slaves habitually worked naked. The crop they tended was three times the height of anything he had ever seen in England, just as the spiders their cutlasses disturbed were monsters set beside their English cousins. There was a kind of surrealism about the view from his jalousie window that was Swiftian in its savagery. That sea of black faces and glistening flesh was occasionally traversed by white women in broad hats, on their way by carriage to neighbours in the next parish, there to dawdle the afternoon away in idle conversation. Their speech was heavily inflected by the Creole they used towards their servants.

All this was exciting and there was even an element of delirium about such a crudely obvious society. Lady Nugent, who kept a far better diary than Samuel Baker, was astonished at the number of 'mulatto levees' she was obliged to attend. It dawned on her at last who these spiteful and fractious hostesses were – 'they are all daughters of Members of the Assembly'. Baker kept his counsel. There was one aspect of the Jamaica journey that was impossible to ignore. If he raised his eyes a little, away from the sex with slaves and the endless schooners of rum punch, he could see enticingly blue and green waters stretching all the way home to Bristol. For the first time in a generation, they were free of warfare. The whole great ocean – and every other ocean – would be under British dominion for a hundred years, just as men of his own class and wealth would be the envy and despair of the entire world.

Victory in Europe and undisputed sea power handed Britain a trading advantage that would last out the century. Baker might listen to old Jamaica hands who prophesied doom for the sugar industry and rebellion among the former slaves – both of which things happened all too soon – but when he looked over the heads of his blacks and the rustling canes in which they worked he could see, for himself and his children, possibilities yet to be articulated, in areas far more demanding and profitable. To seize these chances, a man did not need to be university-educated, or, come to that, the scion of a noble house. Dangerous money, bloodstained money, had its own savour. If Jamaica taught him anything, it taught him this.

It happened that the poet Matthew 'Monk' Lewis had properties adjacent to Baker that he had inherited in 1812. He was visiting Jamaica at exactly the same time. Lewis was a friend of Walter Scott and Byron. He gave his slaves a day's holiday when he arrived and another when he left. He also declared, to black mystification and the irritation of the overseers, an annual holiday to honour the birthday of the Duchess of York. In Jamaica's brutal atmosphere Lewis was an effete curiosity. Tainted by his supposed friendship with the abolitionist Wilberforce, ridiculously sentimental in his dealings with his workers, and undermined by his references to friends – mere writers – the planters had never heard of and had no wish to meet, Lewis cut a sorry figure. He rode right round the island and what he saw dismayed him. As soon as he got back to Europe he amended his will, with the intention of 'protecting' his black workers. (One of its provisions was that his inheritors should be made to live on Jamaica for three months once every three years, simply to keep abreast of what was happening.) The new will was witnessed one brandy-soaked night in the Villa Diodati by Byron, Shelley and Polidori. True to his intentions, Lewis returned to his properties in 1818. More holidays, more idealistic promises and more contempt from the planters. At the end of this second visit, like many another before him, he contracted yellow fever. He was buried at sea on his way home. He was forty-three.

It was a sad story but a predictable one. The ship's company that saw Lewis over the side were lucky not to have followed him. Even on Jamaica, in country that had been cultivated for 150 years, there was something impermanent about affairs, something of the stage set. Young Sam Baker came to realise that while there might be honest men on the island, there was no one of any great merit. (Monk Lewis was surely the only man ever to have visited Jamaica who had also shaken Goethe by the hand.) Most of the time was taken up with mere survival. Better to be a good shot and a two-bottle man than any learned gentleman. It was an incurably eighteenth-century point of view and – for a young man with eyes in his head – the society that supported it was dangerously moribund.

But then, as Sam Baker realised, Jamaican men and manners were not there to please but to make people like himself wealthy. It was this, as much as the thick red rum that lubricated every meeting, that proved so intoxicating. Perhaps, in the very crudity of the island's leading figures, their brutal jollity along with their lack of principles, there was an additional frisson. He was being given a lesson in ruthlessness. The missionaries could say what they liked about the rights of man but how were empires made unless by some cruder, less reflective set of ideas?

Samuel Baker came home and married Miss Dobson, the daughter of another industrious and acquisitive merchant, Thomas Dobson of Enfield in Middlesex. She gave him five children, all named for existing or former members of the family and all raised in a hearty, rumbustious and almost careless way that left them – like their father – not specially well educated but quick. They were also fearless. University, the professions, a parliamentary seat – none of these things was held out to the Baker boys as worthwhile. Samuel Baker intended his sons to be doers, and makers. A generation after he himself stood at his Jamaican windows, looking out on the empty ocean, the world had shrunk, but only a little. The greatest parts of it were still wide open. For a determined and resourceful man there was nothing in it to fear. Life, if it was conducted in the right way, was an adventure. The trick was not to be tied by convention, never to apologise for being rich, always to seize the main chance. The young Bakers knew this by family example. God the Englishman had helped their father do exactly what he wished in life. Samuel Baker, Esq., was the owner of Lypiatt

Park in Gloucestershire, chairman of his own bank and an honoured member of the board of Great Western Railways. Now it was the children's turn.

ONE

On 3 August 1843 the Reverend Charles Martin married two of his daughters, Henrietta and Elizabeth, to the two eldest boys of Samuel Baker. The double wedding took place in the parish church of St Giles, Maisemore, then a small village just outside Gloucester. Across the river was a handsome stone-built property called Highnam Court, formerly the Baker home. After a boisterous reception the two sets of newly-weds were driven away on the road to Bristol, each in their own carriage and four. As he watched them go, Mr Martin could reflect with pleasure on his daughters' good fortune. John Baker, who had married Elizabeth, was a steady young man and a warm friend to his younger brother Sam. The boys – the entire family – were hearty in an old-fashioned way but that was no bad thing either. If there was a cloud over the day's proceedings it was that John and Elizabeth, after a honeymoon in Clifton, would take ship the very next month for the island of Mauritius. For them it was an adventure, but for Mr Martin and his wife a considerable wrench. The couple were to sail in one of old Sam Baker's vessels, the *Jack*, and it did not seem to bother anyone that this flea of a ship, a mere 100 tons, was to carry them on a passage that commonly lasted three months.

John Baker was being sent to Mauritius to manage the family sugar estate there, which was called, encouragingly, Fairfund. Yet who in Maisemore knew much of anything about Mauritius before this happy day? Wedding guests learned there was a newly installed governor, Sir William Maynard Gomm, a Waterloo veteran (it went almost without saying), a man who had been gazetted a lieutenant in the army before he was ten years old. (He ended up a field marshal and died in 1875 at the ripe old age of ninety-one.) Both Sir William and his predecessor on Mauritius, Sir Lionel Smith, had Jamaica connections that Mr Martin might secretly reprehend: it was not exactly a blot on the character of his new in-laws that they were sugar merchants, though recent Jamaican politics did speak of a rough and brutal society such as the rector himself had never met with in the calmer waters of the Bristol diocese.

Though the story was hard to follow in detail, the bones of the matter were simple enough: the distant and unlovely Jamaican Assembly had taken the recent law enacting the full emancipation of slaves extremely badly and refused to ratify it until pressed to do so upon pain of dissolution by the mother country. This insult by a gang of ruffians was surely an affront to the new queen's dignity. Mr Martin did not insist upon the matter – how could he with a man as deeply involved in sugar as old Sam Baker? However, he was gratified to hear that Mauritius was a very different case and Gomm the pleasantest man imaginable. It was also some comfort to Mr and Mrs Martin that their second daughter, Henrietta, would go no further than London after the wedding, where young Sam Baker was to be placed in his father's office in Fenchurch Street.

Of the two brothers, Sam was far the better candidate for a life in the colonies. Not especially tall, he was barrel-chested, muscular and loud. All the Bakers were jolly but, though he was only twenty-two, Sam was the epitome of an old-fashioned squire. He could ride, botanise after a fashion – and he could shoot. He loved shooting. It was the wonder of the family that he had gone to Gibbs of Bristol for a muzzle-loading rifle made to his own design, requiring a massive charge and firing a three-ounce bullet of pure lead. As he pointed out with delight, this whole set-up was 'preposterous to the professional opinions of the trade'. The great weapon weighed twenty-one pounds and could knock down animals not to be found in the New Forest, or anywhere else in England. Sam was a prime shot, and slaughter, it seemed, was never very far from his mind.

His father had lately sent him into Germany to be tutored. It was one of the peculiarities of the family that old Sam Baker distrusted public schools and had raised all his children at the local grammar school and then, as necessary, with the assistance of tutors. As a consequence none of them was markedly bookish. This was not considered a failing. One of the best stories at the wedding breakfast told how Sam had persuaded his brother John to pay court to the Martin girls by sailing across the river that separated the two parishes in a bath tub. These were two self-willed and, to a certain extent, self-educated young men with a fine disregard for convention. John was the more biddable, but the exuberance of his brother Sam was a joy to everyone who met him. It was by no means clear how an office in Fenchurch Street could contain him.

It did not. The following year, after presenting the rector and his wife with a grandson and with Henrietta pregnant a second time, Sam set off with his family to join his brother. An important part of his luggage was his collection of guns and sporting rifles.

The Portuguese first discovered Mauritius in 1505. Ninety years later the Dutch conquered it without too much trouble and then, when they saw a superior advantage in occupying the Cape of Good Hope, abandoned it just as lightly. In 1715 the arrival of de la Bourdonnais' fleet made it French. It was swiftly garrisoned and the lowlands cultivated. On its westerly side the island is guarded by steep cliffs leading to mountains the French *colons* dismissed with a Gallic shrug as being inaccessible. The value of Mauritius was in its handsome anchorage. From Port Louis royal ships and many rapacious privateers harried the lumbering East India trade. Following the capture of one such vessel, the *Osterley*, bound for Calcutta, the governor emptied the hold of its cargo of blue and yellow cloth and ran up fetching new uniforms for his black garrison. They marched about some impressive fortifications, for Port Louis had anchorage for fifty men-of-war and was comfortably considered impregnable to attack by sea.

The French called their island, with justifiable pride, the Île de France. One of the curiosities of the place was its polyglot population. An eighteenth-century visitor, the novelist Bernardin de Saint-Pierre, was entranced by the hinterland and its well-cultivated estates.

> What pleasure to see over there the negro from Guinea growing his bananas, there a black from Madagascar gathering in the grain, while in another plantation a girl from Bengal cuts the sugar cane, as a kaffir shepherd leads his flocks out into the forests, singing. Here we may see a Malabar woman spin cotton under the shade of the bananas, there a Bengali weaves and the little valleys resound with the singing of these different nations, repeated in their echoes. Ah, if the concerts of different birds in the forest are so charming, by how much more the voices of different nations in the same countryside!

Saint-Pierre may have had a sentimental eye but he was reflecting a general truth about the calm and prosperity of the island. He set the enormously popular novel *Paul et Virginie* in an enchanted glade overlooking Port Louis. The two lovers grow up in a state of nature – Virginie serves a not very sympathetically drawn de la Bourdonnais at table wearing a skirt made from banana leaves – and are only parted by money and the implacable demands of social position. Saint-Pierre was a gifted disciple of Rousseau. There are slaves in his story but they are benign. Like Paul and Virginie, they too are closer to nature than their masters. Saint-Pierre makes a sly point in depicting how Virginie celebrated her mother's birthday every year. The night before, she ground and baked wheaten cakes

> that she sent to the poor white families born on the island, who had never tasted European bread and who without any help from the blacks were reduced to living on manioc in the middle of the forests, having, to support their poverty, neither the stupidity that comes with slavery nor the courage that flows from education.

The possession was noted for its tranquillity and the docility and loyalty of its workers. They were relatively well looked after. Governor Dumas reported in 1767:

> The black here is almost like a Polish peasant in the Russian Pale and is commonly content with his lot. We are speaking generally of a more humane attitude towards the slaves than at St Domingo or Martinique. Every creole thinks of himself as a citizen and is not humiliated by the inferiority of his colour.

However, the idyll was not made to last. On 29 November 1810 the British invaded the island with a combined operation mounted from India. Three infantry divisions under General Abercrombie were landed on an open beach and, marching inland to attack on the land side, easily secured the capitulation of Port Louis and its 200 cannons, all of them facing the wrong way. Bottled up in the harbour by Admiral Bertie's fleet were six frigates and another thirty smaller vessels, while in the arsenals and go-downs below the ramparts the victors discovered a huge quantity of stores. All this had been won for a loss of only twenty-nine lives, as swift and complete a victory as any in the war against the French.

There was an unexpected bonus to the victory. As the conquering heroes fanned out into the countryside, they discovered, setting aside an understandable surliness on the part of the conquered French plantation managers, an *ambiance* as unlike that of the Caribbean slave islands as it was possible to imagine. Governor Dumas had been right. Mauritius was a calm and unbloody model of the plantation system that was – on the part of the whites at any rate – difficult to fault.

Under the second British governor, Robert Farquhar, the island began its struggle with the slavery issue. Back in 1807, Farquhar, a devout Christian, had published a pamphlet which suggested ameliorating the effects of abolition in the West Indies plantations by importing indentured Chinese labourers. (When the experiment was tried, it was greeted with dismay. In such a brutal environment the Chinese seemed effete beyond words. Locals took exception to their pattering manner of walking and unconscious air of superiority. Farquhar had asserted that it would not be necessary to import women, since the Chinese did not much care with whom they co-habited. He was wrong about this, too.) Here on Mauritius the governor found, in a different setting, pretty much the policy he had advocated in the West Indies.

The island's principal export was, like Jamaica's, sugar: though the soil was not specially fertile, the crop did very well. The climate was good and Europeans considered the air particularly healthy. The only real town, Port Louis, had a stock of several thousand stone-built houses. De la Bourdonnais' residence, built in 1738, filled one side of the tree-lined Place d'Armes and from its windows a gentle succession of British governors looked out on a view that breathed style and sophistication. Altogether, Mauritius was not at all an unpleasant posting, an English possession where the common language was French. Colonel Draper, for example, a lackadaisical adornment to colonial rule, was at one time commissioner of Mauritius police. He had got himself into no end of trouble in Trinidad in the bad old days but on Mauritius things went better. He married a Creole beauty and contributed to the island's amenities by inaugurating horse-racing. Left alone – and the home government's hold on affairs was tenuous – the British might have succumbed completely to the island's charms.

An instance of the ambling pace of life was the introduction of Indian convicts to build the roads and connect the scattered hamlets. They lived in unsupervised camps and no power on earth could prevent them from co-habiting with the Indian women they found in the plantations. Though they were prevented by law from owning property, many of them found work in the evening and at the weekends. These convicts joined a rainbow of races – to Bernardin de Saint-Pierre's euphoric picture of the concert of voices in the forest could now be added Tamil, Chinese, French and hallooing English. Officially there was a strict separation of races and classes. Unofficially things muddled along.

The only fly in the ointment was the falling price of sugar and the fate of the former slaves, now converted to indentured labourers and what were euphemistically designated 'apprentices'. Mauritius had a taste of how difficult this last issue was in the appointment of John Jeremie as *procureur-général* in 1832. Jeremie had previously been chief justice on the West Indies island of St Lucia, where his high moral tone and pronounced abolitionist views incensed the local planters and led to his resignation. When he brought the same opinions to Mauritius, he found his reputation had preceded him. Colonel Draper was one among many who found him objectionably narrow-minded on the troubled subject of total emancipation.

In his capacity as chief of police, Draper prepared the new chief justice less than a hero's welcome. Jeremie's ship made its gun salute to the governor and dropped anchor. Fussing with his baggage, anxious to go ashore and make his first good impression, Jeremie ran slap into farce. For two days he was prevented by the chief of police from landing at all, despite furious representations. This was done, Draper explained suavely, out of consideration for his personal safety. Poor Jeremie. He rightly concluded that he did not have a friend on the island. He was finally taken ashore with a file of marines to protect him and marched – a terrible moment, this – past shuttered houses through the empty streets of Port Louis. A fortnight later he presented himself for his swearing-in. Not one of the judges on the island would come forward to conduct the ceremony.

Stoned by the mob and without a friend to help his cause, Jeremie was advised by the governor to go back home. After a twelve-week passage, he arrived in England and posted at once to London. If he was looking for sympathy, he got none. An infuriated Secretary for War and the Colonies ordered him to turn round and go straight back. This time, as soon as he was successfully sworn in, he set about his fellow judges, accusing them of complicity in illegal slave dealings and of irregularities in sentencing. This proved too much for the governor. Mauritius was not to be dictated to by some blue-light double-shotted canting lawyer, nor was a veteran of Waterloo and a god-damned general to be told how to run his administration. After less than a year in office Jeremie quit. With a gallows sense of humour, London first knighted him and then posted him to Sierra Leone to reflect on slavery at its source. The fever took him off in 1841. (By coincidence, his arch-enemy, Colonel Draper, had died in post on Mauritius the previous night.)

The Baker brothers arrived in more peaceable times, John in 1843, Sam a year later. Sir William and Lady Sophia Gomm were every bit as pleasant as they had been advertised. Now that the threat of war, or war on the scale the world had known it, had receded, the more ferocious military cast of mind had gone, too. There were schools and colleges for the white population, a Protestant cemetery, excellent Botanical Gardens; and a large theatre building, open every night for balls and other recreations. French bakers and pâtissiers, milliners and seamstresses added to the little elegances of life. There was talk of an observatory and Lady Gomm, with a delicate touch, had put herself at the head of a subscription list to build a statue and memorial to one of her husband's French predecessors.

There was certainly a problem with emancipated slaves, who showed not the slightest wish to continue in the cane fields as wage labourers, but this was offset by the importation, just at the time the Bakers arrived, of 45,000 indentured Indians. As a consequence sugar production jumped by a third in a single year. (In the three years from 1843 to 1846 it more than doubled.) On the Baker estate at Fairfund the refinery was working flat out and for the youthful managers everything about the colony had the attraction of the new.

The same was not quite so true for the wives, the rector's girls. Mauritius was after all an island – or, as these young women might have thought of it, only an island. The London Missionary Society, founded in 1795 to bring the blessings of Christianity to the world at large, had been dismayed – and perhaps disappointed – by the religious fervour it discovered already pre-existing in this tight little community of Catholics, Hindus and Muslims. It withdrew in 1833 and there remained only two Anglican clergymen in the whole colony, both comfortably situated in Port Louis. One of the most agreeable companions to be had nowadays was the indefatigable surveyor-general, John Lloyd.

He was a man after Sam Baker's heart. When he arrived in 1831 the Pieter Boitte Mountain was pointed out to him, the one the French *colons* considered unscalable. Lloyd cut his way through the jungle approaches and – aided by ladders – made the first ascent, which he celebrated by planting a Union Jack on the summit. The Victorians held this to be the origin of British rock-climbing. (One of the people to leave an impression of Lloyd's affability is Charles Darwin, who called at Mauritius on the way home from his epic voyage in HMS *Beagle*. Lloyd had an elephant he let the delighted naturalist ride.)

For Sam Baker, the place had only one drawback: there was nothing worthwhile to shoot. He might have overcome this disappointment but there were also family problems to contend with. His sister-in-law Elizabeth miscarried twice after arriving on Mauritius and was unhappy. She was almost certainly homesick. Baker was acute enough to have noticed an essential difference between the French on the island and themselves.

> You cannot convince an English settler that he will be abroad for an indefinite number of years [he wrote]. With his mind ever fixed upon his return, he does little for prosperity in the colony. He rarely even plants a fruit tree, hoping that his stay will not allow him to gather from it.

The remark might have been directed without rancour at Elizabeth Baker. By comparison, he noted, the French planter came to stay.

> The word 'Adieu' once spoken, he sighs an eternal farewell to 'La Belle France' and, with the natural lightheartedness of the nation, he settles cheerfully in a colony as his adopted country. He lays out his grounds with taste, and plants groves of exquisite fruit trees, whose produce will, he hopes, be tasted by his children and grandchildren. Accordingly, in a French colony there is a tropical beauty in the cultivated trees and flowers which is seldom seen in our own possessions.

Sam soon came to believe that, pretty though the island was, the women were right and there was something of the second division about it. After a visit to Réunion did nothing to calm his wanderlust, he set off in 1847 for Ceylon, travelling alone, having awarded himself a year's shooting.

He was going to the right place: recent report was that three gentlemen had killed 104 elephants there in three days of slaughter. The trusty Gibbs rifle was at his side when he landed at Colombo and hastened to introduce himself to two of the locals in the modest comforts of Seager's Hotel. He explained that he was there for the sport. The reaction was totally unexpected. '*Sport?*' one of them cried incredulously. When Sam mentioned elephants his companion was even more scathing. 'There *are* no elephants in Ceylon. Maybe there used to be, but I have lived here years and never seen one.' These two were what he called 'Galle Face planters' – men who hung around Colombo and the racecourse, whose land was farmed for them by managers in the hinterland. They must have been exceptionally stupid (or delivering a colossal snub) for there was an established trade in elephants, captured and trained in Ceylon and then exported to the mainland as draught animals. It seemed to Sam they took their cue for a life of ignorance and indolence from the governor himself. 'The *movements* of the Governor cannot carry much weight,' he commented acidly, 'as he does not move at all, with the exception of an occasional drive from Colombo to Kandy. His knowledge of the Colony and its wants and resources must therefore, from his personal experience, be limited to the Kandy road.'

Though Colombo had a small harbour, the East Indiamen and those ships bound for China, including all Royal Navy vessels, were of too deep a draught to enter it and instead rode at anchor out beyond the surf. It was both commentary and metaphor for the faintly makeshift and dilatory atmosphere Baker thought he could discern. The sleepy and peaceable town, still with much of the Dutch influence about it, including its mouldering and unimproved fortifications, did nothing to rouse his spirits.

Instead of the bustling activity of the Port Louis harbour in Mauritius, there were a few vessels rolling about in the roadstead, and some forty or fifty fishing canoes hauled up on the sandy beach. There was a peculiar dullness throughout the town – a sort of something which seemed to say 'coffee does not pay'. There was a want of spirit in everything. The ill-conditioned guns upon the fort looked as though intended not to defend it; the sentinels looked parboiled; the very natives sauntered rather than walked; the bullocks crawled along in the mid-day sun, listlessly dragging the native carts.

These observations left Sam Baker with the idea that Ceylon was a hundred years behind Mauritius in development. The island traded in palm-oil, cinnamon and tobacco as well as coffee, yet all with the same want of energy he found so offensive. Much larger than Mauritius in surface area and with a population estimated at a million and a half, its interior, with its dizzying gorges and granite peaks, was, he soon discovered, largely unexplored. Trade and government rested chiefly at sea-level. The Cinnamon Gardens, which suggested at the very least something worthwhile to inspect, turned out to be an untended forest of low scrub. The dense groves of palms stretching back from the shoreline were hardly more alluring. There were scarcely more than 25,000 Europeans in the whole colony: Ceylon was asleep and, as it seemed to this hyper-active and boisterous young man, it begged to be awakened.

His own movements were soon settled. Quite by chance he fell in with 'an old Gloucester friend', Captain Palliser of the 15th Foot, a regiment then stationed on the island. Palliser, who had something of Sam's own tastes and energy, took him up-country and there the Gibbs soon came out of its case. The jungle ravines were teeming with game and there were elephants to be had in plenty. The newcomer blazed away and plunged enthusiastically into the greeny dark for days and sometimes weeks on end. At the same time he began to demonstrate his innate intellectual curiosity, for the loud and hearty sportsman he loved to personate was also a keen naturalist and, perhaps even more unusually for the British on Ceylon, a patient and thoughtful explorer.

Baker had a very sharp eye for landscape and was impressed with the ruins of an extensive civilisation buried beneath the lianas.

In particular, he saw how water had once been gathered and stored. This led him to estimate the amount of land that had once been under cultivation and the size of the population it had supported. The tone in which he reported these reflections was robust – few other Europeans on the island at that time could have written this:

> The ancient history of Ceylon is involved in much obscurity; but, nevertheless, we have sufficient data in the existing traces of its former population to form our opinions of the position and power which Ceylon occupied in the Eastern Hemisphere, when England was in a state of barbarism. The wonderful remains of ancient cities, tanks, and watercourses throughout the island all prove that the now desolate regions were tenanted by a multitude – not of savages, but of a race long since passed away, full of industry and intelligence.

A partial description of Ceylon had been published in 1821. The author was a credulous Dutchman called Haafner and the information contained in his *Travels on Foot Through the Island of Ceylon* was already twenty years out of date when it was finally translated into English. Haafner came to the island at the turn of the century as an escaped prisoner of war from Madras; his travels, which were more like aimless wanderings, emphasised the awesome nature of the mountains Sam Baker was now exploring. Everything bad that could happen to the unwary white man happened to Haafner, sometimes to comic effect. In one incident, he set his lonely camp fire under a sheltering tree and was rewarded by a drenching shower of tiny frogs that tumbled out of the branches. Leaping up in disgust, he retreated to ground where he felt safer, only to sink in it past his ankles. He returned to his fire and built it up to a mighty blaze, with the intention of bringing down every last frog in the tree. They continued to fall, plopping into his food and making his life a misery.

The few other Europeans in Haafner's story are, like him, overwhelmed by the sheer ferocity of nature in the raw, so much so that they come to believe that no place in the interior is safe and no stick or stone is what it seems. Snakes, spiders, every kind of charging animal, including the rampaging elephant, are greeted for the most part with blind panic. As for the natives – the 'koolies' who carried Haafner's kit and led him about in his wanderings – they are beings without personalities, human mud.

> When it became necessary to bring water for preparing our supper, the Koolies were so terrified at the idea of being attacked by the crocodiles, that they with one voice refused to approach the river, though we offered to accompany them with torches and our pistols in our hands. What surprised us most, was that their obstinate and determined refusal inspired us with the same terror, so that instead of a supper, we were under the necessity of contenting ourselves with a glass of liquor and some biscuits.

Haafner's sensibilities were essentially eighteenth century: what he could not name left him in superstitious dread. For him the world was huge and had no edges, the dark led into the dark; and only among other white men was there any sense of place or purpose. Adrift in the Ceylon jungle, Haafner always looked to a town as his ideal destination – somewhere furnishing lights, recognisable and familiar cuts of meat, wine and white men's conversation. His feeble explorations had taken him to the foothills of what was later called the Great Wilderness of the Peak – that is, Adam's Peak, the highest point on the island, where a rock was said to bear the imprint of the first man. Even in Sam Baker's time, the Society for the Diffusion of Knowledge, founded in 1827, had in print a map of Ceylon in which the site of the supposed biblical Paradise was indicated, regretfully, as 'unknown mountainous region'.

Having arrived to shoot big game, Sam found himself instead exploring the empty spaces of a map. It suited his personality to be first, to set his foot where no white man had been before. The Great Wilderness (which, after all, existed on an island only 280 miles long) held no fears for him but, rather, encouraged a native obstinacy. His explorations also cocked a snook at received opinion on the island. He had a young man's pride of life, which included in his case a marked anti-authoritarianism; but there was more to him than this. Haafner could never have sat in patience beside a jungle track and let his mind wander as fruitfully as these words indicate:

> How little can the inhabitant of a cold or temperate climate appreciate the vast amount of 'life' in a tropical country! The combined action of light, heat, and moisture calls into existence myriads of creeping things, the offspring of the decay in vegetation. 'Life' appears to emanate from 'death' – the destruction of one material seems to multiply the existence of another – the whole surface of the earth seems busied in one vast system of giving birth.

With the placing of those fastidious inverted commas, the big-game hunter and accidental explorer gives way to someone Huxley or Darwin could have understood and commended. Baker, though he did not yet know it, would find enemies enough in Victorian England, who mistook his unrepentant love of slaughter for a sign of the old brutalism that had animated their fathers. The thoughtful and enquiring side of him comes into view almost apologetically and at times is hidden by a lifetime penchant for schoolboy humour, as in this extract about the activities of a naturalist troubled by midges.

> A cigar is a specific against these small plagues, and we will allow that the patient entomologist has just succeeded in putting them to flight, and has resumed the occupation of setting out his specimen. Ha! See him spring out of his chair as though electrified. Watch how, regardless of the laws of buttons, he frantically tears his trowsers from his limbs – he has him – no he hasn't – yes he has – no, no, positively he cannot get him off. It is a tick, no bigger than a grain of sand, but his bite is like a redhot needle boring into the skin. If all the royal family had been present, he could not have refrained from tearing off his trowsers.

Sam roamed the high places for months on end, with no one but a Muslim bearer, Tamby, for company. It was an unusual and unpopular thing to do. To spend so much time in the unwelcoming and fever-ridden mountains – more baldly, to fail to ingratiate oneself with the society that clung to the littoral – was looked at askance in Colombo. Nobody likes a loner. In the colonial nine-teenth century, standing apart from the rest was a particularly grievous social crime. Moreover, the administration of Ceylon, which Sam so cheerfully disparaged, was especially nervy, for it knew itself to be making a sorry contribution to trade statistics. It was not a very achieving sort of place at all.

The new seriousness that flowed down from the queen and her prosy little husband had spread into a lake that soon enough became a general style, extending to the furthest colony. It became the strident conventional wisdom that man and society could and must be improved. In 1845, for example, Ceylon installed its first bishop: he was not there to strike an amiable interdenominational balance, much less to dispense tea and sympathy, but rather to insist on the role of the church as evangelical crusader, the power-ful auxiliary engine of change. Trade might follow the flag but it needed gingering. The scourge of colonial administration for many years was the permanent under-secretary for the colonies, James Stephen. His clerks referred to him fearfully as 'King Stephen', for he more than any political appointee ran the colonies. The verb is not excessive. Stephen's wife was Harriet Venn, whose father was a leading member of the Clapham Sect, that group of evangelical Christians who gathered round Wilberforce. No colonial bishop – come to that no governor – could ignore this connection.

Sam Baker was never a reformer in this sense. Bishops bored him. He distrusted missionaries with a vengeance and parliamen-tary and church politics passed clean over his head. All he knew was what he saw for himself. As the weeks turned into months and he tramped the high jungles he realised he had found somewhere to challenge his restlessness. What was more, he had arrived just at the moment when there was a drive to attract settlers. Land was being offered by the government at £1 an acre. Nevertheless, he might never have thought seriously about staying on in Ceylon but for the accident of falling ill from what he calls 'jungle fever' after an orgy of shooting. He had probably contracted malaria. Weak and wasted, he took himself off to recuperate on a plateau called Newera Eliya, 6500 feet above sea-level and overlooked by

Ceylon's third highest peak. Immediately, he fell in love with the place.

It was not entirely virgin land. A former governor, the bullish Sir Edward Barnes, a Peninsular and Waterloo veteran, had built himself a stone house on the plain reputed to have cost £8000 and there was also a ruined sanatorium for the island's troops. More romantically, the landscape was pitted with diggings, sometimes holes, sometimes deeper shafts, where the ancient kings of Kandy had searched for rubies. The place-names were evocative. The road up from Badulla was called the Valley of a Thousand Princes and the plateau itself was known as the Royal Plains. Barnes may have built his own house and the sanatorium so high up with the intention of replicating Ootacamund in India, the hill station to which the Madras presidency took itself in the summer months. This dream died with him. When Sam Baker first set eyes on it, Newera Eliya was no more than a forlorn relic.

He arrived more dead than alive and within a fortnight felt his strength returning. There was nothing under the plough and no stock to be seen. The few whites who lived there permanently ran hotels and rest-houses in a wildly romantic landscape where leopards were bold enough to snatch dogs from the veranda and rats ate any crop that was planted. The full bestiary of Newera was awesome, in fact, though not to a man who had spent a year wandering through ravines and climbing mountains, shooting game too heavy to carry and announcing his kills by tooting on a bugle to attract the indigenous Sinhalese in the rice paddies far below. Sam Baker found himself entranced. He plunged, and bought a thousand acres of this wild and uncultivated upland, jamming his walking stick into the turf at the eastern end of the plain. His scheme, cooked up in a fevered brain, was twice as grandiose as Governor Barnes's desire to have his own hill station. On this remote plateau Baker intended to settle a model farm in the good old English style, to be staffed by stout-hearted Gloucestershire men and women and grazed by imported sheep and cattle. Coffee would not do: the site was too high for coffee and anyway he wanted nothing to do with the existing planter society. What he had in mind was a piece of the West Country set down in the tropics, with the added attraction of seemingly inexhaustible big-game shooting on the doorstep.

This decision, so swiftly arrived at, discussed with no one else, was an act of social rebellion. Newera Eliya was about as remote from the governing class of Ceylon as it was possible to get. To buy land there was almost as exotic as purchasing a desert island, yet Sam Baker was not planning to run away from existence. Instead, he would show the world how a life in action should be lived, on a site the colonial government had practically forgotten. It was a challenge much more appealing than watching sugar cane grow back on Mauritius. The naturally combative side to him was stirred into a fine indignation.

> Why should this place lie idle? Why should this great tract of country in such a lovely climate be untenanted and unculti-vated? How often I have stood upon the hills and asked myself this question when gazing over the wide extent of undulating forest and plain! How often I have thought of the thousands of starving wretches at home who here might earn a comfortable livelihood!

He stayed no more than a fortnight before setting out for the coast and a ship to take him home. Once things were under way in London, he easily persuaded John and the womenfolk that their destiny also lay in Ceylon. His son Charles had died an infant's death on Mauritius; his second child was a girl called Jane who had not taken to a tropical climate. There was another new-born son who was the apple of his eye. His brother's wife was still child-less: maybe the miraculously invigorating air would do for everyone else what it had done for him. It seems they thought so too. A jubilant Sam went down to Lypiatt Park and communicated the same torrential enthusiasm to his younger brother, Valentine, a stocky and rather gloomy boy of nineteen. Then he looked around him for servants to the enterprise.

His first hiring – and he was to rue the day he made it – was a one-eyed groom from his father's estate called Henry Perkes. Per-kes had the unfailing confidence that came from being a pub wit.

Sam may not have noticed at first that he was more often drunk than sober. As bailiff Baker chose another West Country man, a tenant farmer called Fowler, who came with a homely wife and a beautiful daughter. He found a local blacksmith willing to follow him. This man had as his wife 'a cheerful knockabout woman' perfect for the job in hand – she could swing an eighteen-pound hammer as powerfully as her husband. Since the whole of the Gloucestershire countryside was talking about the repeal of the Corn Laws and the coming ruination of agriculture, Baker had arrived at an opportune moment. Altogether, excluding family members, Sam persuaded nine others to join him.

We can get some idea of what was in play from Charles Kingsley's novel, *Yeast*. The story commenced publication in serial form in 1846 and has the distinction to be among the worst constructed novels of any century; all the same it has strong resonance with the scheme Sam Baker had taken into his head. What Kingsley was trying to dramatise was the disaffection and intellectual confusion of the governing class – or at least their young – set beside the sharply observed miseries of the rural population in a time of agricultural slump. Kingsley's hero, Lancelot Smith, learns from the honest poor how to be a man. He has a university education and £2000 a year at his disposal but no purpose. Love is not the answer to his problems, nor is rick-burning or radical politics. The true path lies in the search for the Kingdom of God. His first steps are guided by the giant gamekeeper and hedge philosopher, Tregarva. Then, towards the end of the book, he meets the mysterious Barnakill, who proposes the two of them desert England altogether and retire to some utopian community 'in the land of Prester John'. (Barnakill does not mean Ethiopia but Russia. In a very necessary epilogue Kingsley modifies this startling proposal further by suggesting that the location of this earthly paradise is more metaphorical than geographical.)

Educated at Cambridge, Kingsley was deeply influenced by the Christian socialism of F. D. Maurice and a great admirer of Carlyle. *Yeast*, as it unfolded, suggested to some people a dangerous radicalism. It was published in book form in the revolutionary year of 1848 and its author attracted some passing notoriety. However, Kingsley was no more a firebrand than his fictional hero. He was in fact a country parson of donnish tastes who saw nothing noble in the lives of his own parishioners and made no great inroads towards their well-being. By 1860 he was appointed professor of Modern History at his old university and was for a brief time tutor to the Prince of Wales. Even a modest amount of bourgeois comfort was enough to placate the Lancelot Smith in him. In the last fifteen years of his life he became an ardent naturalist and reconciler of faith with science: he became, in short, a representative Victorian, genial, a little muddled and, when called upon, a friend to the established order.

Sam Baker needed no Barnakill to show him the way out and, unlike Kingsley, he was first and foremost a man of action. To go and settle halfway up a mountain on an island very few of his followers could have found on a map was a colossal undertaking for such a young man, given that he was remembered in his home county as nothing more than a jolly young giant with a passion for shooting. Moreover, as everyone knew, he had recently inherited a small fortune from his grandmother and could if he chose buy almost any property in the west of England. From there he could indulge his taste for adventure by expedition. That would have been his father's advice, for old Sam Baker risked very little in *his* life and was perfectly aware that the honours and dignity he sought in his old age had to be purchased. He was, when it came down to it, only a merchant – a rich and generous one, but famous only in Gloucestershire and among other London merchants. It was true the family had Tudor courtiers in its background, but in early Victorian England such an ancestry needed to be refurbished with sons who had been to university and made political connections that would last them through life.

Sam Baker's indifference to such a world and such a career is marked. His father's ramshackle way of educating him aggravated this but it was not the cause – he was an outsider by temperament. In later life, when he had proved himself a great explorer, he was fond of defending his eminence in stiff little sentences like this: 'I do not love to dwell upon geographical theories, as I believe in nothing but actual observation.' This is a vain man speaking.

It was soon clear to the farm workers he recruited that he had very great organising abilities. The colonists were to take ship in the *Earl of Hardwicke* with many tons of equipment, including a newfangled power saw and a patented compost-maker. There was a small ark of animals to be stowed before the mast. If he minimised the element of risk – and he had already discovered several different ways of suffering injury and sudden death on the Royal Plains – that was only in his nature. As the plans went forward, he paid a visit to Beattie's, the gunsmiths in Regent Street, and ordered from the firm not one but four double-barrelled rifles. From there he walked down to Paget's of Piccadilly and bought an impressive knife. 'The blade is one foot in length and two inches broad at its widest point and slightly concave in the middle. The steel is of the most exquisite quality and the knife weighs three pounds.' In due course, Baker used it to dispatch at a single blow a charging wild boar weighing 300 pounds. The knife split the animal open from the spine to its pizzle.

In the book he wrote about the Ceylon venture, *Eight Years in Ceylon*, Sam Baker says he did all this merely to have the pleasures of a country estate without the harassment of his neighbours' gamekeepers, which may have been the echo of a jocular family accusation. Young though he was, he had a very clear view of what he must do to get what he wanted – and the wit to set out in advance of his little band of colonists to prepare for their arrival. He built them all handsome little cottages with wood cut from the enclosing jungle and began the laborious business of clearing his land. He was wide-eyed about this, too. Every root, every stump was dug out. He knew that the soil, which looked so promising on the surface, would never amount to anything without manure. It lay on a bed of pure white clay. Baker was undeterred. He was prepared to add another £10 an acre in costs to clear and sweeten his land. Such long-sightedness was rare in Ceylon. The elevation of Newera and its exposure to the long months of the monsoon, when the rain and mist seemed to sit on the landscape for ever, made it an unappealing investment for the faint of heart. The real land-rush was lower down the mountain in lush grass country. Characteristically, Baker spent his money and energies on the more difficult option.

Things began badly. His daughter Jane died at sea on the passage from Mauritius and the toddler son on whom he doted was poisoned by a servant shortly after he set foot on Ceylon. The argosy from England arrived safely enough but trouble began immediately after debarkation. Among the animals fetched from England was a prize Durham cow, intended to mate with a half-bred Hereford bull. Sam arranged for it to be carried up in all its pomp in a cart that local craftsmen assured him would transport an elephant. The cow promptly fell through the floor. It was accordingly driven on foot and died of exhaustion halfway up the mountain. Perkes, whose official designation was that of groom, ran a brand-new carriage over the cliff. Baker reproduces an approximation of his letter of apology:

> Honor'd Zurr,
> I'm sorry to hinform you that the carriage and osses has met with an haccident and is tumbled down a preccipice and its a mussy as I didn't go too. The preccipice isn't very deep being not above heighty feet or thereabouts – the hosses is got up but is very bad – the carriage lies on its back and we can't stir it nohow. Mr— is very kind and has lent above a hundred niggers, but they aint no more use than cats at liftin. Plese Zur come and see whats to be done.

He was drunk when the accident happened. One horse had to be destroyed and another died the next day. They had been sent from Australia expressly to weather the climate. Perkes then excelled himself. Sent down the mountain to the accident site with an elephant, he overcame the protests of the mahout and took him off at a fine gallop. Refreshed by brandy and water, and finding his offers of help declined, the groom took off again back up the pass. In his own words, he 'tooled the old elephant along until he came to a standstill'. Shortly afterwards, the beast keeled over and died. Perkes was, as Baker grimly observed, 'one of the few men in the world who had ridden an elephant to death'. When he finally caught up with him, the groom was being pushed round the nascent plantation in a wheelbarrow, his mate as drunk as he.

There is a clue to Baker's unique temperament in a couple of lines of *Eight Years in Ceylon*. Apart from the damage done by Perkes (whom he quixotically describes as 'honest and industrious') there was an early mini-revolt of his tiny colony against the authority of the bailiff, Mr Fowler. It reached a climax when the white men refused to obey orders in front of the 150 natives Baker had hired to uproot the trees. 'I was obliged to send two of them to jail as an example to the others,' Baker remarks. 'This produced the desired effect and we soon got regularly to work.' One can make too much of this incident but it demonstrates Baker's supreme self-possession.

Most of *Eight Years in Ceylon* was written by palm-oil lamp at the end of Sam Baker's stay on the island. It is not a blueprint for how to set up and manage a model farm – as with the earlier partnership on Mauritius, John, the older brother, assumed most of the day-to-day responsibilities. Nevertheless, it was Sam's energy that transformed the plateau. The soil was bad, the rats ate all his first crops; and his two rams, on which he depended for a flock, fought a bad-tempered duel to the death. The bull, cheated of his Durham mate, was put to serve the puny local cattle and produced a strange hybrid, easily outstripped in strength by the elephants Baker trained to drag a plough or trundle not one but three harrows. However, the crossbred cattle showed some surprising qualities. A leopard got into Fowler's byre through the thatched roof and the poor man went out by lantern light to evict it armed only with a pistol, to be chased out of the place by an enraged cow well up to the challenge from a mere big cat.

Both John and Elizabeth Baker were, years later, buried at Newera Eliya and the Baker family did not sell the prosperous tea estate the original farm finally became until 1947. Even then, the head of the family retained the freehold on the ruined old houses which his grandparents had built. If there is a spirit of the hearth that still dwells there it is assuredly that of Sam Baker. He would not have been human if he had not preened himself a little on his sang-froid. What gave him the calm to face down beasts intent on killing him was indivisible from his general manner.

> There cannot be a more beautiful sight than the view of the sunrise from the summit of Pedrotallagalla, the highest mountain in Ceylon, which, rising to the height of 8,300 feet, looks down on Newera Ellya some two thousand feet below on one side, and upon the interminable depths of countless ravines and valleys at its base.

This is the language of the proprietor, which Baker certainly was. The passage places him alone on his eminence, for though he loved his family, he was still a young man and in the whole of his narrative his wife Henrietta scarcely merits a mention. It continues:

> There is a feeling approaching the sublime when a solitary man thus stands upon the highest point of earth, before the dawn of day, and waits for the first rising of the sun. Nothing above him but the dusky arch of heaven. Nothing on his level but empty space – all beneath, deep beneath his feet. From childhood he has looked to heaven as the dwelling place of the Almighty, and he now stands upon that lofty summit in the silence of utter solitude: his hand, as he raises it above his head, the highest mark upon the sea-girt land: his form above all mortals upon this land the nearest to his God.

The greater part of *Eight Years in Ceylon* concerns the sport he had set out to find there, but it does include this lyrical passage:

> Comparatively but a few years ago, Newera Ellia was undiscovered – a secluded plain among the mountain tops, tenanted by the elk and the boar. The wind swept over it, and the mists hung around the mountains, and the bright summer with its spotless sky succeeded, but still it was unknown and unseen except by the native bee-hunter in his rambles for wild honey. How changed! The road encircles the plain, and the carts are busy in removing the produce of the land. Here, where wild

forest stood, are gardens teeming with English flowers: rosy faced children and ruddy countrymen are about the cottage doors; equestrians of both sexes are galloping round the plain and the cry of hounds is ringing on the mountain-side.

A little over thirty years after his father gazed out on his cane fields in Jamaica, the young Sam Baker had performed a double trick, of creating an Arcadia equal to Saint-Pierre's in *Paul et Virginie,* but almost wholly independent of the colony in which it stood. Towards colonial government in general Baker exhibited a fine contempt. Its dilatoriness was exhibited, Baker thought, in such obvious matters as the Botanical Gardens in Colombo, which had been set up as a cultural attraction – the jungle tamed – and which also doubled as a handy site for flirtation and intrigue. Baker pointed out that since most settlers came out to make their fortunes and had no capital to spare for experiment, the government would do much better by using its gardens as a base for scientific investigations. (He was proved right: the introduction of tea to Ceylon eventually came about from crop trials made there.)

Very few men inside or out of any of the colonial governments of the day had gathered so comprehensive an understanding of a land, its indigenous inhabitants and its potential. *Eight Years in Ceylon* is teasingly short on domestic detail but cannot be faulted otherwise. Sam Baker took as his canvas not just his own estate, nor the game he found, but the whole island. He saw everything with an explorer's eye.

Then, in 1854, something truly unexpected happened. Racked with fever, Sam staggered down from the mountains without his horse and having buried his gun-bearer. With as much suddenness as he had shown in his original impulse to buy his thousand acres, he now quit. The little community was astonished to learn that all four of the Bakers, with Sam and Henrietta's four surviving children, had decided to return to England, leaving Mr Fowler in place as manager. Poor Fowler. His wife had died on the plain and was one of the first tenants in the graveyard of the new church. She joined Sam's own baby son.

There is an old tree standing upon a hill whose gnarled trunk
has been twisted by the winter's wind for many an age, and so
screwed is its old stem that the axe has spared it, out of pity,
when its companions were all swept away, and the forest felled
... The eagle has roosted in its top, the monkeys have gam-
bolled in its branches; and the elephants have rubbed their
tough flanks against its stem in times gone by; but it now throws
its shade upon a Christian's grave.

This is the only passage in the book when he comes anywhere
close to admitting the full price for his adventures in Ceylon. Ill
though he was, his wife was being dragged down with him. They
had lost two sons and a daughter to the enterprise and the long
monsoon months from June to November were hard to bear. Without light – without sun – the transition that took place in Newera
just at a time when a distant Gloucestershire was bathed in plenty
was hard to bear. Baker concluded his paragraph on the church-
yard with this unexpectedly pietistic sentence: 'The sunbeam has
penetrated where the forest threw its dreary shade, and a ray of
light has shone through the moral darkness of the spot.'
    They took their leave of Fowler and the others and sailed home
together. Old Sam Baker had remarried after the death of his first
wife and had given up Lypiatt Park: there was nothing left for them
in Gloucestershire. John and Elizabeth settled for the time being
in Rugby; Valentine and the youngest brother James were in the
army encamped before Sebastopol. Sam took his family to a rented
house on the Atholl estate in Scotland. Towards Christmas, the
weak and listless Henrietta allowed herself to be carted off to the
French Pyrenees to get well again. Her husband also had it in mind
to hunt the black bear he had heard roamed the winter slopes.
The couple took their four children with them.
    Henrietta Baker died at Bagnères-de-Bigorre on 29 December
1855. Since her marriage to Sam she had lived almost a third of
her life in the tropics. She died in a room where deep snow lay
outside the window and melted into the icy black waters of the
Adour. One of the unmarried Martin sisters, Charlotte, who was
only twenty-two, came out to France to rescue the children.

She found her brother-in-law stunned and almost completely helpless. He had arrived at Bagnères with the utter confidence that being a Baker was of itself a cure against ill. Henrietta would buck up, the children would scratch out a few words of French and in some snowy ravine behind the town the black bear would present a perfect shot. His own animal high spirits would act as tonic and emollient – things would soon be as they should be. But the *maire* of Bagnères was also a crack shot and had been into the mountains before him. One of the sights Charlotte Martin winced at seeing was Sam's gun cases in the hotel bedroom, still buckled, still with the protective tampons of lint tucked into the weapons' muzzles. Couldn't it be said that he had dragged the family south to Bagnères simply to satisfy himself? No doctor would have prescribed such a trip to an out-of-season spa. *C'était tragique, la mort de cette pauvre Anglaise, mais vous savez . . .*

The widower who ate alone at his restaurant table was thirty-four years old and a casual eye might have added another ten to that. Something had happened to this man that was as unexpected and humiliating as flinching in the face of danger. The sheer ordinariness of death, its artless sprawl, had tripped him up. Henrietta had died not from the exhaustion that had brought her to this Christmas card spa town, but from typhus, caught from bed lice somewhere along the road. It was an awful outcome and might have ended another man's career there and then.

TWO

Valentine Baker, always called Val in the family, was named for his naval grandfather. There is a photograph of him as a young man in Ceylon: he wears a high collar and stock, his hair is long, his arms are folded composedly across his chest. His moustache is in the experimental stage and has yet to find its voluptuous curves. It is the eyes that tell the story. What is most striking about Val's expression is its calm. If the camera represents the outer, public world, then he is looking into it with an eerie self-possession. That same look in the eye of a wild animal would have sent an instant warning signal to Sam Baker, tightening his finger on the trigger.

A boy among men, Val came out to Ceylon on the *Earl of Hardwicke* with the rest of Sam's party in 1845. From the beginning he was only ever a lukewarm farm colonist. For example: after a season or two on the plateau Sam Baker invented for himself a sort of woollen suit for his jungle explorations, the fabric dyed a muddy and streaky green by the juice of plants. It was cinched at the waist by the belt that carried the killer knife. He wore this kit without embarrassment and was always eager to press its advantages on others. It is not possible to picture Val ever wearing anything like it, even if it stood between him and sudden death.

He was at school in Gloucester during the Mauritius years and still only nineteen when he came to Newera. A windswept plateau halfway up a mountain was never going to satisfy his curiosity about life in the tropics. In any case, Val was only in Ceylon under licence – his father had long wished that he and his youngest brother James should enter the army. The family was rich and had worked its way into becoming part of the landed interest in Gloucestershire; and so, to old Sam Baker, the way forward for his youngest sons pointed to service in the Guards or, better still, a good cavalry regiment. Looked at in this light, Val's journey to Ceylon was no more than a jaunt. Unfortunately, as his photograph shows, there was very little of the jaunty about him.

To have a soldier in the family was a fatherly ambition that could turn out, under the wrong circumstances, to be ruinously expensive. The army offered its officer elite the opportunity of a plural life such as some parsons had enjoyed in the eighteenth century – they were gentlemen first and soldiers only afterwards. In the fashionable regiments no officer, however cautious in his habits, could subsist on his pay alone. His path to senior rank was choked by elderly and often grievously incompetent men who saw the purchase system, by which everything from a cornetcy to a colonelship could be bought and sold, as a guarantee of their pension. The first step in a military career – the right regiment – was the most important one. Thereafter, deep pockets helped – Lord Brudenell raised himself by reckless purchase from cornet to command of his own regiment in just eight years. As Earl of Cardigan he is reputed to have spent a further £10,000 annually to ensure the 11th Hussars remained among the most fashionable (and reactionary) of British cavalry regiments. Cardigan's manic personal vanity made him a particularly vivid example of what was, in a dozen or so regiments, the norm. The Guards, the Household Cavalry and certain favoured Hussar regiments had become, in effect, the junior branches of the aristocracy in uniform.

If this was old Sam Baker's ambition for his son Val, it must have caused consternation when news came that he had ridden back down the mountain only a few months after arriving at Newera and purchased an ensignship in that very undistinguished foot regiment, the Ceylon Rifles.

*　　*　　*

Touching the role of a young officer in times of peace, Thackeray wrote woundingly: 'The professional duties of a footman are quite as difficult and various.' He had this further to say in his *Book of Snobs*, published in 1846, the year Val joined the Rifles:

> When epaulets are not sold; when corporal punishments are abolished and Corporal Smith has a chance to have his gallantry rewarded as well as that of Lieutenant Grig; when there is no such rank as ensign and lieutenant (the existence of which rank is an absurd anomaly, and an insult upon all the rest of the army), and should there be no war, I should not be disinclined to be a major-general myself.

Val had joined as modest a regiment as could be found, tucked almost out of sight at the bottom of the Army List. His decision may have seemed inexplicable in Gloucestershire but a motive based on local conditions suggests itself. Up in Newera Sam, in his blustery and good-humoured way, was developing his role as the social outsider, a reputation he enjoyed and did his best to burnish. By joining the Rifles Val indicated an alternative. An ensign's duties might be mostly comprised of smoking and lounging but what they also offered was the pleasure of belonging. The elements of obedience and submission implied by regimental life were handsomely offset by the sense of fraternity engendered. A man who purchased the queen's commission anywhere was joining a select, if embattled, club. This desire to conform would become Val's tragedy.

The immediate consequence of his move to the coast was to open a window on to the part of Ceylon his brother had made such a point of ignoring – conventional Colombo society. As Val soon discovered, while the island might be a paradise for big-game hunters, its administration was a mare's nest. As with every other outpost of Empire, social recognition hung upon favourable notice by the governor or his commander-in-chief. To be invited to this or that ball; there to be presented to a general on his way to a more distant posting, or to a savant of the Royal Society being carried to the ends of the earth – all this gave the appearance of upholding a civility whose wellspring was in London.

The spirit of empire was not so sturdy that it did not need continuous reinforcement. When HMS *Beagle* came to Sydney in 1836, Charles Darwin found it 'a most magnificent testimony of the power of the British nation. Here, in a less promising country, scores of years have done many times more than an equal number of centuries have effected in South America.' Such generous sentiments were received with gratitude by his hosts, as was the conclusion he drew from them, a desire 'to congratulate myself that I was born an Englishman'. He had not been so kind towards New Zealand, describing the English there as 'the very refuse of society', but in Australia, young though he was, he had done the right thing.

The colonial enthusiasm that greeted the arrival of every ship flying the British flag and honoured its passenger list down to the least of its officers was demonstrated by people a long way from home, it was true; but that was not the only reason to feast strangers. The governor's residence, which was always the distinguished visitor's first port of call – in Colombo it was called, archaically, the King's House – was the amplification chamber of a distant murmur. What were they saying in London? The home country's desires and wishes were not always clear and congratulation was a rare commodity. As a consequence there was no such thing as stale news. Rumour and gossip were quite as closely attended as official dispatches.

Such was early Victorian society that well-bred strangers in conversation with each other were seldom at more than two or three degrees of separation from common acquaintances, by marriage, by regiment or by country seat. For the governor and his entourage, this was a second and more anxious reason to flatter the latest new arrival. By indirection, they were trying to find out how they stood personally. Colonial appointments, far from being sinecures, were very much movable feasts. Since 1840 five governors had packed their bags and quit Colombo. Sam Baker pointed out in *Eight Years in Ceylon* how this constant shifting around of administrators, their secretaries and military advisers did nothing but harm to emerging colonies, denying continuity and cohesion to their governing class.

Val was lucky – or circumspect – in his choice of Colombo

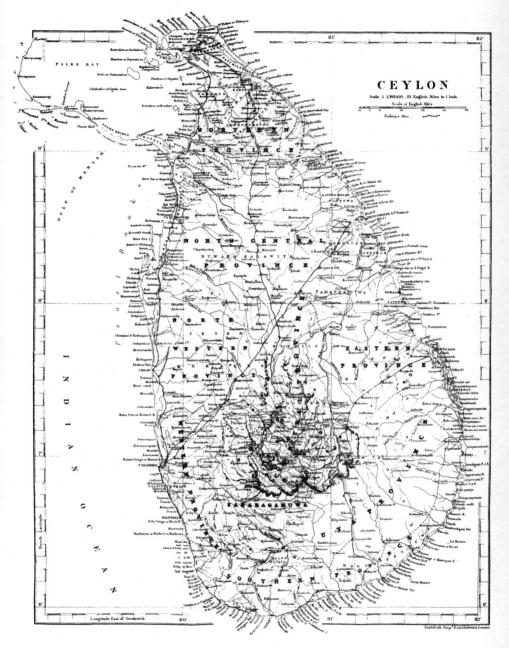

Ceylon as it was in Skinner's day.

friends, striking up acquaintance with a young man not entirely unlike himself. The chief justice of Ceylon was a man called Sir Anthony Oliphant, none too happily married to a powerful but neurasthenic woman who spent most of her summer months in a cottage by the lake at Newera. The couple were notorious evangelicals. Their only son Laurence was two years younger than Val and had been raised on the island as something of a wild child. In 1846 Sir Anthony and his family went home to England on a two-year leave, with the intention of leaving Laurence to study at university. Instead, the boy threw over his place at Cambridge to follow his father and mother back out to Ceylon.

When he and his mother pitched up at Newera, he found the Bakers in the full flood of setting up the model farm. Sam, in his breezy and open-handed way, took Laurence shooting. They camped together deep in the forest and the older man taught Oliphant, among other things, how to catch and dispatch a crocodile: you tied a live puppy to a wooden crucifix and, when the predator's jaws were jammed wide open by the indigestible element of the bait, you hauled him in and took a sporting shot through the eye.

Oliphant was completely sanguine about butchery of this kind; nor was he fazed by the other privations of a Baker jungle expedition. Courageous and resourceful, very quick-witted, he would later be one of the most enigmatic figures of the nineteenth century. His mother, whose address at Newera was 'The Turtle Dovery', was twenty years younger than her husband and liked nothing more than to be congratulated on her youthful appearance – and, on occasion, to be mistaken for her son's sister. She clung to Laurence with almost a lover's tenacity.

The two young men – Oliphant and Val Baker – were at first glance very alike. They were good looking, athletic, perhaps a little too sketchily educated, but obedient to the usual conventions of society. Each had an interesting background. Strangers who had heard something of the Oliphant family and came looking for a mummy's boy in Laurence were surprised to meet a blond but already balding giant, energetic and voluble. Those Colombo planters who felt themselves snubbed by the maverick Bakers up in Newera discovered in Val not an unhappy deserter, but a family member with the same trademark self-possession.

An astute observer might have found more intriguing shadows in Laurence Oliphant. He was one of those men made to be a secret agent – spontaneous and effusive on the outside, but inwardly tortured. Born at the Cape in 1829, brought up haphazardly in Ceylon by a succession of private tutors, he nevertheless – to the surprise of his father's distinguished dinner guests – spoke five languages. Dissembling his feelings in order to accommodate the war between his parents had made him a master of disguise. Never the milksop his mother seemed to want to cherish, and certainly not the evangelical saint of his father's imagination, Oliphant was a complicated young man. On his way out to Ceylon in 1848 to join his family, he found himself in Naples in the middle of the Italian uprising.

> I shall never forget joining a roaring mob one evening, bent upon I knew not what errand, and getting forward by the pressure of the crowd and my own eagerness into the front rank just as we reached the Austrian Legation, and seeing ladders passed to the front and placed against the wall, and the arms torn down.

He helped drag the hated emblem of foreign occupation to the Piazza del Populo and assisted in its burning. This is worthy of Byron or Shelley. At Messina his hotel was bombarded by the king of Naples's fleet and when he came back up to Naples he was in the square in front of the palace when King Bomba ordered his troops to fire into the crowd. Laurence escaped injury by crouching behind an arch. He was nineteen years old.

Val Baker's life to date had been a great deal less exciting. He had manners, he was dutiful, yet he was to others merely an officer in an undistinguished rifle regiment, a young infantry subaltern who knew a great deal about horses. His military duties were almost ludicrously undemanding. The faintly effeminate nature of the indigenous population that made it so difficult to recruit also made the island easy to govern. There was, as it happened, an outburst of civil unrest just at the time Val came down to the coast. Everyone knew that, in the event of a serious threat, the place would be flooded with troops from India. In the ordinary course of things, soldiering in Ceylon was about as taxing as taking up watercolours, or butterfly-hunting; and it had been this way since the brief Kandyan wars of 1817–18.

There was one Ceylon Rifle officer known by name at least to everyone on the island. Thomas Skinner joined as an ensign in 1819 when he was fifteen years old. To great amusement, he attended his first parade in civilian clothes, no uniform being found small enough to fit him. Skinner proved to have a genius for road-building and, by teaching himself the use of the theodolite, went on to produce the first accurate survey of the island's interior. (Little monuments to him are scattered along the roads of Ceylon to the present day.) His career is an example of how the purchase system worked.

After he had spent some years as a lieutenant, Skinner's fellow officers clubbed together to provide the purchase price of a vacant captaincy, an exceptional mark of respect for his talents. Out of pride (both his father and father-in-law were colonels) Skinner declined the money and so lost eleven long years of seniority. His promotion eventually came about in a particularly grotesque way. There was in the Rifles a Captain Fretz. One afternoon Fretz lev-elled his musket at an elephant and had the block blow back in his face. A chunk of metal over three inches long and weighing nearly four ounces entered his nasal cavity and lodged against his palate. Incredibly, Fretz survived another eight years of service with this horrific alteration to his appearance, astonishing his colleagues when drunk by absently twiddling a screw that poked from what was left of his nostril.

This was the captaincy Skinner waited for so patiently, while at the same time receiving fulsome commendations from the gov-ernor's office for his industry and ingenuity as road-builder and surveyor. They were getting him on the cheap. In the end he gave the island fifty years of service without ever rising beyond the rank of major. The man who benefited from Lieutenant Skinner's original fit of pride and made captain in his place was called Rogers. He was struck by lightning at Badulla, on the road to Newera, shortly after Val joined the Rifles. Skinner observes without comment that Captain Rogers was credited with killing 1500 elephants during his military service on the island.

Since 1840 members of the administration had been encouraged to purchase land and take up coffee-farming, as an inducement to remain in post. This was soon extended to the public at large – Sam Baker was a beneficiary of the policy when buying his thousand acres at Newera. The short-lived land-boom attracted every kind of investor and speculator. For as long as Ceylon coffee was protected by tariff all went well. However, when the tariff was abolished by Whitehall, the price of coffee beans fell from 100 shillings a hundredweight to 45 shillings, or the cost of growing the crop in the first place. Many of the investors were ruined.

It became clear the government had raised huge sums on the sale of land that could not be easily cultivated and for which there was no crop. At the same time the land-grab had brought into the colony men of a very different stamp to Sam Baker. A scramble started for permits to produce arrack, the fiery liquor made from palm-sap. The so-called 'arrack farms' provided a quick return on capital: those who could not afford them bought government licences to open taverns, which soon proliferated in their hundreds. The government derived £60,000 a year from the sale of such permits and licences but it was revenue disastrously acquired. Arrack turned a peaceable, if indolent, native population into a society of drunks. The old trust between the governors and the governed began to collapse. What Skinner identified as 'the native gentleman', that is the native of high caste on whose loyalty and respect for the white man everything depended, now began to be sidelined. There was no question who would win in such a situation. Native Sinhalese society began to disintegrate.

It is a story of greed and opportunism that Val witnessed at first hand, one that goes unreported in *Eight Years in Ceylon*. Skinner, who should have been a hero to Sam Baker, is never mentioned

by him – any more than is Val himself. In 1849 there was a tax
revolt that led to the arrest and summary execution of hundreds
of native protestors. Oliphant's father was kept busy trying some
defendants by legal process while others were shot out of hand in
batches of four. Colombo panicked. The bishop of Ceylon fell out
with his clergy. The governor, Lord Torrington, was hastily recalled
and replaced, not by another soldier but by a senior Indian civil
servant brought out of retirement and given the sweetener of a
KCB to clean up the mess. Laurence Oliphant could not be held
by the island: in 1851, though he had been admitted to the colonial
Bar, he went to Kathmandu on the sort of sudden whim to which
Sam Baker was prone.

In April 1852 Val too made his break with Ceylon. He sold his
commission and purchased one in the 10th Hussars, then stationed
in Kirkee (Poona) on the plains above Bombay. The army, with
which he had toyed in the Ceylon Rifles, now claimed him completely. Belonging, which was the choice Val made in life, was given
a sudden and even brutal codification. He began to follow a path
that diverged from all others in the nineteenth century; and if as
a consequence his portrait seems to us unfocused, to his age he
was a familiar type. That belligerent stare, the capacity to stay silent
when nothing needed to be said, a quasi-aristocratic contempt for
outsiders, was the mark of a Victorian army officer. He already had
the temperament. The cavalry turned it into a style.

The 10th Hussars had something of a royal connection. The
Prince Regent had taken a strong personal interest in the regiment
named for him and had once tried to persuade Wellington that
he had commanded it at Waterloo. He certainly designed its uniform and bullied Beau Brummell to join. (The Beau resigned after
three years when the regiment was posted to Manchester, giving
as his reason his unwillingness to go on foreign service.) Money
got Val into the 10th. His cornetcy cost £800 to purchase at the
official rate, though he probably paid considerably over the odds
to acquire it; now only money or war would advance him higher.
At Kirkee, high up on the basalt plains of the Deccan, he could
covertly study middle-aged captains who, socially eligible though

they might be, were too poor to purchase their way and, like the long-suffering Lieutenant Skinner, waited on luck or seniority to bring them to the top of the pile. The posts they were after could quite as easily be snatched from them by an outsider, a system of arbitrary cruelty but one fiercely defended by the only authority that really mattered. In 1833 the Duke of Wellington had advised the House of Commons:

> It is the promotion by purchase which brings into the service men of fortune and education, men who have some connection with the interests and fortunes of the country, besides the Commissions which they hold from His Majesty. It is this circumstance which exempts the British Army from the character of being a 'mercenary army', and has rendered its employment for nearly a century and a half not only inconsistent with the constitutional privileges of the country, but safe and beneficial.

The 10th Hussars had already been in India for nine years when Val joined them. The officers and men of a European regiment posted abroad were the lords of creation to those around them. With nothing very onerous to do, regiments like the 10th Hussars developed to a fine point the *esprit de corps* on which their identity depended. The regiment was everything. In England it had no particular loyalty to a town or county. At this time there was no fixed brigade or divisional structure. Of the several hundred officers holding general's rank, only a fraction were on the active list. Those who were in the field considered it none of their business to administer a central policy, even had one existed. They were not managers, nor were they strategists. They were simply senior soldiers, whose job was to bring the troops to battle. The affairs of the army as a whole were conducted between harassed scribblers in thirteen separate departments – there was no general staff and no War Office. The British army, as Prince Albert concluded sourly, was 'a mere aggregation of regiments'.

It was not unusual for units to be posted to India, or elsewhere in the world, for ten or even twenty years. Once there, regimental pride kept the men from going mad or mutinous. Above them was a shadowy and unarticulated concept, 'the Queen's Army'. Below them and at their feet were the natives, the savages, the locals. For the officers, the ambience was part club, part country house. At night, dressed for dinner and with the mess silver reflecting back the candlelight, they found that India faded a little into the background and England – a certain old-fashioned and romantic image of England – was recreated. The talk, the food, the taking of wines were all carefully prescribed. Though some wives came out with their husbands – more and more since the introduction of the first steamer services – it was essentially a man's world. At Kirkee the officers built themselves a racquets court and kept up a dusty and zealously rolled cricket pitch. Every cavalry regiment encouraged racing. Shooting and fishing were a common interest – a man would have his own guns and his favourite rod with him as a matter of course.

It was not all an idyll of knightly companionship. Sir Charles Napier had only recently quit India for the second time, such a hero to his age that *The Dictionary of National Biography* gives his occupation simply as 'Conqueror of Sind'. Born in 1782, Napier had fought his way into the affections of the British army as a courageous soldier and a supreme strategist. Short-sighted and faintly querulous in appearance – with his silver spectacles and umbrella he resembled a country parson more than anything else – he was religious by temperament and radical in outlook. In a widely unpopular farewell address given in 1850, in place of the usual sentiments he castigated the officer class in India for its fondness for gambling, drinking and running up debts against the locals. Napier had the courage to point out that not every officer was a gentleman. His criticisms were directed against the Indian army but were deprecated by the entire officer caste. This was breaking a deeply cherished code of conduct: the army did not criticise its own. Napier died shortly after in 1853. As can be read on the plinth to the statue by George Canon Adams in Trafalgar Square, the greater part of the subscriptions to erect it came from private soldiers.

Val was twenty-three when he joined the 10th Hussars, a little old for such a junior officer. However, the pace of his life soon accelerated. After only a year with the 10th he sold his commission to a man called Carrington and exchanged without purchase to the 12th Lancers, a sister regiment. He went down to Bombay and sailed to join his new colleagues at the Cape. In so doing, he joined the greater, other, world at a time when Sam and John Baker were still living in a dream. Val came to realise years before his brothers that Ceylon – both the romantic landscape and the mess the admin-istration was making of it – was a long way from the heart of the beast.

For what they had at the Cape was war.

Armchair strategists of the sort that shared their port with elderly generals had long seen the Cape as being the true gateway to India, an opinion derived from their fathers at the time of Nelson. In the years since, a sea-borne threat to the colony had disappeared, possibly for ever. All the trouble came from inland. What was more, the introduction of steam on the Suez–Bombay route had changed even the basic premise of the argument: Aden and its stocks of coal was now quite as important as Cape Town. The new metaphor was not of gateways but of hinges. Right at the other end of the continent, Egypt was gradually acquiring its significance as 'the hinge of Asia'. The Cape was, like Ceylon, an example of a colony that could neither pay its way nor devise what was called in the language of the day a forward policy.

Val's little war was against the Basuto and was counted the eighth 'Kaffir War' to be fought for possession and extension of the colony's borders. The other seven had been against the implacably hostile Xhosa, who carried in their ranks the ancestors of Nelson Mandela. In April 1853 William Black, assistant surgeon to the forces in South Africa, commented on the nature of the adversary.

> The Kaffirs evidence very few, if any, moral attributes; their minds are made up of strong animal passions, not under the control of, but ministered to by a stronger intellect than most native tribes in Africa possess. They inherit a national pride from this state of mind, which little adapts them for the recep-tion of the benign influences of Christianity.

The Xhosa and the Basuto could be forgiven for taking that to be a description of the whites they had come across. The situation in the Cape was complicated by the Boers, whose Christianity was not exactly benign. The Boers liked the British not much better than the blacks and, in an attempt to find themselves new country, pushed the colony's borders ever further northwards. The British found it all very exasperating. Another Napier, no relation to the general, had written his suggestions for policing the Cape borders in 1851. Lieutenant-Colonel Napier commanded the irregular cavalry which tried to fight fire with fire by adapting its tactics to those of the enemy. After pointing out how difficult a boundary the Fish river was, he proposed

> that all Kaffir tribes be driven beyond the Kye [Kei]; that river to be then considered as the boundary of the Eastern Province; that after the expiration of a reasonable period, every male Kaffir above the age of 16, caught within this limit (whether armed or unarmed) be put to death like a beast of prey; or if taken alive that he be removed to the vicinity of Cape Town, there to work as a felon on the public roads.

This was the world in which Val and the Lancers found themselves. There were about 2000 troops already engaged in the war and the Lancers had come out with the Rifle Brigade to settle matters. Val was astonished and disgusted by what he found.

> I remember at the Cape, during the Kaffir War, seeing a regiment march into King William's town ... They were without a vestige of the original uniforms. They had all been torn to pieces, and the men had made coats out of blankets and trousers out of anything they could get. A tight, well fitting jacket is all very well for a dragoon to wear whilst walking about a country town, or making love to nursery-maids, but this is not the purpose for which a soldier is intended ...

Val's own troopers wore cavalry overalls so fashionably tight that, once dismounted, they could not get back up into their saddles without help. Soon enough the wait-a-bit thorns and acacias made a mockery of their turnout as well. Campaigning in the Cape was a bad-tempered muddle, from which only a few things emerged as beyond dispute. The Boers were excellent shots, the Basuto incredibly brave. The British marched this way and that, pinched by economies imposed by home government and maddened by the heat, the flies and the heroic obstinacy of their enemy. Scapegoats were found. Sir Harry Smith, the governor-general, was sent home. The army seethed. In its own ranks, the readiest explanation of the trouble the Kaffirs were causing was that they were egged on by the hated missionaries, who would keep telling them they were as one with the white man in the sight of God. 'We treat the Kaffirs as a power like ourselves to be treated with and to make war against as highly civilized and humane people,' complained Major Wellesley of the 25th, who though (or perhaps because) he was an Etonian wrote an English all his own. 'We are taught this by Exeter House and the Aborigines Protection Society, divine laws do not go to this length, and in return for our humanity the Enemy murder us in their old accustomed barbarous manner, and we spend several millions yearly.'

This was written in camp at the Little Caledon river in December 1852. A mile or so away was a mission house and, in the hills to Wellesley's front, Chief Moshoeshoe's kraal. It was in this tawny landscape that Val Baker took the first crucial step in his military career. It was the moment of which every subaltern dreamed. At this otherwise nondescript place, called Berea, the Lancers went into action. It was just before Christmas and the engagement was short and, on the Basuto side, bloody. Berea ended the war and was reported in the British papers as a great victory. It did not matter much that the Lancers had been ambushed when they were in the act of driving off 4000 head of cattle that did not belong to them: the black man one had in one's sights at a moment like that was indisputably from an inferior race and needed to be taught a lesson.

Not for another twenty years would Sam Baker turn his rifle against a human being, and then only with the greatest reluctance. Yet as Val discovered, Africa was a far more powerful example of 'the moral dark' than Ceylon. The action at Berea, which ended the eighth 'Kaffir War', was an unequal contest between men with spears and men with rifles. It was war on the smallest scale – the casualties on the British side were no more than fifty-four killed and wounded – but it was war all the same.

Once Moshoeshoe had sued for peace, the 12th Lancers marched south and were placed under orders to proceed to Madras. Val left the Cape with the approbation of his senior commanders, a medal and a locally bred horse, Punch. Exchanging from the Hussars to the Lancers had done him no harm at all and he returned to the languors of barracks life in the green and beautiful city of Bangalore with a story to tell. Never particularly demonstrative, nor the most approachable of mess members, he had all the same made his mark.

Less than a year later the colonel himself raced into the officers' lines waving a sheet of paper that announced a very much greater affair. Fate had dealt Val the high card. The 12th Lancers were ordered to the Crimea.

They were already three months behind the game. War was declared by Britain against Russia on 27 March 1854 but, because of the tardiness of communications and the chronic incompetence of military organisation, the regiment did not leave Bangalore until July, marching by slow stages across country to Bombay. Though they chafed at the delays, they were lucky. The regiment missed the horrors of the winter campaign and arrived at Balaclava in April 1855. No sooner had they landed than Val Baker, raised to a captain's rank, was detached from general duty and sent to serve on Raglan's staff.

The 12th Lancers arrived late at a military and diplomatic debacle that had been years, even decades, in the making. The arthritic deformation of the army that had begun before Val was born was now revealed in all its pathos. Very few general officers were under sixty – the British commander-in-chief, Lord Raglan, was sixty-eight when he took the field. The men responsible for servicing the expeditionary force once it was in the Crimea had forgotten, if they ever knew, how to do their jobs. James Filder was brought unwillingly out of a lengthy retirement to be commissary-general, in charge of the civilian contractors to the war. Like Raglan he was in his late sixties. Assured that all that was being asked of him was to supply something akin to a small colonial engagement, Filder was drawn deeper and deeper into disaster. The clerks who worked under him had no grasp of the practical needs of an army. During the campaign an officer who went down to Balaclava to requisition a couple of sacks of vegetables for his squadron was turned away with the explanation they could only be issued by the ton. A more seasoned soldier who needed a handful of nails to roof a hut was issued with and accepted twenty barrels. Things like clothing, ammunition and, above all, medical supplies were harder to come by.

The effects of mismanagement and military incompetence were everywhere. Val could ride out on the ridge that looked down on Balaclava, past thousands of items of familiar kit lying scattered and half-buried, along with bones and the rags of uniforms. The one thing not to be found anywhere was a scrap of wood, or anything else that could be burned. In the winter of 1854 soldiers had stripped the dead of their boots to use as fuel: they even tried to cut their frozen meat ration into strips of kindling. It was said that because Lord Raglan refused to allow starving horses to be withdrawn from the line, the animals ate first their harness, then each other's tails, until they perished. Men froze to death at their posts. Elizabeth Davis, who had been with Florence Nightingale at Scutari, came up to the General Hospital at Balaclava. The first case she attended was of frostbite – all the patient's toes came off with the bandages. In a neighbouring bed a comrade's hands fell off at the wrist.

For a cavalryman, the greatest of all the horrors was the destruction of the Light Brigade the previous October. Val's brother James was a cornet in the 8th Hussars and was snatched from disaster at the very last minute. Just before the charge he was told to report to Raglan's staff. The order saved his life. Tennyson's sombre valediction was published only three weeks after the battle, and while the public swallowed whole the idea that something glorious had taken place, something that threw credit on the English character, military judgement differed. A huge blunder had occurred, one that immediately turned Raglan into a lame-duck commander. Though the Prince Consort sent out Roger Fenton to make a photographic record of the campaign, the results were painterly and anodyne group portraits that told people next to nothing. It was William Russell's dispatches for *The Times* that satisfied the country's taste for blood and, along with it, revenge on the senior commanders. The army despised Russell for having committed the gravest offence it knew – 'croaking' – yet many officers were not above doing the same thing. Responsible men, driven to it by despair, betrayed their commanders with anonymous press comments or the publication of their private correspondence.

The botched campaign led to the fall of a ministry. In January 1855 Lord Aberdeen went out and Palmerston came in. He offered Lord Panmure the post of Secretary at War and he lost no time in shifting the blame from the government to the army itself. Panmure's society nickname was 'the Bison'. He put his head down and charged Raglan full on. It brought forth this remarkable reply:

> My Lord, I have passed a life of honour. I have served the crown for above fifty years; I have for the greater portion of that time been connected with the business of the Army. I have served under the greatest man of the age more than half of my life; have enjoyed his confidence and have, I am proud to say, been regarded by him as a man of truth and some judgement as to the qualification of officers; and yet, having been placed in the most difficult position in which an officer was ever called upon to serve, and having successfully carried out most difficult operations, with the entire approbation of the Queen, which is now my only solace, I am charged with every species of neglect.

So comprehensive was the criticism of Raglan and his senior officers, only the young could come out with any credit. Some of the names thrown up from the mud and ice of the Crimea were destined to become famous for as long as the century lasted. Garnet Wolseley was only twenty-one when he came out and had already been wounded and mentioned in dispatches while serving in

Burma. He was twice wounded in the campaign and again mentioned in dispatches. The French gave him the *Légion d'Honneur.* He was promoted captain in the field and after the war became a colonel at the age of twenty-five. By the time he celebrated his fortieth birthday Wolseley was a major-general and the subject of Gilbert's affectionate lyric in *The Pirates of Penzance.*

Another man who had an outstanding campaign was a twenty-one-year-old lieutenant of Engineers, Charles George Gordon. In the end he, even more than Wolseley, was to personify the new soldier-patriot. Gordon's background was impeccable. He came from four generations of officers and both his father and his brother Henry became generals. He was brought up within the walls of Woolwich barracks, where his father was Inspector of the Carriage Department of the Royal Military Academy. As a child Gordon was rumbustious and anti-authoritarian, and it was an uncomfortable surprise to his later admiring biographers to learn that at fourteen his dearest wish was to become an eunuch. The strange worm that ate away at Gordon all his life had made its first appearance.

He joined the RMA and proved to be a gifted cadet. Academically he could not be faulted. The problem lay with his temperament. Gordon was a quarrelsome young man, so much so that he lost a year's seniority for striking a colleague. There was a greater punishment still. Instead of joining the Artillery as he wished, he was commissioned into the much less glamorous Engineers, of whom it was said that their officers 'were either mad, Methodist, or married'. He served eighteen months at the depot in Chatham and then was posted to Pembroke, where the docks were being hastily fortified against the latest French invasion scare. There he met the mysterious Captain Drew, a fellow Engineer and devout evangelical Christian. Drew changed his life. After many fevered and prayerful conversations with this officer, Gordon went out to the Crimea in the simple but distressing hope of meeting his Maker.

To attract God's attention, he showed the kind of bravery in the campaign that was almost obligatory for a subaltern but which he burnished in his own fashion. He would carry out hair-raising reconnaissance of the Russian positions alone and unarmed and give himself any duties that exposed him to the greater risk. He would not accept parcels of food or clothing from home and extended this contempt for personal privation to the men serving under him, who he thought had only their own stupidity to blame for any suffering they endured. He was at last wounded. Had he died, he would have been remembered only by the sappers in his unit as the most colossal prig. Unfortunately for them, ten days after receiving his wound he returned, ready with more of the same maddening self-righteousness.

The generals at last obliged Charlie Gordon with the sort of action that should have carried him off for good – the second assault on the Redan Redoubt of 18 June 1855. It was a sapper's day out, for the plan called for ladder parties and scaling equipment. The abortive infantry attack was led by General Eyre, with whom Val Baker had served at the Cape; and there was another Cape hand in the main Engineers party, Colonel Richard Tylden. Garnet Wolseley also took part in the attack. Another lieutenant of Engineers and Gordon's friend, in so far as he had any, the giant Gerald Graham, was awarded the VC for his part in this action. Lord Raglan, who had only ten more days to live, watched the assault from an exposed position, while earnestly entreating his staff officers to seek cover behind a battery wall.

The day provided one of those telling stories by which the nineteenth-century army is illuminated. Led away from the carnage by Garnet Wolseley, Raglan paused by a wounded officer on a stretcher. 'My poor young gentleman,' he murmured with his trademark courtesy, 'I hope you are not badly hurt.' He was inviting the wounded man to think in those detached terms with which a true Briton faced death and mutilation – after all, he himself had left his right arm at Waterloo, struck by a musket ball that could as easily have done for the great Wellington, who was standing next to him. Instead of giving a smile or a feeble hurrah, the poor devil craned up from his stretcher and blamed his commander-in-chief for every drop of blood shed that day. Wolseley was outraged. It would, he said, have given him satisfaction to run his sword through the 'unmanly carcass'.

The adjective tells the story. It was not one Raglan himself would have bothered using. Like his chief, the Iron Duke, the Waterloo veteran required nothing more of his troops than that they stood their ground and took the consequences. They could be scoundrels or cowards, heroes or braggarts – it was all the same in the end. Of course he would have preferred the dying man to thank him for the courtesy of his enquiry, but if instead he screamed abuse, what had had been gained or lost? Hundreds were dying all around. It was Wolseley who thought enough of the moment to remember it later with such incandescent anger.

A week or so later Val was part of the huge funeral cortège that followed Raglan's coffin down to the sea. All four of the allied commanders-in-chief marched in the parade. There were detachments from every British regiment and the way was lined two-deep with soldiers who had not been paraded but came anyway to pay their last respects. As the bands played the Dead March from *Saul*, and even the Russian guns fell silent, what was passing was the death of the old army and its sentimental connection to the distant and almost forgotten wars against Napoleon.

As a member of Raglan's escort, Val had been placed above the battle with a highly privileged view of the conduct of the campaign. A more ambitious – or indiscreet – officer might have attempted something in print or, if not that, written letters to his family intended for posterity. That was not Val's nature. In the three short years since leaving Ceylon, the principal military virtue Val had acquired happened to coincide with his private character. As he rode down the hill following Raglan's coffin, he kept up that social mask which is the hardest of all to maintain, an implacable and chilling *visage de bois*. He was twenty-eight years old and not about to croak.

In the late summer of 1855, when the war had reached stalemate and no one could stomach the idea of a second winter campaign, the British ambassador to Constantinople came up to Balaclava with an embassy retinue. His purpose was to tour the battlefields and distribute medals. To Val's complete surprise the ambassador's private secretary was none other than his friend Laurence Oliphant, whom he had last seen heading for Kathmandu.

Val gave him dinner in the cavalry camp. Loquacious as ever, Oliphant swiftly took charge of the evening. Yes, he had been to Nepal, but then, three years ago, at the time Val was fighting at the Cape, he made a semi-secret journey from St Petersburg down the Volga and along the Black Sea littoral. This was a restricted military area, about which the Russians were (understandably, in the light of circumstance) very sensitive. It turned out that Oliphant was one of the few Englishman ever to have penetrated to Sebastopol itself, over which so much blood had been spilt. Disguised as a German farm-hand, he skulked round the streets with his eyes wide open, taking particular interest in the massive fortifications. He correctly identified the Malakhov redoubt as the key to the city's defences. When he came home, he wrote a book about his travels, published a few months before war with Russia was declared. The point of the story was in its coda. Oliphant had been secretly summoned to the Horse Guards at the end of 1853 and quizzed by Raglan about what he had seen – and this, he declared complacently to Val, was why they were all where they were now.

Three years had changed these two men to a remarkable degree. The hare was dining with the tortoise. Oliphant had been presented at court in 1852 – the queen fixing him with a peculiarly intent stare, though why she should do so he left Val (and us) to guess at – and he also let fall offhandedly that literary London considered him one of the better young writers of the day. Only recently he had reviewed *Eight Years in Ceylon* for *Blackwood's Magazine*. In fact, he remembered now an interesting and recent anecdote about Sam that his brother might like to hear.

It was a tale told with all of Oliphant's penchant for mystery and intrigue, and it began on the boat taking him from Marseilles on his way to take up his post at the embassy in Constantinople. On the same ship was a fellow called James Hanning Speke, a captain in the 46th Bengal Infantry, a native regiment that Oliphant did not for a moment suppose Val had ever come across. Speke was something of an amateur explorer and towards the end of his service in the Punjab had taken the idea of shooting in Central Africa. In 1854 he was on his way home to England to volunteer for the Turkish contingent when he stopped off at Aden. There he met a Lieutenant Richard Burton of the 18th Bombay Native Infantry.

They met by chance in the only decent hotel at Steamer Point. The Baker connection to the story was apparently very slight: Sam was staying at the same hotel, on his way home with his family from Ceylon. The three men, very different in personality but all of them interested in the empty spaces on the map, fell to discussing Africa together. Burton, very much the more finished article as an explorer, let it be known in his languid, mocking way that he was thinking of setting up an expedition to Somalia. Had Sam Baker not just given up one romantic dream, it was exactly the sort of challenge he would have jumped at. Instead, Speke begged to go.

The expedition nearly killed him – he was stabbed eleven times by a fanatic's spear – and he found he did not like Burton half as much as he supposed he would; but seeing Africa for the first time left him with an impossible dream, one which Oliphant winkled out on the ship from Marseilles. When the present war was over, he was determined to return to Africa with Burton and discover the source of the Nile, believed to be located in some as yet unknown inland sea. If the sea was there, as some ancients supposed, no white man had ever seen it. To find it was the Holy Grail of geography. If such a thing could be accomplished, and the discovery claimed for Britain, it would be the sensation of the century.

As the bottle emptied and the conversation dwindled, Oliphant may have come to his senses and remembered where he was – in a sea of unmarked graves with a soldier for his host. Both Speke and Burton were soldiers too, of course, but nothing like this tight-buttoned young cavalryman with his unsmiling eyes and severe manner. Though a huge bell had chimed from the future, the story had fallen horribly flat. Val had made his choices in life, and they did not include crack-brained schemes to look for the source of the Nile, least of all with Indian officers from nondescript regiments. Long before the evening ended, Oliphant realised he had been talking to the wrong brother.

Val still had a war to fight. He took part in a cavalry battle to the east of Sebastopol in the swamps of the Tcherneya river and then, on 5 September, a three-day bombardment commenced that signalled the end of the campaign. The Malakhov redoubt, the one that Oliphant had spied in 1853 as the key to the fortifications, was taken by the French. As soon as he saw the tricolour flying above the carnage, the Russian commander, Prince Gortschakov, began the systematic destruction of Sebastopol – in a series of huge explosions, the docks and harbour, every arsenal and store was blown up. And then the Russians left.

Even at the end the British blundered. Their part in the final battle was to make yet another assault on the Redan. For what he described as their honour, General Simpson, who had succeeded Raglan, ordered the attack to be made by those regiments who had tried with the Redan twice before. Simpson, like Raglan, was a veteran of Quatre Bras and it seemed to him only proper to extend his troops this courtesy. Most of those who took part were raw recruits, terrified replacements for those who had already fallen. Contrary to the ideas which had animated the old army, regimental pride could not be relied upon completely. The last hurrah at Sebastopol was mingled with yet more accusations of incompetence; and, shockingly, cowardice. As for the prize itself, when Val and the Lancers rode down into the city, they found nothing but streets blocked with fallen masonry and the smoking ruins of the port and harbour.

Though the war did not end until the following March, both sides had reached an exhausted stalemate. Val and his younger brother James left the plains above Balaclava without regret. In the new cavalry camp set up at Scutari they took a stone-built house that looked across the straits to Constantinople and there they invited Colonel Tottenham of the 10th Hussars as house-guest.

This return to the pleasures of a good table and decent wines, exclusively military conversation, was the world Val had chosen over the picture held out by the restless Oliphant. The main topic of discussion was the role of the cavalry, for the destruction of the Light Brigade had opened up a debate not simply about tactics and strategy, but about basic organisation.

Tottenham was one of that minority of senior officers who admired the tragic figure of Louis Nolan, the man who had ridden screaming up to Cardigan to try to divert the Light Brigade into the right valley, only to be blown to bits. Now that the war was as good as over, the post-mortem judgements were flying in thick and fast. Val, like his former commanding colonel, held that while Nolan was a very brave man, that was not the whole of it. He was also a brilliant horseman. His short book on the cavalry, drawn from his experiences of service with European armies, was a manual that should be taken to heart. Nolan's point was simple – gallantry and courage were not enough. In these virtues, as the Light Brigade had shown to such terrible effect, Britain lacked nothing. Val saw that it was time for a continuation of this root and branch reappraisal of cavalry, not as a social class – about which of course there could be no criticism – but regarding men and horses, the weight they rode, the saddles they sat, everything down to the last details of their equipment. Colonel Tottenham was encouraging. When the 12th Lancers were ordered back to India, Val retransferred to the 10th Hussars and went home with them to England. Once there, he immediately sought leave of absence to go to Europe and see what Nolan had seen.

THREE

—◦—

Laurence Oliphant's musings on Africa were prescient. What Speke had told him on the passage from Marseilles to Constantinople was no more than an explorer's tale about adventure and camping out under the Somali stars – along with a great deal of grumbling about his companion Burton. However, the idea of an expedition to discover the source of the Nile, which for Speke was simply a desire to shine in the world's admiration, had a much wider political and cultural importance. Famously, the Greek historian Herodotus had penetrated as far as the Nile's first cataract in the fifth century BC and stood pondering on the origin of all that water boiling over the rocks. The eighteenth century closed with Napoleon's military expedition to Egypt in 1798; this time it was Citizen General Belliard who peered through eyes inflamed by desert ophthalmia at the same puzzle. The rocks of the cataract, he wrote to his diary, 'seem to signify that here are the limits of the civilised world. Here nature seems to bar our route and to say to us, *Stop, go no further.*' So far as Napoleon was concerned this was indeed the southern limit of his conquest. The disastrous expedition to Syria followed. Only a year later, left stranded by the Corsican, it was the unlucky Belliard, now back in Cairo, who surrendered the city to the British without a fight.

Despite the screw gunboats of the Royal Navy nosing along the lower reaches of the Congo and the Niger, or the Boer caravans trekking north from the Cape Colonies, the interior of Africa lay for the most part unexplored, a whole continent without, in the European sense, a history. The greater part of it was a geographical blank, often imagined as a sandy and largely empty wasteland. Relentless agitation had kept one African issue to the forefront of British interest – the west coast, considered to be the cradle of slavery. The Anti-Slavery Society was founded in London in 1824 and soon claimed 1300 branches. These and the readership of its monthly magazine became the conscience of the whole country in the matter. At Exeter Hall in the Strand, premises it shared with the Bible Society and other temperance and philanthropic organis-ations, the Anti-Slavery Society set as its aim the abolition of slavery not simply in the British Empire, but everywhere on earth. Such a moral crusade called in the end, whether the pious realised it or not, for guns.

It had them. Since 1834 slow-sailing squadrons of the Royal Navy had been patrolling the west African coast in an attempt to suppress the sea-borne trade. It has been estimated that at one time one in six of all Royal Naval vessels were engaged in blockade and stop-and-search duties. Sometimes the results elevated an unknown to the ranks of the Christian heroes. William Laird Clowes's *History of the Royal Navy* mentions one.

> On August 13th, 1844, being off Fish Bay, on the West Coast of Africa, in a four-oared gig with but one spare hand, Mate John Francis Tottenham, of the Hyacinth, 18, Commander Francis Scott, pursued and ultimately drove ashore a Brazilian slave brig of 200 tons, carrying two 4-prs., and a well armed crew of eighteen, four of whom were wounded by the fire from Tottenham's musket. For this service, Tottenham was made a lieutenant on December 27th following.

Only three years earlier Tottenham had been in the South China seas aboard the *Hyacinth*, engaged in actions at Canton and Macao. He was exactly the kind of heroic figure the anti-slavery movement wanted to hear about, for the popular idea of Africa was as a place of moral horror. All that most Britons knew of this vast continent was death by fever and the cruel and almost casual snuffing out of Christian good. Since the end of the great European wars millions of flintlock muskets had disappeared into Africa, a great number of them manufactured in Birmingham. Who knew what foul purpose they served, except to fire on honest tars or terrorise a thousand peaceful villages? This was the great challenge. If anyone was going to turn such a situation around by moral example, it should ideally be an Englishman, one of God's chosen.

History provided a Scot. In December 1856 a hitherto unknown missionary returned to England and caused an immediate sensation. This taciturn and apparently unassuming man had walked Africa from coast to coast, not merely a great feat of exploration but also a stunning demonstration of human will and physical endurance. He could hardly have had a better curriculum vitae. Sent to work as a child of nine in Blantyre Mills, David Livingstone spent his first week's wage on Ruddiman's *Rudiments of Latin*. Slowly and painfully, he educated himself enough to qualify as a doctor, with the intention of becoming a medical missionary. The Opium Wars prevented him from going to China, and in the year Sam and John Baker were married (1843) he accepted a post to go and do God's work in southern Africa. He lived and worked there in complete obscurity, exploring the Kalahari, map-making, discoursing with witch-doctors, tramping the unknown. Whether he ever came home again, or was instead fated to leave his bones under a small pile of rock or in some sandy desert grave was a matter for God and the London Missionary Society.

Livingstone's *Missionary Travels* was published in November 1857 on the back of considerable hysteria worked up by the Royal Geographical Society, which had already awarded the author its coveted Gold Medal. A second edition of the book was called for even before the first 12,000 copies went on sale. After so many years of nonentity David Livingstone found himself a national hero. Mayors tumbled over one another to give him the freedom of their cities. A public subscription fund was opened. The queen received him in private audience. Not many of his most fervent admirers realised how rich he was – the press saw him as some sort of apostolic figure wandering in the wilderness who had been brought back to London to blink in the unaccustomed light of hero-worship. During his travels he had almost forgotten how to speak English.

His book delighted by its close detail and conversational tone. There are many fine touches. At the court of the chief Shinte Livingstone learns there are two other visitors expected who may also be European. He is galvanised. 'Have they the same hair?' he asks, hardly daring to breathe. Shinte's messengers look at the explorer with new interest. 'Is that hair? We thought it was a wig.' In Zambezi country he is distressed to find the Batoka hopelessly degraded from their addiction to smoking *mutokwane*, which Livingstone identified as cannabis sativa.

> They like its narcotic effects, though the violent coughing which accompanies a couple of puffs appears distressing and causes a feeling of disgust in the spectator. This is not diminished on seeing the usual practice of taking a mouthful of water and squirting it out together with the smoke, then uttering a string of half-incoherent sentences, usually in self-praise.

Anecdotes like this made the book unputdownable. The interior of Africa was not after all a desert populated only by snakes and nomads. On the contrary, Livingstone's savages and aborigines were on the whole perfectly amiable people – wrong-headed, careless about dress and deportment, but educable. There was even more. He wrote with the complete assurance of a man who might well be a missionary but who could also identify his country's interests and speak to the nation's concerns. In Livingstone's Africa the Portuguese might leave their consuls to languish at some river's edge, their black mistresses sweeping the porch with laconic passes of a handful of reeds, but the true Briton had a duty to report as well as to endure. The question was not so much what (for example) the Zambezi basin was like, but what it could become, under a wiser stewardship and with the improving genius of a dominant power guided by God.

With his hideously scarred arm, mauled by a lion only six months after he set foot in Africa, his idiosyncratic peaked cap, gruff Scottish accent and taste for hard beds and simple foods,

Livingstone was a walking advertisement for the *Travels*. He was forty-four years old and looked every day of it. He was several times mobbed in the street and on his visits to church men would scramble back across the pews for the honour of shaking him by the hand. Though there was a strong element of hysteria in this, he was giving back what his readers were most hungry to have – a sense of their God-given purpose. The word slavery first occurs thirty pages into his text and those of his readers who liked to believe in the actual superiority of black over white, innocence over experience, seemed to have found their man.

> We cannot fairly compare these poor people with ourselves [he warned], who have an atmosphere of Christianity and enlightened public opinion, the growth of centuries, around us, to influence our deportment; but let anyone from the natural and proper point of view behold the public morality of Griqua Town, Kuruman, Litaklong and other villages and remember what even London was a century ago, and he must confess that the Christian mode of treating aborigines is incomparably the best.

The interpolated phrase about London is a strong clue to the times. What was exciting about missionary Christianity was how fresh and charged it was, how it borrowed nothing from the past. Missionary work *was* discovery – those who had been lost were found. Men like Livingstone were surely the divine instrument by which the mysterious Griqua Town had been transformed from squalor and ignorance to a state of grace. If it could work there, then why not round the next bend in the river, or in some even more distant kraal? Livingstone was pushing on an open door – his audience wanted to believe him almost before they opened the pages of his book. Its popularity was easily explained. By 1860 more than half of all voluntary contributions to charities went to Bible and Home Missionary societies and their fellow-workers (and competitors) the Foreign Missionary societies. In the eighteenth century there were nine such institutions. This number had risen to seventy-one. Twenty-seven had been founded in the previous decade.

*　　*　　*

Six months or so after Henrietta's funeral, in the autumn of 1855, a chastened Sam Baker went out to visit his soldier brothers in the house at Scutari. His mood was sombre and vacillating. He had even begun to think of entering the church himself. Richard Hall, his most sympathetic modern biographer, suggests he was close to a nervous breakdown and this may have been caused in part by the suspicion that his ship had sailed without him. What he had done in Ceylon was now an old story – a war and Henrietta's death had been struck parenthetically into the text.

He had not seen Val for four years and his youngest brother James for much longer than that. Sam could be in no doubt that he was an interloper. He had come out with some idea of exploring the Black Sea littoral – but that was already being undertaken by the army, which had new frontiers to survey and chart. As to his guns, it was almost an indecency to bring them. Even to be drinking wine and looking out towards the domes and minarets of Constantinople was a strange holiday for a widower with four young children to care for.

There was news of friends and acquaintances to catch up on. He remembered meeting Speke and Burton in Aden and listened intently to Val's update. Everything Oliphant had said about Speke's impossible dream had come to pass. He had resigned his commission with the Turkish contingent and gone back to Africa, summoned there by Burton to set out in search of Lake Nyassa. Sam smouldered. He certainly considered himself quite the equal of Speke. As for Oliphant, that strange will-o'-the-wisp, he too was gone. A San Francisco journalist named William Walker had hit on the bright idea of seizing Nicaragua and making himself president. That was where Val's restless friend was headed now, probably under cover for the Foreign Office. These stories hurt Sam. Here was this larger-than-life figure, wined and dined in the camp of the victors and struck down by an overwhelming hesitation. It was a life programmed for high adventure that had in the space of a year been rendered shapeless.

When he first came home from Ceylon Sam had gone to Scotland and taken a lease on a small property called Lochgarry House.

One day on the Duke of Atholl's estates, in the presence of the duke and several carriage loads of ladies, he ran down a stag with a pack of dogs in the Ceylon manner. He dispatched it not with a rifle but with the famous hunting knife, up to his waist in water in some Highland stream. 'Weel,' commented the duke's gillie Macarra sourly, 'you've just ruined the dogs forever, and there'll be nae hauding them frae the deer noo. They'll just spoil the flesh and tear the deer to pieces.' Much did Sam – or come to that the duke himself – care. It was an advertisement for something that class valued almost as much as prudence and sagacity. Baker had shown an overweening pride of life, an almost animal intensity that was the polar opposite of middle-class propriety. There were undoubtedly some aristocratic landowners who took Macarra's view, but they were balanced by those whose taste for eccentricity extended even to deer-stalking. Men who murdered horses by putting them at impossible obstacles, who placed extravagant bets on themselves to swim lakes or jump from roof to roof in Cambridge colleges were always memorable. They were like men who ruined themselves at cards or went into voluntary exile after some imprudent elopement. Their credo was never to explain, never to apologise. In such a world as this, apolitical and self-indulgent, Sam Baker might have found his niche. He was rich, he was talented and he owed no man his allegiance. Killing his stag by running it to a standstill and then wrestling its head round while he severed its spinal cord with a single thrust was a story that could travel round Scotland. Then came Bagnères.

Sam returned home from the Crimean holiday looking for meaning and direction. One of his few fast friends in Ceylon had been Edward Stuart-Wortley, whose grandfather had been Lord President of the Council and a noted Whig minister. When Sam saw the immense public reaction to Livingstone's travels, he asked Stuart-Wortley, now back in England himself as the second Lord Wharncliffe, to help him get a post with the explorer when he made his much-heralded return to Africa. It was a despairing piece of over-reaching. Letters he himself wrote to Livingstone went unanswered or were deflected with a few noncommittal words;

Wharncliffe reported that the Foreign Office was unsympathetic.

Though he did not know it, Sam was trying to force himself upon a very delicate situation. The proposed Zambezi expedition – or Livingstone's Return – was clearly the blue riband of adventure – the *Missionary Travels* had done their work and there was no man with a higher standing in the world of African exploration. Livingstone was not the first to have crossed Central Africa from coast to coast, not even the first white man, but he was of course the first Briton. That he had done it in a spirit of such long-suffering piety, on a salary from the London Missionary Society of £100, gave his story enormous allure. He was without doubt the society's most famous missionary, credited with conversion of the heathen on an unprecedented scale. Those who had direct dealings with him found him difficult to handle, but then if he was doing God's work, what did a few rough edges matter?

There was, however, a devious side to Livingstone. Understandably enough, he considered he held the future of the southern continent in his hands. The LMS plans for him were simple: he should go back and carry on quietly with God's work, forswearing all other ambition. The society had a strong interest in keeping the Livingstone legend within its own control but its secretary, Mr Tidman, also guarded a well-kept secret. His investigations had shown that, far from converting Africans in their hundreds, Livingstone had succeeded with just one. Southern Africa was not ablaze with Christianity after all.

Captain Peyton and the officers of HMS *Frolic*, which lifted Livingstone off the coast at the mouth of the Zambezi at the end of his epic walk, also had an interesting story to tell, one that would further dent the reputation of the great missionary if it ever came out in all its detail. When he said goodbye to his bearers, the explorer reluctantly agreed to take to England with him his interpreter and right-hand man, Sekweku. The African had never seen the sea and when he first set eyes on it he found himself staring at line after line of unbroken surf. Captain Peyton sent two boats across the bar to bring off the two men. Livingstone feigned cheerful indifference and in any case he knew enough of the ways of sailors to put his trust in them completely. Sekweku was terrified. He knew all about canoes and was a good swimmer but being rushed into a boat in a cloud of spray and spume on this tumultuous, God-forsaken beach must have had the air of finality about it. Livingstone described the passage out to the *Frolic*. 'The waves were so high that, when the cutter was in one trough, and we in the pinnace in another her mast was hid. We then mounted to the crest of the wave, rushed down the slope, and struck the water again with a blow which felt as if she had struck bottom.'

However, once on the ship and under way, both the missionary and his servant were treated with such kindness that Sekweku calmed down. Livingstone had previously warned him that he would die of cold in England, to which he replied, 'That is nothing, let me die at your feet.' All this was forgotten as the *Frolic* set sail for Mauritius, where Livingstone was to pick up a passage home via the Red Sea. The crew liked Sekwetu, he grew a little more used to the ocean, and altogether things looked better. Several times he said to Livingstone, 'Your countrymen are very agreeable.' However, when the ship hove to at Mauritius, having sailed into a dead calm, Sekweku tried to stab a seaman and then, in the most grotesque form of suicide imaginable, leapt overboard and hauled himself hand over hand down the anchor chain. His body was never recovered. Such an ugly and inexplicable death was a strange commentary on the civilising capacities of the white man.

Despite Mr Tidman's urgings on behalf of the London Missionary Society, the explorer had no intention of going back as a medical missionary on a pittance. Was there anyone in London who could see the bigger picture and respond to the Scot's mixture of naivety and worldliness? There was. The president of the Royal Geographical Society was a geologist, the sixty-three-year-old Sir Roderick Murchison. It was through his efforts that Livingstone had been talked up as the greatest explorer since the Elizabethan age. Never before had the society's Gold Medal award been the subject of such press interest. Livingstone was the man of the hour, and Murchison the man to exploit him.

At its foundation, the RGS had been a modest affair, more of an explorer's club than anything else. Murchison had turned around its fortunes with a long and patient campaign and was now in his fourth period of office as president. Though he was a moderate scholar, his true gift lay in politics – he was a consummate fixer. In a secret correspondence Murchison persuaded Livingstone to end his allegiance to the London Missionary Society. The explorer now arranged to go back to Africa under the aegis of the RGS with the additional endorsement of the government, which furnished him with a £2000 treasury fund and a salary of £500. Livingstone, the saver of souls, would be a nominal British consul to the Portuguese possessions on the east coast, while at the same time exploring the Zambezi with a view to opening it up to European settlement.

Sam's proposal was that he should attach himself to this second exploration. He was finally turned down both by the Foreign Secretary and by Livingstone himself. Lord Clarendon's motives were perhaps to avoid, in terms of temperament, one of the greatest mismatches of the century. He may also have inclined a little to Livingstone's own dismissal of Sam Baker's application, which the missionary derided in a single damning phrase – Baker was 'a mere nimrod'. The two men never met. Sam was astute enough to have grasped something about Livingstone that he already realised about himself. They were both loners. With Livingstone it was almost an obsession. He was an indifferent geographer. The Zambezi, which he assured Murchison was navigable all the way to the Victoria Falls, was interrupted in its passage to the sea by a series of cataracts, the largest of which was the Kebrabasa Rapids. It was the one stretch of the river that Livingstone had not surveyed and ignorance of it was to prove fatal to the expedition.

Had Sam gone with Livingstone, he would certainly have fallen foul of him within a few weeks. Commander Bedingfield RN, who later rose to be an admiral, was in charge of river transport and was a practical man of action in the Baker mould. Bedingfield was quite appalled to find the Zambezi nothing like it had been described and the expedition leader a man incapable of making sound decisions. Livingstone, who had a fetish about evacuating the bowels regularly, wrote the commander a magisterial note.

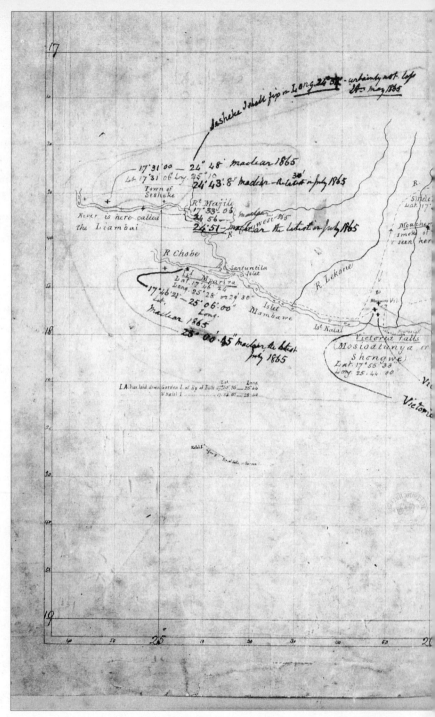

Livingstone's detailed annotations of the course of the Zambezi, 1865. His note on 'the river here was not seen' (centre) led to the disastrous navigation of the impassable Kebrabasa Falls.

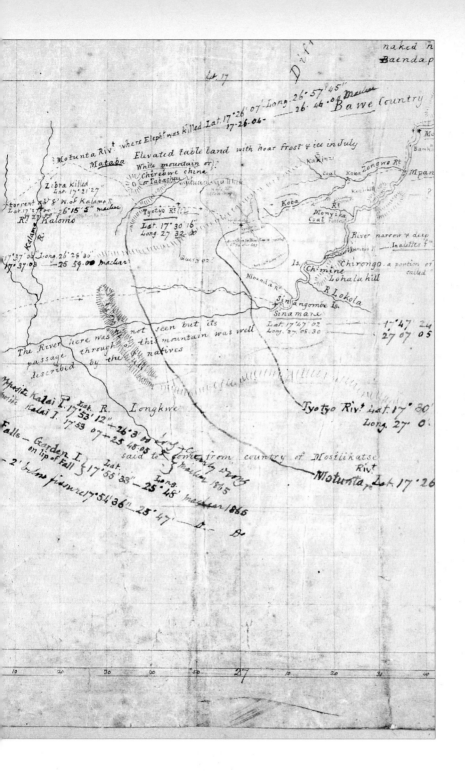

naked n
Baendap

Lat 17

Dift

Lat. 17°26′07′ Long. 26°57′45″
17.26.04   26.44.00 maclear

Bawe Country

Motunta Rivt where Eleptt was killed Lat. 17°26′07′

Elevated table land with hoar frost & ice in July

Mataba

White mountain or
Chirebwe chine
or Tabachu

Zebra killed
Lat. 17°21′27″

Kakinzu

Coal Koba Zongwe Rt Mpan
Kezzi hill Bank

torrent 2b′ 8′ W. of Kalamo R.
Lat. 17°3′00   26°15′5″ maclear

Koba Rt
Monyika Coal field

Rt. 11 Kalomo

Tyotyo Rt

Lat. 17°30′16″
Long. 27 32 30

River narrow & deep
In dittes f″

17°37′00 Long. 26°28′30″
17.37.00   25.59.00 maclear

Guery oz!

Is. Chi·mine Chirongo a portion of
called
Lohala hill
R. Lokola

Moenda R

Sinangombe Is.
Sinamare
Lat. 17°47′02
Long. 27°05.30

1°47′24
27 07 05

The River here was not seen but its
passage   through   this mountain was well
described   by the   natives

Opposite Kalai I. 17°53′12″ 26°3′00 Lat. R. Longkwe
Kalai I. 17°53′07 25°48.05 maclear

Tyotyo Rivt lat 17° 30′
Long. 27 0.

Falls – Garden I. Lat. 17°55′33″ 25°48′ Long.
17°54′36″ 25°47′ maclear 1865
2′ below fissure D   D

said to come from country of Mosilikatse
maclear 1866

Motunta, Lat. 17°26

A pretty extensive acquaintance with African Expeditions enables me to offer a hint which, if you take it in the same frank and friendly spirit in which it is offered, you will on some future day thank me and smile at the puerilities that now afflict you. With the change of climate there is often a peculiar condition of the bowels which makes the individual imagine all sorts of things in others. Now I earnestly and most respectfully recommend a little aperient medicine occasionally and you will find it much more soothing than writing official letters.

Bedingfield considered himself and his rank insulted and left soon after. In time the expedition claimed all but one of Livingstone's officers – and the death of his wife Mary. There were collateral disasters. In dumping the London Missionary Society, Livingstone was obliged to find a replacement for himself in a mission among the Makalolo people. Two couples and their children arrived at the place designated by 'Dr L.', armed with every assurance from him that the work would go well and their ministry prosper. Eight Sundays after their arrival three of the adults and five of the seven children were dead. Those who followed Livingstone fared little better. Bishop Mackenzie, a high churchman in the very image of muscular Christianity, brought out a Universities Mission of similarly hearty and sporty young men. Cruelly misled as to the nature of the Zambezi, Mackenzie lasted almost exactly a year before dying of emaciation.

Sam had far superior organising ability and a better grasp of how to manage men than ever Livingstone possessed. His view of the 'native' was likewise more realistic and clear-eyed. And although Livingstone was a medical doctor, the elephant-hunter was a better practical first-aider. It was fortunate for him that his face did not fit. Death or the social stigma of having let the great patriot down would have been sure to follow. As it was, life had something more in store for him. Africa beckoned – but first there was an adventure of an altogether different kind. It took place not on the Zambezi, but the Danube.

* * *

In March 1849 Lord Dalhousie annexed the Punjab and declared it a British province. From this transaction the queen got a territory the size of Italy, the Koh-i-noor diamond and the deposed maharaja, a young boy called Duleep Singh. The Koh-i-noor was recut and reset and Duleep Singh was sent to court at Windsor, where the queen took a shine to him – in 1854 she commissioned a full-length likeness by Winterhalter, showing the young prince in exotic costume, his turban sparkling with gems. Singh was, by general consent, as pretty as his picture, a willowy and androgynous youth with olive skin and liquid eyes. One bemused American described him as 'opening like a tulip'. Lucky boy: God now claimed him as an Englishman.

He was the first of many Indians it gave Victoria pleasure to contemplate. Though he was prone to occasional fits of the giggles, he was so pliant and winsome, so quick a study, that he made an enviable comparison with the queen's own eldest son. Until he came of age he was given a state pension and a tutor and guardian was found for him in the person of an old Punjab hand, Dr – later Sir John – Login. Like the queen herself, the young man took a liking to Scotland. Every autumn he rented Menzies Castle in Perthshire, where he indulged his passion for shooting. It was only a matter of time before this fantastical figure met his neighbour in Scotland, the unconventional slayer of deer, Samuel White Baker. Sam was home from the Crimea with nothing but his guns for solace. It occurred to both of them that what was needed was larger game than was available in Scotland. Duleep Singh had an additional impetus in that Sir John Login's guardianship was legally at an end: he wanted to do something in his own right.

The two men hit upon the idea of going down the Danube together and hunting for bear. The prince would travel incognito and without an equerry. This plan alarmed the queen, the more so when she learned that in Lady Login's opinion Sam would make a very dubious chaperon. To begin with, there was a seventeen-year age-gap between the two sportsmen. Mr Baker was completely unknown at court, nor did he have, for expeditions of this kind, the useful reassurance of a military background. Moreover, though on good days the prince was all that could be expected of a Christian gentleman, there was a tendency in him to backslide. He was capable of a distressing eastern turpitude, lit by flashes of blind anger. Finally, though he was a devoted falconer, Duleep Singh was something of an eccentric shot. He had once astonished some aristocratic hosts by standing up in a moving carriage and loosing both barrels at a sitting bird, narrowly missing his companions. On another occasion on the way home from the braes he had from sheer *joie de vivre* shot a widow woman's cat sitting peaceably on a doorstep.

Until he met Sam, the prince's life had been flattered by an amused sycophancy. One of his dear friends was Lord Hatherton, who held estates in Staffordshire. Inside the parish church at Penkridge the Hatherton family pews were taken out and replaced by armchairs and a working fireplace. At the beginning of the service curtains would be drawn round this cosy scene and his lordship would stand warming himself in front of the hearth and reading *The Times,* rattling the pages to indicate when the sermon had gone on long enough. The noisy and bearded Mr Baker was obviously a very different kind of acquaintance.

The young prince supposed that Sam would use the connection to his own advantage at some time in the future; that was the way of things. Meanwhile, shooting bears in snowstorms was not the only pleasure he had in mind. The sporting tour would finally swing south to Constantinople and after that Rome, where the youthful Prince of Wales would be waiting to receive his friend and (hopefully) have relief from the boredom of an educational visit got up by his father. Lady Login also intended to be in Rome. She wanted Duleep Singh to meet the lissom but indolent Princess Victoria Coumura, with a view to marrying her.

They set off in late December of 1858, their luggage making an agreeable mountain on the platform at every change of train. The prince travelled as Captain Robert Melville, an incognito that did not last very long. In Vienna the emperor himself greeted them and took them shooting on the Esterhazy estates. Everyone understood that Singh was wealthy, possibly incredibly wealthy. He was also, as Sam Baker was beginning to discover, not quite as sporty as he liked to make out. There was hunting and there was hunting. When they set out from Vienna on a converted grain barge crammed with champagne crates, a girl the prince had picked up went with them. On 16 January 1859 the Vienna *Fremden-Blatt* announced: 'The Maharajah Duleep Singh, well known in English fashionable circles, has chosen unto himself a bride at Pest. They are now resting at Semlin. The marriage will take place at Galatz and after the ceremony the young couple will proceed to India.' Apart from the presence of the girl, not one word of this was true, least of all the return to India, a political and diplomatic impossibility, as Duleep Singh was to find out. Meanwhile, Sam installed three stoves on the leaky and decrepit barge and the days passed in drinking champagne and staring out at the blinding snow as they careered south and east along the Danube.

After successfully shooting the famous Iron Gates, the love-boat struck an ice floe and began to break up. The travellers came ashore on the Turkish side of the river at the fortress city of Vidin. Albanian mercenaries terrorised the filthy streets, the local pasha suspected the shipwrecked sportsmen of being spies and only the presence of Austrian and Russian consuls gave them security from arrest. Hotel accommodation was basic, few houses had window-glass and dirt and rubbish were thrown directly into the frozen streets. Vidin in deep midwinter was no advertisement for eastern exoticism. It had minarets but they overlooked a terrible squalor. For the prince there was little to see or do. Only a month or so earlier he had been dining with the queen at Windsor. Now, even with the solace of a lady companion, he was bored. There was only one upcoming attraction – the Vidin slave market.

Of the two travellers, it might be supposed that Duleep Singh would find the buying and selling of young white slaves the more diverting spectacle. There was nothing dissimulated about the business: what was on offer was youth and beauty, drawn from as many as half a dozen nationalities. Some were vassals of the Turkish Empire, some had fled across the river from revolutionary politics in Europe. The market was an expression of Balkan chaos, a trade in displaced persons. The Turks who attended were not looking for boys to draw their ploughs or girls to sing at their work in the dairy. The British and French had long put pressure on Constantinople to curb this traffic in sexual slavery. It was said that the khedive of Egypt had a ship specially commissioned to cruise the Ionian shores in search of young flesh. A girl could be bought at auction for as little as £5.

It requires a great feat of imagination to picture what happened at the Vidin auction. Muffled up to the ears in scarves, warmed by a piratical beard, Sam began bidding. The lot in question was a slim, broad-faced young teenager, her blonde hair piled haphazardly on the crown of her head. She spoke German but was actually Hungarian, something that only came out later. The auction room is easy to recreate – leaky stoves, the babble of languages Sam could not speak, the prurient interest of his neighbours. The girl was hardly parading before him in harem trousers with a jewel stuck in her navel: there were beggars on the street outside who looked just like her, dressed in rags, lips blue with cold. To buy a human being in the presence of a hundred other sweaty and shoving men was one thing. To do so watched by the maharaja of Punjab, with whom you are already falling out, was a form of social suicide.

He bought the girl. She was named, or he named her, Florence. How much she knew or could remember of her origins we shall never know. She was seventeen years old. Whatever she told him in the only language they had in common – German – was probably a sanitised version of the truth. She was an orphan, of that she was sure. In the background was war and revolution. It is possible to conjure from all this a philanthropic gesture on his part – he bought her to save her from a fate worse than death at someone else's hands. And this of course was the net outcome. He saw a waif. She saw a large man with a striking black beard and guns for company. What happened next, in the weeks or months ahead, was beyond her control. For the time being, to have clean new clothes, stockings and boots, to bathe in hot water and have pins and combs for her hair, to be treated with respect – all this was enough.

The hunting expedition came to an abrupt halt. The four of them posted in a ramshackle coach to Bucharest, where the prince's girl was paid off and the two men made a dry-eyed parting. There is no doubt that some of the facts did leak out in time – for example, in the account Lady Login made to the queen of Her Majesty's young favourite and his winter journey, his doughty companion is never once mentioned. Victoria was not slow to seize the point. There was another source of potential gossip. The British consul in Bucharest, Robert Colquhoun, made a shrewd guess at what was going on. It happened that Colquhoun owned a house in the Forest of Atholl and knew Lochgarry House well. It was entertaining to this elderly bachelor to swap fishing stories with Sam, but he was the first to indicate how much of a sticking point Florence was. He was, he regretted, quite unable to receive her. But then why should Sam want to put her to the inspection of Mr Colquhoun? The answer was he was in love.

It was wonderful, but it was much more dangerous than shooting bear. There were limits to even Sam's disdain of conventional morality – what he had done and what had happened in the bedroom since was unforgivable, even by his own family. Florence was a quick learner but she needed a much more plausible background than the one she had been able to furnish. Colquhoun was right to balk at meeting her. She was fifteen years younger than Sam. She might be Hungarian, she might again be Armenian. Sam reflected. If he merely wanted a temporary Balkan solace, she would do very well. If he wanted a more permanent liaison, he would have to find a way of reinventing her, teaching her English, above all smoothing a way for her to meet his four children. For the time being, it was clear, he was more or less forced to stay where he was in the Balkans and try to keep the whole business secret.

As it happened, an opportunity existed. After the Crimean War there was a rush of venture capital to Turkey. The sultan was a great enthusiast of railways – he bought locomotives from Leeds long before there were rails for them to run upon. However, a company had recently been formed to build a rail-link from Constanta on the Black Sea to a point near Bucharest, so

as to unlock the grain harvests of Walachia and Moldavia. One of
the directors of this enterprise was a sporting friend of Sam's,
William Price, MP. Three brothers called Barclay were the contracting engineers. Sam applied for and got the post of managing
director.

Even without Florence, this was a job after his own heart. The
workforce was recruited from thirty-two ethnic groups, overseen by
English and Irish navvies. So primitive was the land over which the
track was laid that anyone on horseback was instantly perceived as
a tax-collector: the population fled until the danger passed. There
were no roads to speak of and it was hard to find any village larger
than a few flea-infested hovels. Constanta, on the coast, was more
interesting. Here Ovid had been exiled. One of the first cuttings
made for the railways was through the Roman town-walls on which
the poet had strolled, now cheerfully vandalised in the name of
steam.

The Barclay brothers were young men with a vicarage background. George Barclay later wrote a facetious and charmless book
about the building of the railway. Foreigners were funny because
they were so stupid. Shepherds along the tracks seemed to believe
that a train could stop in its own length, leading to hilarious incidents where they and their flocks were bowled over and mangled.
The company put up fencing to guard the track and the locals at
once stole the pickets for firewood. Barclay's labour force was similarly uneducable. Workmen stepped off trains moving at thirty
miles an hour as if getting down from carts and were tumbled
under the wheels. It seemed to him exceptionally comical that
they blessed new sections of the line by sacrificing a cockerel and
sprinkling blood on the track.

Included in this catalogue of nonsense was some account of the
character of the managing director, ensconced, as Barclay pictured
it, in his love-nest in Constanta. Sam was actually a very resourceful
manager and might have made something of these three young
Barclays. The problem was Florence. When the railway was finally
completed, Sam's name was not included on the list of invitees to
the official opening. The young engineers had ratted on him. They

did not like his duck-shooting excursions and they did not like his domestic arrangements either.

Great events were happening elsewhere. In April 1859 Speke and Burton were back in Aden, exactly where Sam had last seen them. Speke's dream had come to pass. He had looked on the waters of a great lake – which to Burton's intense irritation he had unilaterally named Lake Victoria – and was convinced he had discovered the source of the Nile. Burton had not gone with him those last crucial miles and the discovery was Speke's alone. In making it he had nearly killed himself and was dragged back from death by his companion, who with a dry wit diagnosed his problem as hydrophobia. They set sail from Zanzibar with Speke still very weak. A few days after they arrived at Aden HMS *Furious* put in and offered them the voyage home. Speke at once accepted, but Burton delayed, in order to smoke a hookah or two and swap stories with an old friend. According to him, the last words ever spoken between the two men were these. Speke said, 'Goodbye, old fellow. You may be quite sure I shall not go up to the Royal Geographical Society until you come to the fore and we appear together. Make your mind easy about that.' They shook hands on it.

But Speke had a worm of ambition inside him he could not control. He ran over in his mind all the little instances of his friend's disdain, the hundred petty insults it seemed he had been offered in the long months of marching through the wilderness. The *Furious* docked on 8 May and the very next day Speke posted to London and was closeted with Sir Roderick Murchison. Although Burton himself came home only thirteen days later, by then it was too late. Murchison did for John Hanning Speke what he had done for Livingstone. He made him an instant celebrity. Burton, who had been the leader of the expedition and who undoubtedly saved Speke's life, was airbrushed out of the picture. His protests that Speke may have been overhasty in declaring the source of the Nile – which were made out of not petulance but simple realism – suppose there was a river running *into* Lake Victoria at its southern end, where would that leave things? – were swept aside.

Murchison – who was getting nothing but bad news from his other protégé, Livingstone – needed a hero. He immediately busied himself with raising public and private funds for Speke's return to the great lake. This time the explorer chose as his companion yet another Indian army officer, Captain James Grant, a giant of a man whose greatest recommendation to Speke was that he was very happy to be the lesser partner in the enterprise. They sailed from Portsmouth on 27 April 1860. (Burton consoled himself by marrying and taking his bride off to Salt Lake City.) The plan of exploration was simple, at any rate on paper. They would retrace the steps of the first expedition, look for the outfall of Lake Victoria and then chart the unknown river or rivers to the point where the waters could be definitely identified as the Nile. To walk from Zanzibar to Khartoum was going to be a feat that called for exemplary fortitude. More than this, it was, if it succeeded, a coup of the greatest diplomatic significance. Here was a challenge fit for Britain – to slice the continent open like a ripe peach and in so doing lay bare the iniquities of the Arab slavers. It was adventure of the highest order and, like Livingstone's travels but on a far bigger canvas, it was also the expression of a moral imperative.

Sam arrived in London a month after Speke and Grant had sailed. He came alone. Part of his purpose was to visit his four children, whom he had not seen for four years and who were being raised by his sister, Min. The greater reason for coming home was undoubtedly to chase the glory of the hour. Like everyone in Europe within reach of a newspaper, he had heard of the discovery of Lake Victoria. For the second time in his life he was no part of a great story. It occurred to him now, after it was too late to volunteer his services to the expedition, that if Speke was intending to come northwards along the Nile, he might set out from Cairo and meet him at some point along the way. He told no one in the close family about this but went to consult William Cotton Oswell, a fellow big-game hunter.

Oswell had considerable experience of southern Africa – in fact he had helped Livingstone a great deal in the days of his obscurity, to the extent that the missionary named one of his children after him. Without Oswell's wagons Livingstone would never have succeeded in crossing the Kalahari, which was then held to be impassable. Together they had discovered Lake Ngami. An accidental explorer, Oswell was a legend among big-game hunters. He was rich, he was completely fearless, and cheerfully insouciant in matters of social reputation. He was in fact Sam Baker under a different hat.

Oswell had knocked around the world a great deal – undertaking shooting expeditions to North and South America – and though he was modest and unassuming to a fault, he was more of a political animal than Sam. After lengthy and genial discussions between the two men, it was considered a good strategy not to involve Murchison. Instead, Sam would go to Africa as a private citizen, bearing the costs of his trip out of his own pocket. When they heard of it, the RGS took panic at even this proposal and asked him to confine his wanderings to the east bank of the Nile below Khartoum; in particular, to stay well away from the White Nile, down which they fondly hoped to see Speke and Grant sail in a year or so. There is something comical in picturing men in top hats discussing huge tracts of Africa as if they were London parishes. Francis Galton, the secretary of the society, had actually been where Baker was going when he was a student and left his name on one of the pyramids of Merowe. That was the sort of area he had in mind for Sam to wander. He should certainly keep away from a place called Khartoum, a barracks town barely twenty years old.

Sam returned to Constanta and told Florence of his plans for them both. So it was that, two years after being rescued from the Vidin slave market, she landed at Alexandria, the indispensable lieutenant of what on the face of it was to be a walk in the bush, hunting for elephants. She was nineteen years old. Despite her protector's visit to London, no one in the family dreamed of her existence.

FOUR

⟨⟩∘⟨⟩

In July of 1857 Lord Palmerston answered what seems today suspiciously like a planted question in the House of Commons. Mr Berkeley, member for Bristol, rose to ask whether the government had any objection to M. de Lesseps' scheme to dig a Suez canal. Palmerston's reply was an attempt to kill the idea immediately.

> Her Majesty's Government certainly cannot undertake to use their influence with the Sultan to induce him to give permission for the construction of this canal, because for the last fifteen years Her Majesty's Government have used all the influence they possess at Constantinople and in Egypt to prevent that scheme from being carried into execution. It is an undertaking, which, I believe, as regards to its commercial character, may be deemed to rank among the many bubble schemes that from time to time have been palmed off upon gullible capitalists . . . I believe, therefore, that those who embarked their money in such an undertaking (if my honourable friend has any constituents who are likely to do so) would find themselves very grievously deceived by the result.

De Lesseps, who had been touring Britain drumming up interest in the scheme, considered his honour and that of France had been impugned. He could not call out the Prime Minister, but placed himself at the disposal of Robert Stephenson, who had spoken in support of Palmerston. The great engineer's son, who only ever spoke in the House on technical questions, was genuinely mortified and wrote a handsome letter of apology. A duel was sensibly averted: nevertheless, de Lesseps resolved from now on to proceed as far as possible without British capital. He already had the concession from the viceroy of Egypt in his pocket.

The viceroy was a gargantuan figure called Mohamed Said. At the Gabbari Palace His Excellency had the parade ground covered with iron plates to keep the dust from his Paris-tailored clothes. He liked all things French. There was an alarming side to him, however; easily bored and not always the statesman de Lesseps liked to promote, Said occasionally distracted himself by making his court wade through loose gunpowder with lighted candles in their hands. An English traveller called Cameron added another much more telling anecdote. To amuse himself, Said once made a bonfire of eighty million piastres of local tax, extracted from the long-suffering fellahin by whips. Burning state money on this scale was a particularly bad joke. The Ottoman Empire staggered under £20 million of debt to foreign bankers and its most important province, Egypt, was flirting with public bankruptcy.

However, the sultan and his viceroy, both of them such huge and fleshy sensualists, were playing poker with aces in their hands. For as long as the threat to peace was perceived as Russian expansion southwards, such as might one day threaten India; or westwards towards Poland, Prussia and the Austrians, then for just so long the ramshackle remnants of the once-glorious Ottoman Empire would be kept in being. It was a Russian tsar who called Turkey the 'sick man of Europe' and when British parliamentarians talked about 'the Eastern Question', this was what they meant. Though very few European statesmen could speak about Turkey and the Turks without a faint shudder of disgust, the need for a stop to Russian ambition at the eastern end of the Mediterranean was pressing enough. After all, a war had just been fought on the issue, one with the unusual consequence of uniting Britain and France. It was a joke against Raglan that during the campaign he had to be reminded several times that the French were not his enemies but his allies. Most people in Britain – if they were going to have to fight anyone – would have preferred to fight the French.

Sam's visit to Egypt and the Sudan was entirely private and his instinct was to remove himself as soon as possible from the politics of the country. The newly appointed British consul-general was that same Mr Colquhoun he had met in Bucharest. Sam persuaded him to provide a firman from the Egyptian government giving him freedom of movement, without realising its limited value. Under a system of what were called 'capitulations', foreign nationals were the responsibility of their own consular officials. Comfortably, they were above local arrest and taxation; and criminal charges could not be laid without the presence of the consul in person. Contrariwise, their only redress for injuries done was by the same system. Should Sam or Florence be murdered as they sat at their table in Shepheard's Hotel, it would require Mr Colquhoun to leave his office and come to the scene of the crime. If the murderer was, say, an American, *his* consul also had to be present. If the American was subsequently found to be hiding out in the house of a Frenchman, then three consuls would be involved before the door was smashed down.

Cairo was made tolerable by hotels and carriages, champagne and bottled beer, the pleasures of a full *table d'hôte* and the company of faintly bewildered compatriots, some of them tourists, most on their way out to India. There might be sand on the carpets of the hotel and a vile smell from the bathroom arrangements; on the other hand there were servants at every turn of the stairs, an English or at least a Mediterranean menu, Greek cashiers, French receptionists, burly Armenian bell-captains to do one's bidding. Gazelles wandered the gardens and nuzzled for titbits. Exotic birds hopped about the branches of the dusty trees. That this was not Cairo but a version of it suitable for moderately rich Europeans did not matter. The city and the ruins that rose from it were there to be inspected in the early mornings, when the light was so appealing. The most apt contemporary description of Cairo was by Sophie Lane Poole, who wrote a book about it in 1842. It seemed to her that the city resembled one that had been unoccupied for a century or more, and was now re-peopled by a bustling and frantic

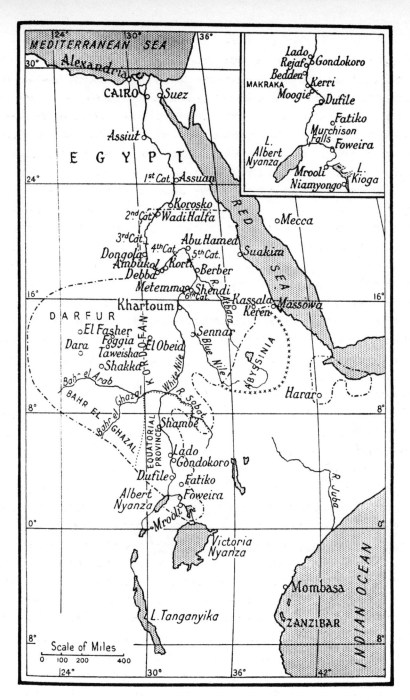

Egypt and the Sudan. The Sudanese place names describe no more than
tiny forts created by Gordon.

community unable to repair the damage and restore the fabric. Things went pell-mell in Cairo, at any rate on the surface: every small transaction, like finding a hotel room or hiring a carriage, directing a porter or booking tickets for a train, was a noisy battle between those who wore watches and had timetables to keep and those who did not. Edwin de Leon, the American consul in Sam's day, left a picture of Shepheard's Hotel as it was when the Bakers were passing through:

> A black Berber Bowab, or doorkeeper, in primitive arab dress, was squatted on his kafass, or arab substitute for a bedstead – his seat by day, his bed by night – just in the doorway of which, at night, he was the guard. Outside, the donkey boys held high carnival; whilst gorgeously clad Dragomen strutted or buzzed like greedy dragon flies around the newly arrived travellers, enticing them to the bazaar, in anticipation of a three months trip in a dahabiah, the gondola of the Ancient River.

De Leon seems to have relished the scene, which represented the sort of comfortable exoticism enjoyed by British tourists. They were catered for by the burly and faintly coarse Shepheard himself, whose portrait was painted by Frederick Goodall in 1859, dressed in Turkish clothes while at his ease on a divan. His hookah is at his side and a parakeet perches near his shoulder. Shepheard could afford to look self-satisfied. Cairo's foreign hotel trade was in boom. Murray had already published a guide to Egypt – a few years later, in 1873, at the invitation of the khedive, Thomas Cook opened offices for those who wished to explore the Ancient River under British management. De Leon continues:

> In front of the hotel were no houses, but stretching across to the Hotel d'Orient for many acres of space was the old Ezbekieh, planned and planted by Mehemet Ali, the primitive Hyde Park of Cairo, with its gigantic trees and thick shrubbery, with Arab cafés and cafés chantants at intervals, filled nightly with Egyptians of every rank and race, smoking Narghiles and chibouques and sipping coffee and raké and chattering like a flock of magpies . . . There you saw men of all shades of colour, different types of race and varieties of costume; the half-naked fellah, or

peasant, the stark-naked Santon, or saint, the richly clad Turk, the Arnaut soldier, a walking arsenal, the coal black Nubian, the coffee coloured Abyssinian, the copper coloured Arab and the straitlaced Englishman.

A thousand miles upstream, guarded by six impassable cataracts, was Khartoum. 'A more miserable, filthy and unhealthy spot can hardly be imagined,' Baker thundered when he got there. The governor-general of the Sudan was a man called Musa Pasha – 'a rather exaggerated specimen of Turkish authorities in general, combining the worst of Oriental failings with the brutality of a wild animal'. His minor officials, who governed a territory without boundaries and almost without maps – were indolent and rapacious by turns. The desert encroached on all sides and the only way in and out was via Berber, a hundred miles down the river. There the traveller heading north could cut across the desert the Arabs called the Belly of Stones to Korosko, above the first cataract; or ride by camel east to the Red Sea at Suakin. Khartoum itself was hardly more than a barracks. Where the imagination might raise pictures of somewhere exotic and glamorous, this was an African town of buildings fashioned from mud bricks. Their whitewashed walls hid dreadful and shameful secrets. The few Europeans who made their way there, like the Bakers, quickly discovered there was only one topic of conversation.

The town had been an entrepôt and barracks from the time the Turks came south in 1820. The world market in ivory was controlled from there but, lucrative though it was, buying and selling ivory was nothing more than a front for another more sinister trade. Thousands, hundreds of thousands, of black slaves had passed through the place on their way to the Red Sea – indeed, the man who might be considered the founder of Khartoum in its present state, the Egyptian viceroy Mohamed Ali, had only come to the Sudan to recruit such slaves as soldiers for his army.

It has been calculated by the economic historian Patrick Manning that between ten and fifteen per cent of the population of the eastern Sudan was enslaved in the nineteenth century. At the time the Bakers arrived, the trade was approaching its peak. Twelve and a half thousand slaves came down the Nile to Khartoum each year, to which figure must be added those who did not survive their capture, or were destroyed in the tribal wars caused by the trade. Just whereabouts this rape of the country originated was a closely guarded secret, though a child taken from a village out in the high savannah to the south could expect to walk a thousand kilometres before being shipped from Suakin to new masters in Arabia. He would be walking in the footsteps of hundreds of thousands of his forebears.

What was new in Khartoum was the realisation that a great deal of moral indignation against slavery was being generated, no longer just in Britain but throughout western Europe, accompanied by the deep suspicion that the province only continued in being as a consequence of it. This last point was well-founded. Said visited Khartoum in 1857, accompanied by Ferdinand de Lesseps. He professed himself disgusted with what he found. De Lesseps records a strange incident that took place one night in the miserable palace placed at the viceroy's disposal. Said was in a turbulent mood.

> Scarcely were we settled at the dinner table than I saw his expression harden. He again deplored the impossibility of finding a way to undo the evil which his people had wrought, and said that nothing remained but to evacuate the country. I reminded him that he had the means to repair the damage and do good; that with his absolute power he had only to will it and it would happen. For a few moments he remained silent. I saw the blood darken his face. Abruptly he got up, unfastened his swordbelt, detached the sabre and threw it against the wall. His fury was unbounded. He told me to go to my room.

Lesseps, who always liked to say the right thing, had clearly made a big mistake. He was on tenterhooks in his room, listening to Said rage up and down. At three in the morning the viceroy called for a bath. He would leave the Sudan at once. What had been uncovered at this fateful dinner was something Said understood only too well and his French adviser simply did not grasp; or, if he did, chose to ignore. Without slavery, the Egyptian economy would collapse. It was the one brick that could not be pulled out of the wall. Said the moderniser, the manipulator of European interests, the Mediterranean statesman, needed the horror of slavery quite as much as – and, in purely domestic terms, more than – he needed the canal.

In the book Sam Baker wrote about his Sudan journey, *Albert Nyanza, Great Basin of the Nile,* he describes taking himself off to the east above Khartoum, there to spend a year learning Arabic. This he intended to do downwind of an elephant with a gun in his hand but first he had to explain to his readers the presence in the story of 'one whose life yet dawned at so early an age that womanhood was still a future'. This was more than mere gallantry. Florence's courage and calm played a key part in his travels – she was quite as resourceful as any man he might have engaged to follow him and probably better than most. But how to present her? He chose the simplest way and described her as his wife.

> I shuddered at the prospect for her, should she be left alone in savage lands at my death; and gladly would I have left her in the luxuries of home instead of exposing her to the miseries of Africa. It was in vain that I implored her to remain and that I painted the difficulties and perils still blacker than I supposed they really would be: she was resolved, with woman's constancy and devotion, to share all dangers and to follow me through each rough footstep of the wild life before me.

If the marriage and the safety of a family home were fictions, the rest was not. Leaving aside where she would have waited if he had gone up-river alone, she was not going to be without him and that was that. Casting himself as Naomi, Sam found an appropriate text to woo his female readers.

> 'And Ruth said, Entreat me not to leave thee, or to return from following after thee: for whither thou goest I will go, and where thou lodgest I will lodge: where thou diest I will die and there will I be buried; the Lord do so to me and more also, if aught but death part thee and me.'

Two things stand out in the pages of *Albert Nyanza*. The first is what a consummate storyteller Sam is. The book is peppered with

Sam Baker's sketch of himself and Florence on expedition.

close descriptions, through which his own personality shines. We are in the presence of an amateur, not just of exploration but of life itself. Any book about the interior of Africa was expected to be a catalogue of danger and misfortune – brought about by native treachery, wild animals, fever and starvation. Sam had all these ingredients in his own tale, but also an unfailing eye for landscape and weather (as well as pretty girls) and a style that is conversationally unaffected and direct. Here he parleys with a local chief.

> Commoro could not possibly understand my object in visiting the Latooka country: it was in vain that I attempted to explain the intention of my journey. He said, 'Suppose you get to the great lake: what will you do with it? What will be the good of it? If you find that the large river does flow from it, what then? What's the good of it?'
>
> I could only assure him that in England we had an intimate knowledge of the whole world, except the interior of Africa, and that our object in exploring was to benefit the hitherto unknown countries by instituting legitimate trade, and introducing manufactures from England in exchange for ivory and other productions. He replied that the Turks would never trade fairly: that they were extremely bad people, and that they would not trade ivory in any other way than by bartering cattle, which

they stole from one tribe to sell to another. Our conversation was suddenly terminated by one of my men running in to the tent with the bad news that one of the camels had dropped down and was dying . . .

This abrupt transition from high ideals to the plight of the camel ('poisoned by a well known plant that he had been caught in the act of eating') is a stroke worthy of a novelist. Comorro is left to his savage opinions while the narrator leaps to his feet exactly as he did in life. In another passage he is hunting with three of his men when the air suddenly cools and there is a tropical rain-storm. Sam exults in the luxury of being cold and soaking wet 'in the English fashion'. When he looks back, his gun-bearers are struck to the ground like daffodils, cowering under thorn trees and utterly miserable. What comes through is an immense pleasure derived from simple circumstance.

His pen portraits of Africans are masterly. Katchiba is an ancient and decrepit chief who is usually carried about his village piggy-back, accompanied by a wife with a gourd of beer. Sam makes him a present of some 'sun-goggles' and, emboldened, Katchiba asks to ride the explorer's horse, Tetel.

The horse, recognising an awkward hand, did not move a step. 'Now then,' said Katchiba, 'go on!' but Tetel not understanding the Obbo language was perfectly ignorant of his rider's wishes. 'Why won't he go?' enquired Katchiba. 'Touch him with your stick,' cried one of my men: and acting upon the suggestion, the old sorcerer gave him a tremendous whack with his staff. This was immediately responded to by Tetel, who, quite unused to such eccentricities gave a vigorous kick, the effect of which was to convert the sorcerer into a spread eagle, flying over his head and landing very heavily upon the ground, amidst a roar of laughter from my men, in which I am afraid Mrs Baker was rude enough to join.

There is both geniality and contempt in his writing about Afri-cans. It is balanced out by a second quality to the book – the interest its author has in all things practical. *Albert Nyanza* is the story of a highly resourceful man who can recognise native skill when he sees it and has his own to contribute. He can re-step a mast, fashion new rigging, care for the pack animals, mend guns, both his own and his hosts', organise his escort along semi-military lines, shoot for the pot as well as for pleasure, act as a veterinary surgeon and doctor as required and, when the occasion demands, become a full-scale military commander. It is only fair to recall here that Livingstone's *Missionary Travels* is also rich in anecdote: the difference in the two works is nevertheless striking. The missionary puts his trust in God and rational argument. Sam is by comparison an adventurer. Livingstone more than once sits in some threatening situation with a shotgun on his knee, waiting for the Lord to resolve his problem. Sam's way was to stride into the thick of the fight – his whole expedition was dogged by the threat of mutiny among his bearers – and clout the biggest and ugliest man he could find. At his back Florence would generally lay out on a cloth the arsenal of weapons he carried with him. She was his unflinching lieutenant. He had a phrase for her that caught on with his public – 'She was not a *screamer.*'

It never was Sam's intention to confine himself to the Abyssinian tributaries of the Blue Nile. What sort of an adventure would it have been to come home saying, 'Yes, I was in the general area when the two heroic explorers Speke and Grant passed through on their way to Cairo and worldwide fame'? His plan was to go up the White Nile as far as boats would allow and wait for Speke. If he failed to show up, he would go and look for him on foot – ideally, rescue him. On the visit to London, when he had missed the explorers' departure by only a few days, Sam made sure he found and introduced himself to a Welshman called John Petherick, who had fifteen years' experience of the Sudan as an ivory-trader and was back in England to marry and, if possible, have himself made British consul to the country. (His representations to the Foreign Secretary on this subject led Lord John Russell to liken him to a wild horse, or hippopotamus.) Petherick was big and bearded and a great shot – a man in Sam's own image. He was a much more valuable contact – and more easily duped – than someone like Murchison. Once in the Sudan, the Bakers made sure they kept in touch with the Pethericks by letter and, when they arrived in Khartoum, went straight to the consulate. It was empty. Petherick and his wife had headed south on the very mission Sam had reserved for himself: to find and greet the two explorers Speke and Grant.

Musa Pasha and the Turkish officials in Khartoum were deeply suspicious of the new arrival. His Arabic was good, his stores and supplies were on a heroic scale and he did not suffer fools gladly. This was no big-game tourist, nervous of his surroundings. On the contrary, he was alarmingly well-organised, perhaps too much so for a private individual. The slave trade had reached the point where the whole of the south was in uproar. Was it not possible that the man and his boyish consort had motives other than exploration and discovery? And even if he had not, was this the time to help fit him out for a trip into country that was virtually in a state of civil war? Instead, Musa Pasha amused himself by placing endless obstacles in his path. For six months Sam stomped up and down Khartoum in the unwelcome guise of a petitioner, drinking coffee and getting nowhere. There were no boats; no porters could be found; something called the Sudd, a vast lake of impenetrable weed, had blocked the Nile as a waterway. The trip was dangerous, Mrs Baker was too young and delicate for what lay ahead, the elephants her husband wished to slaughter could be found in greater abundance in the country from which they had just arrived. It was a stand-off Sam did not intend the Turks to win. The only friend he made among the other Europeans in the town was a deliberate affront to the rest – a broken and rachitic Bavarian carpenter called Schmidt, who scratched a living supplying animals to zoos.

Then Murchison and the Royal Geographical Society unwittingly gave Sam a card it was hard for Musa Pasha to trump. The RGS had heard rumours that Petherick and his wife had perished somewhere out there in the wilderness. Maybe Speke and Grant had suffered the same fate. It was typical of Khartoum that the news had gone first to London before coming back to Sam but the upshot was clear. The only man on the spot who could be trusted to find out what had happened to these four Britons was Samuel White Baker. The society wrote to enlist his assistance.

Murchison's letter gave Sam's position a double legitimacy. To begin with, his dealings with Musa Pasha were put on an entirely new footing. It could hardly be claimed any longer that he was a spy – the fate of British nationals was concerned. Admittedly there were only four to consider (six, if the Pethericks still lived), but they were, after all, the *only* Britons between Khartoum and Zanzibar. Negotiations for boats went on with the same maddening dilatoriness, but Sam knew that what he wanted would sooner or later have to be granted. There was a second reason for congratulation as he looked out of the consulate windows at stars juicy as pomegranate seeds, or woke each morning in Petherick's bed. From being a mere nimrod, a man judged unfit to follow Livingstone, he was now a player. The question that had split Speke from Burton, that had electrified the intellectual community and given Murchison so much political kudos, was now in his hands. He had come out to Africa with a vague hope in his mind of doing something memorable for his country. Events had conspired to throw this prize into his lap. If Speke and Grant had indeed perished, he had been gifted their mission.

He left Khartoum on 18 December 1862. Just before casting off, Musa Pasha demanded a poll tax on all his porters. Sam ran up the Union Jack, paraded his men on deck and offered to throw any official who came on board into the river. Perhaps by arrangement with the authorities, his boat was then run down and his oars smashed by a vessel arriving from the south. The captain of the new boat was

> a gigantic black, a Tokrouri (native of Darfur) who confident in his strength, challenged anyone to come on board, nor did any of my fellows respond to the invitation. The insolence of Turkish Government officials is beyond description – my oars were smashed and this insult was the reparation: so stepping smartly aboard, and brushing a few fellows on one side, I was obliged to come to a physical explanation with the captain, which terminated in a delivery of the oars.

Baker's sketch of Galla slave girls, for whom he had an unfortunate
predilection. They were 'the Venuses of Abyssinia'.

He had started as he meant to go on. Six hundred miles or so
to the south was the only other permanent settlement on the Upper
Nile, Gondokoro. It is a place-name that has disappeared from
modern maps, for Gondokoro never was a town, but a huge
seasonal camp to which thousands of slaves were brought each
year. The Austrians had established a mission there, the fate of
which was unknown. The thing that made Gondokoro important
was the intelligence it gathered about tribal wars, particularly in
the Bahr el Ghazal to the west, and the fate of slavers and anyone
else who travelled there. If the Pethericks were alive, their whereabouts would be known at Gondokoro. If Grant and Speke had
not perished, they would have to pass the place on their journey
north.

Baker arrived at Gondokoro on 2 February 1863, after a very
sharp learning curve in handling a big expedition. All his men had
been paid five months' wages in advance, as was the custom. It did
not buy their loyalty, let alone their friendship. What struck the

Nile explorer was the complete ingratitude of Africans, which derived from the absence of any sense of contract in their culture. Their behaviour towards Sam was to extort as much as possible from him and then, when no more was forthcoming, desert him. The Arabs he had with him were exactly the same, though with a greater capacity for dishonest fawning. When he at last saw the mountains that lay behind Gondokoro, Sam took pleasure in the sight only because it meant he could walk on dry land again after the hell of the Sudd.

The Sudd, which in Khartoum Sam may have discounted as a fiction dreamed up by Musa Pasha to keep him where he was, was one of the Nile's cruellest jokes. In the wet season it had a surface area the size of England, a vast sea of floating vegetation, grey-green and menacing, without a single fixed point. To be lost in the Sudd – to choose the wrong channel – had much the same consequence as being trapped in ice had for polar explorers. Sam and Florence came across the beginnings of the problem on Boxing Day.

> Floating islands of water plants are now very numerous. There is a plant something like a small cabbage (*Pistia Stratiotes*, L.) which floats along until it meets a comrade; these unite and, recruiting as they float onward, they eventually form masses of many thousands, entangling with other species of water plants and floating wood, until they at length form floating islands.

On this passage they were lucky, for the river was low. Many days passed with nothing but reed and tangled masses of lotus plants to gaze on, and on occasion neither the oars nor the sails of their boats were of any use: men had to wade in the crocodile-infested waters dragging the vessels. Sam described the landscape as a series of 'interminable marshes' but the full horror of the Sudd was reserved for another season, another expedition. Johann Schmidt, the Bavarian animal-hunter who had begged to accompany the Bakers, died early, on the last day of 1862. He was breathing blood and, as Sam bathed his face for hours on end, flies walked across his eyeballs without him even flinching. Sam asked if he had relatives who should be told of his passing. Schmidt muttered that there was a girl, someone he held dear. When they asked for her name, he muttered, 'Krombach.' It was the name of the village where he had been born.

Everybody in Gondokoro was drunk. The slave barracks were not yet filled but the jailers passed the time by abusing the girls they had already captured and firing off rifles at random. A boy sitting on the gunwale of one of Sam's boats was accidentally shot in the head, toppling into the river and leaving his brains behind on the deck. The Austrian Mission was deserted and its tumbled clay bricks had begun to revert to dust. Poignantly, the only sign that civilisation and the word of God had ever passed this way was in the grove of limes and citron the missionaries had planted round their ruined church. Nobody had a use for the fruit, which lay shrivelled in the dust. The whole of Gondokoro would be abandoned in 1875: even now, at the height of the slave trade, it was no more than a scratch on the surface of Africa. The local people were called the Bari and Sam found much to admire in them, with their neat houses and regular enclosures. They were the terrified neighbours of a sprawling, violent camp that stank of slavery and blood. Any Bari causing the slightest problem would be taken to a low cliff and flung to the crocodiles; and this is how they lived among this 'colony of cut-throats'. Every day and all day long the slavers fired off shots at random. At night howls and screams rent the air.

It was to such a place that Sam had brought Florence. It raised the question: what was worse – to be the only Europeans in an unpeopled wilderness, hacking at waterweeds and driven mad by mosquitoes, or to be party to a scene like this? Just as you could not teach an African an obligation, neither could you persuade an Arab slaver that your purpose in being in this forlorn back country was disinterested. For such men, exploring for the sake of it was meaningless. Sam's very presence made him an enemy; perhaps soon enough an actual target. Maybe a stray bullet would find its way to the interloper's boat, just as had happened with the unlucky cabin-boy. Maybe worse: the men Sam had brought with him might kill him and then defect to the slavers who, though they might not have hampers furnished by Fortnum and Mason, as had the white man and his blonde wife, were rich in girls and the massy Austrian silver coins that were the currency of the country. There was, however, one piece of good news for the Bakers – Petherick and his wife were reported to be alive, trading ivory somewhere on the western bank. Their boat lay moored and empty, attended by the men who had brought them there. They had been last seen two months ago.

On 15 February 1863 Sam heard musketry to the south and the first of a party of slavers arrived. He strolled out to see them approach and then broke into a trot and then an exultant run. When he was fifty yards away he stopped and bellowed from the depths of his chest, 'Hoorah for old England!' With the caravan, their clothes in tatters, their eyes burning with fever, were Speke and Grant. It was not a meeting to compare with that between Stanley and Livingstone, perhaps, but it was momentous all the same. Speke and Grant expected to meet *someone* who would get them north to Khartoum, even if it were only an Arab trader on his way there with slaves. The person they most expected to see was Petherick.

Speke was in an ecstasy of self-congratulation. It was now absolutely certain in his mind that he and he alone had discovered the source of the Nile and he felt himself entitled to whatever honours there were to be had in this hellhole. Though he was delighted to see Sam, therefore, Speke was intensely put out not to find Petherick there in his capacity as consul. He knew, from letters received from Murchison on his way from Zanzibar, that Petherick had been offered the proceeds of a £1000 public subscription to 'find' him. That was entirely in accord with the ambitious way Murchison thought – two Britons meeting under the Union flag in the middle of nowhere. An official ceremony and then a judiciously muted celebration, in which mention of the queen might be given an honoured part, possibly with some further remarks on the sagacity and foresight of the president of the Royal Geographical Society.

Unfortunately, this was also the way Speke saw things happening. As he staggered north, he had rehearsed over and over the famous phrase he would use to his patron Murchison: 'The Nile is settled.' Though he happened to be right in principle, as a geographer Speke lacked many qualities. He was bad at learning languages – he had no Arabic and, as Burton first pointed out, did not even speak French. He lacked the empathy Burton had for natives, although at the court of King Mtesa, where he and Grant had rested some months, he had shown a keen interest in measuring the girls' busts and limbs with a tape. He called this, with ghastly facetiousness, his 'engineering'.

(One of the secrets both men kept from the Bakers was that Speke had fathered children in Mtesa's court.)

Speke's biggest shortcoming from the point of view of academic geography was that, if he saw a lake that stretched away to vanishing point, it was for him illimitable. If a few days or weeks later he saw more water, it was accounted the same geographical feature. Once he had found the outfall of Lake Victoria, any river, if it flowed north, was always the Nile. Speke had come to prove a point. The facts were made to fit or, if they did not, were cheerfully ignored. He might be a brave man, but he was a crude and careless investigator. Murchison might love him, but there were others in the Royal Geographical Society already disposed to feel dubious about the detail of his claims.

It was good to go aboard the Baker boat and dig into the last of the delicacies, and Sam was nothing if not a sympathetic ear; but the vindictive streak in Speke made him harp on about the unlucky Petherick. What sort of a British consul was it who put his pocket before his duty and the chance to welcome the greatest discovery of the century, as great as any in the second millennium? Grant meanwhile was casting sidelong glances at Florence. He knew that she could not possibly be married to Sam. A small picture of what it was to be British in 1863 emerges. Speke simply would not give up the sense of slight he felt at not being received by the queen's appointee, even in this utterly remote and desperate place; Grant found it almost impossible to be civil to the young blonde who waited on him with wine and biscuits. Meanwhile the Arab muskets cracked and whined; the stench of slavery drifted down from the stockades; and across the river the Petherick boat still lay empty, its patched and tattered sail wrapped around the unshipped yard.

There was always something faintly manic about James Hanning Speke, even when he was at his ease in his London club. Here in Gondokoro, emaciated and flushed with fever, he was hardly able to stop talking, while the more passive Grant (physically the largest of all three men) listened without comment. Speke's most persistent topic was the need to get home as soon as possible – his hunger for fame and glory was burning a hole in him. Without prompting, Sam Baker offered him his boats, a piece of generosity verging on the foolhardy, for how then were he and Florence to return? Speke at once accepted and offered as courtesy payment some topographical notes and a speculative map Grant had made. When they first met, Sam had asked him plaintively, after hearing of his epic walk, 'And does not one leaf of the laurel remain for me?' It did. Somewhere to the south-west was another feeder lake, the Luta Nzige, in the country of the Unyoro people and their fearsome king, Kamrasi. Speke had never seen it but had been told by natives of its existence. According to Sam, 'Speke expressed his conviction that the Luta Nzige must be a second source of the Nile and that geographers would be dissatisfied that he had not explored it.'

That was all he needed to hear. Measured by the sketch Grant had drawn, the outfall of this lake was no more than a hundred miles away. The Unyoro were notoriously warlike, which is why Speke had not diverted his journey north to verify the lake's existence. But now here was a situation in which a third European, Baker, and a fourth, Petherick – both of them healthy giants as well as first-class shots – were on hand to help put this final piece of the jigsaw in place. It would have meant Speke going back on his tracks, perhaps for another six months, but to have done so would have clinched the whole question of the Nile sources. The idea held no charms for him – all he wanted to do was go home.

While they discussed the matter Petherick arrived back from his trading expedition, accompanied by his wife and a Dr Murie. Speke treated him with the utmost contempt. He refused to accept any help from the unhappy consul, commenting icily how he 'did not wish to accept the succour dodge'. He made it clear he would sail to Khartoum in Sam's boats. Kate Petherick saw at once that he intended to ruin her husband. The situation was impossible – seven Britons, two small flotillas of boats, any number of guns and a reasonable supply of trading goods and yet Speke would not talk to Petherick, Grant could not talk to Florence. As for Sam, he had already decided that he and no one else must go in search of the Luta Nzige.

In plain terms, he would claim his leaf of the laurels. What stopped Speke from looking for the lake – the warlike Kamrasi and the Unyoro – held no special fears for him, for he had travelled thus far with no fewer than fourteen guns in his personal luggage. Though he tolerated Speke (enough to suffer the querulous advice that he should marry Florence and make an honest woman of her), he was not overawed by him. And it may be that the grating quality of Speke's petulant diatribes had begun to pall a little on all of them. At times, Speke could behave like someone who had been slighted in the mess. He was touchy in a way that Sam was not. It did not matter to Sam one way or the other whether Burton or, nearer to hand, Petherick, were cads. He did not think like that. Everything he had done in life he had done alone. His expectations of other people were accordingly very modest. Moreover, he was there in Gondokoro entirely at his own expense. It placed him in a powerful position. Samuel Baker was no soldier, but neither was he anybody's servant.

Speke and Grant sailed downstream in the Baker boats on 26 February 1863. A month later Sam and Florence crossed the river an hour or so after sunset with those of the original party who had not deserted; there was no guide and no interpreter.

> 'Where shall we go?' said the men. 'Who can travel without a guide? No one knows the road.' The moon was up, and the mountain of Belignan was distinctly visible from nine miles distant. Knowing that the route lay on the east side of that mountain, I led the way, Mrs Baker riding by my side, and the

British flag following close behind as a guide for the caravan of heavily laden camels and donkeys.

It was a challenge someone like Sam Baker was unable to refuse and there is no doubt that he crossed the river in a spirit of pure adventure. As a bonus, if he came home with a map and description of the hidden lake, he too would write his name in the history of African exploration. He would have done something in his life, satisfied an aboriginal hunger for the all but impossible dream, while at the same time honouring his country. There was a further consideration. Speke's companion Grant had shown him how little Florence was reckoned among men of his own class. He would change that, too. Riding beside him through the dark, slim and unassuming, was the slave-girl he would return to Europe as a heroine in the grand sense. If they got through the next few months together, Florence would become that paragon of all the virtues, a true Briton in her own right. Her real origins washed away in the waters of the Nile, she would be the second Mrs Baker and thus invulnerable to criticism, from Grant or anyone else. The anyone else included his own family and, in particular, his daughters.

FIVE

⟞○⟝

In that same week, a very long way from Gondokoro, Major Charles Gordon was put in orders to command a force of 3000 men. He was barely thirty years old. The contrast between his situation and Sam Baker's was marked. The landscape Sam and Florence marched over with their woeful little party was like a huge and dusty drum, a stretched and bleached skin trembling with anticipation. Under certain conditions mirages bounced like pebbles around the rim. Though the figures in this landscape were often completely naked, there was nothing voluptuous about their ash-smeared bodies. The continual sight of them, unashamed and impassive despite such shocking immodesty, over time became wearying and, finally, intimidating. Even the gentlest part of African 'savagery' had its element of mockery.

Gordon was two continents away in China. The world he looked out on was green and lush, a coastal plain only a metre or so above sea-level and crowded with the brown matting sails of boats moving invisibly along sunken dykes and canals. If there was order in nature it was surely replicated in the industrious and patient habits of the Chinese, even though the nation was presently at war with itself. Gordon looked on this scene with a surveyor's eye. He easily conditioned himself to think of the greater part of the population he met in it as pagan and therefore unimportant – he did not have Sam's winsomeness, nor any of his curiosity. He had come to make war.

All the same, the landscape was more immediately understandable to an English mind than the burned emptiness of the African savannah. Egrets rose from the sharp green of the paddy fields; smoke hung lazily in the air. If the Chinese did not have godliness in the sense Gordon employed the word, they did at least have cleanliness and propriety. In China the word village meant what it did in England – not some twitchy and starving population penned in behind a palisade of thorns, but a place, a locality. The paths were strewn with ducks and chickens. There were even high-arched wooden bridges by which to cross the streams that everywhere abounded. The very road Gordon followed led towards a walled city. In short, he was a figure in a willow-pattern plate. Beside him ran a crowd of children, for whom he always showed an almost feminine sympathy.

He had presence, this foreign devil, in his frogged Engineer's jacket and his baggy mud-stained trousers. His step was light, his back erect. His face reflected a mandarin calm and inscrutability, as befitted his situation. The children crowding round him were excited but respectful, for at his side there walked an actual mandarin, raised up in high-soled boots. Behind these two came a group of round-eyes, by no means as composed and seemingly carefree as their leader. For waiting at the gates to the walled city was a reception committee of theatrically dressed ruffians – also white men – lounging and smoking, some loaded with pistols and cutlasses, some with muskets. While Gordon was still dozens of metres away, these men were startled by the intensity of the stranger's stare and the peculiar economy of his gestures. He carried no weapon but had in one hand his swagger stick and, in the fingers of the other, a cigar. It was the timely arrival of a true Briton into a situation of extreme danger. Even the children understood the dramatic possibilities. These angry and sullen men at the gate could either shoot Gordon on the spot, or listen to what he had to say. If they paused to listen they must inevitably submit.

So began Gordon's first duty in his new post. On the very same day that Sam Baker rode south with the Union Jack at his back, Gordon assembled the European officers of his little army at Sung

Kiang, in the delta country of the Yangtze river. His purpose was to over-ride their determination not to serve under him at any price. Gordon had found for himself the perfect elements to excite his contrary nature – a complicated and sultry terrain and a political situation hardly less straightforward; doubtful allies and a cruel and godless foe. The army he was asked to take charge of had killed one commander and disgraced another; the Foreign Office was almost as afraid of what he might do next as it was of the enemy; and his demoralised and recalcitrant troops rejoiced meanwhile under the ill-fitting Chinese title of Ch'ang Sheng Chi'un – the Ever Victorious Army. On this particular day the phrase was specially ironic. There was, as he discovered, mutiny in the air.

Gordon's hastily assembled headquarters staff – his loyalists – comprised romantically-minded young subalterns and some seasoned old non-commissioned officers who had seen it all before. The officers he had come to convince at Sung Kiang were mercenaries and included American as well as French and German soldiers of fortune. Their Chinese troops would hardly get out of bed for less than an all-out assault on some town or other. Their motivation was very simple: loot. The two previous American commanders had not been soldiers at all – the Ever Victorious Army was merely their engine for making profit out of death and destruction.

The EVA was a rabble that attacked *en masse* and gave no quarter. When it did not think it could win, it did not leave its base. Foreign merchants had brought it into being to protect their holdings in Shanghai and that placed it nominally on the side of the imperialist army and the much smaller allied army of regular British and French troops. The enemy were the Taiping rebels. But then, who could say how long that situation would endure? (When the war was over, Wolseley, Gordon's companion under the walls of Sebastopol, said semi-humorously that, given the same arms and opportunity, he would have made himself emperor of China. This had of course suggested itself to more than one mind among those in the campaign.)

Gordon made his name in China. Nobody – mandarin, mercenary or hapless Taiping general – had ever met anyone quite like him. His reputation for reckless bravery had yet to be established among his army, though its companion virtue, an almost manic self-belief, was evident right from the start. There was, he made clear at Sung Kiang, only ever going to be one way of doing things and that was his. As the Chinese irregulars who formed the bulk of his army quickly came to realise, he was a war-lord fashioned in their own image, remorseless and capable of suffering any degree of privation to see his will enforced. In the past the Ever Victorious Army plashed about in the paddies, led to their objectives by local guides, bullied into position by the sweating round-eyes and soon enough exchanging unspeakable cruelties in the smoking ruins of this or that walled town. For them the war was uncomplicated by strategy: they went only where they could be persuaded to go. A few days' or weeks' marching, twenty-four hours of bloodshed, and then there followed three days of rape and pillage.

All that was now about to change. One of the first surprises about Gordon was his sapper's knowledge of the terrain. Coupled with it was an astonishing contempt for political interference. Neither the Shanghai merchants nor the imperial generals had any control over him. He made it all clear on that first day: what was required of the Ever Victorious Army was their disciplined obedience to him and him alone and then all would be well. There was one other not so small matter: the commander's startling personal probity. Gordon accepted only a third of the pay due to him (this was a vanity that he practised all his life) and his personal luggage was hardly more than a couple of blankets sewn together to make a sleeping bag, his Bible and a travelling bureau. It was a regime he intended to extend to his troops. They would be paid regularly for the first time but forbidden to loot. Whether they liked it or not they would be trained up to that new concept, Christian soldiers.

China itself was the prize. In 1850, flouting the Heavenly Throne of the Manchu emperor, a semi-mystical opportunist called Hung Su-Tsuen proclaimed his temporal sovereignty and three years later occupied Nanking and made it his capital. Since then everybody had fought everybody else, a running war culminating in the sacking of the Summer Palace at Peking by allied troops in 1860. Gordon himself had been present at this.

> You would scarcely conceive the magnificence of this residence or the tremendous devastation the French have committed. The throne room was lined with ebony, carved in a marvellous way. There were huge mirrors of all shapes and kinds, clocks, watches, musical boxes with puppets on them, magnificent china of every description, heaps and heaps of silks of all colours, and as much splendour and civilization as you would see at Windsor: carved ivory screens, large amounts of treasure, etc.

A few days later Lord Elgin, the British ambassador, gave orders to have the Summer Palace and its 200 pavilions burned in retaliation for the torture and execution of four British envoys, including the *Times* correspondent, Thomas Bowlby. (Close readers of this narrative might expect to find Laurence Oliphant present. In fact, this was Elgin's second visit to China. Oliphant had been with the first but declined the second unless he was made head of legation. This the government refused. After briefly meeting Gordon, Oliphant left in a sulk for Japan. As for Elgin, depredations on this scale were something of a family tradition. At the beginning of the century his father, the seventh earl, removed those parts of the Parthenon frieze which became – and have remained – known as the Elgin marbles.)

An orgy of looting followed the burning of the Summer Palace, so intense that many gold items, considered to be mere brass, were flung into the heart of the flames. Gordon tut-tutted but seems to have participated – 'Although I have not as much as many, I have done well.' It was vandalism on the heroic scale. Five years after Sebastopol the French and British allies, who had loved each other so little then, now roamed at will through Peking, their pockets stuffed with loot. Gordon mentions an English officer who bought a string of pearls for 16s. which he sold the next day for £500.

It was clear to even the most obtuse foreigner that China, however shaky the imperial throne, was a country steeped in ancient culture. That cut no ice with Gordon. He deprecated the looting of Peking, though his principal objection was not cultural or histori-cal but practical: he thought pillage sapped the morale of the troops who took part in it. Otherwise, his attitude towards the Chinese seems to have been one of cool indifference. Gordon never classified people as attractive or appealing: there was nothing in the Chinese character that he enjoyed and he seems to have witnessed the crucifixions and mutilations that littered the country-side with a dispassion verging on heartlessness. He was there because he was there and took no views. As to the seductive power that the east held for some men – its languor, or the delirium of its sexual allure – this meant nothing to him.

Five days after assuming command of the Ever Victorious Army, Gordon led them out from Sung Kiang on their first mission. God, it seemed, was more of a soldier and certainly more of an Englishman than Mammon. Together with imperialist and allied troops, the Ever Victorious Army attacked a place called Fushan and was entirely successful. Gordon's force included two or three steamers, including the ingenious *Hyson*, an amphibious vessel that had wheels and could run upon land if the gradient was not too severe. At Fushan he also had a 32-pound gun and other elements of artillery. But what won the battle was his good generalship and disregard for personal safety. The Chinese liked him without in the least understanding him: that suited Gordon very well. He liked to be liked, but at a distance. If he was in any way venal, it all took place within the confines of his tent. To his troops he was a man alone, raised high above their petty appetites. To his fellow officers, who were also excluded from his company, he was touchy, probably a little mad, but a supreme commander. The Imperial Throne thought so too, raising him in rank to a brigadier-general.

God the Englishman loved a just cause. At the next outing of the EVA, to Quinsan, with Gordon leading the attack on board the *Hyson*, 3000 rebels were accounted for in battle, with perhaps another 10,000 drowned and hacked to death by the villagers who rose *en masse* against them. Gordon's losses were two killed and five drowned. The new commander, bearing in his hand the swag-ger stick the Chinese now dubbed the Wand of Victory, had no qualms about shelling cowering and helpless rebels until the dykes and rivers ran red. Nor was he any kind of a soft touch to his own men. After the fall of the city Gordon proposed to move his base of operations there, abandoning the existing garrison at Sung Kiang. His troops refused. Gordon assembled the non-commissioned officers, told them he would shoot one in five until they changed their mind and had a corporal taken out of the ranks and shot on the spot. After an hour to reflect, the remainder fell in as before. Gordon's will was absolute. During the battle an imperialist general, cheated of loot he considered was his, fired on the Ever Victorious Army, killing about 150 of them. Gordon did not hesitate to march on his ally and was only prevented from attacking his own side by the hasty diplomacy of a Surgeon Macartney.

The obvious comparison is with Lawrence of Arabia. The two men shared many of the same traits, not least a penchant for melodramatic resignations. Gordon was a genuinely anguished man, whose chief confidantes were his mother and his devout sister, though even they must have been perplexed by him at times. Much ink has been spilt over whether he was a homosexual or a drunk, or both. The African explorer Stanley was assured one sweaty night by someone who claimed to know all about Gordon that in those days his problem was opium. None of these theories rings true. Gordon was that unusual English phenomenon, an ascetic. It says something about Victorian society that the true place for such a personality was in the army.

There is another possible comparison: with James Hanning Speke. As we have seen, Speke too was a loner. When he promised Burton he would wait for him in London so that they might go up to the Royal Geographical Society together, he was easily talked out of the idea on the voyage home. He confessed to a sympathetic ear that Burton had made sexual overtures to him which left him repelled. The ear belonged to the equally nervy and lonely Oliphant, whose own preferences were just as deeply buried as Speke's. Of course, there were men in railway carriages or in the smoking rooms of spa hotels who flaunted their dangerous desires or confessed to similar sweaty moments of attraction and repulsion: only here the scale is different. Gordon's strangeness, like Speke's, and certainly like Lawrence's, was a highly sophisticated tease. He wanted such questions asked of him, so that he could refuse to answer them.

The crowning moment of Gordon's Chinese career came at Changchow, a city where 20,000 rebels had successfully resisted siege until the arrival of the Ever Victorious Army. There were two incidents at Changchow which were extraordinary enough to change a man's life for ever. In the first Gordon went forward with a Major Tapp well in advance of his own troops to supervise the building of a gun emplacement. It was night and the little party out in no-man's-land suddenly came under a hail of fire from their own troops, the imperialists *and* the rebels inside the walls. Tapp was killed. Gordon, cigar in hand, walked back to his own lines unscathed. Almighty God had directed that the fire that killed Tapp should also spare him.

In the final assault, when the general attack was wavering, Gordon rushed the walls with the Ever Victorious Army, clambered up the breach and stood alone and exultant, urging his troops forward. He was staring down the mouth of a rebel 32-pounder levelled at almost point-blank range and the horrified onlookers waited for him to be blown to a red mist. The gun misfired. Gordon managed a perfect sang-froid about the incident: he was not killed, he explained laconically, only because the Chinese rebel gunner, member of an inferior race, had failed to keep his powder dry. The Chinese he led – *his* Chinese – saw it differently. He was saved because he was above human intervention. It was a perfect Gordon moment: when he looked into the eyes of his men and saw the awe he induced in them, his first instinct was to forswear it. It was all a matter of damp powder and bad gunnery.

There is some form of ecstasy in renunciation of this kind. Any reading of Gordon's life demonstrates that he was conscious enough of his own character to seek such moments out. Changchow ended the war. As the *Hyson* steamed slowly downriver between the massed ranks of three armies, all of them banging gongs, firing artillery pieces and discharging their muskets into the night air, few noticed a package being towed behind the famous little gunboat. It was a beautifully tailored Shanghai suit Gordon had bought to wear on the journey home. He was towing it down the river to give it age and distress. Famous though he was by now, not just in China but all over the world, he must have the outward appearance of ordinariness. He had already kicked in the crown of the bowler hat that society demanded he wore with the suit. Let no one accuse him of putting on airs.

There had been a month of similar renunciations. Gordon refused all the money the Imperial Throne wished to shower on him and reverted to his major's rank. Everybody knew he diverted most of his pay while in the employ of the Chinese to the benefit of his men. This business with the suit was his last triumphant piece of self-abnegation. In a land of greedy opportunism he went home with nothing. It is the almost perfect expression of an all-consuming vanity masquerading as humility. He walked aboard the steamer home in his shrunken and misshapen suit, wearing his battered bowler, the hero in disguise. All that was required to make his happiness complete was to be recognised.

One of the tin trunks that Sam Baker's dwindling group of porters hefted south towards the Luta Nzige contained full highland dress. On one occasion he took it out and, adding a couple of ostrich feathers to the bonnet, graciously received the chief of the Latooka, who was himself completely naked. Later in the day he sat eyeing the principal wife of this chief and their comely daughter – Sam in his Atholl tartan, Florence in ankle-length cotton, her shrinking figure supported by a full bodice: and, on the other side of the Persian carpet that was always unrolled for such state occasions, two totally nude African women. There was an exchange of civilities and small presents – beads and coloured handkerchiefs. Snapping at its pole was the Union Jack, while in the middle distance emaciated dogs ran frantically this way and that. The lowering sun lit heaps of skulls, for in this country the dead were piled outside the village gates and left to rot above ground. Bokke, the chief's wife, suggested to Florence that she would be very much more attractive if the front teeth of her lower jaw were knocked out and a hole made in the flesh of the lip for the insertion of some ornament. Instead, Sam snapped a thermometer and gave the three pieces to Bokke for her own lip.

Such scenes as these are handled with skill and a certain amount of wit in *Albert Nyanza*, though the reader must always be reassured that the storyteller is, by the colour of his skin if nothing else, the superior intelligence. 'There is no such thing as *love* in these countries,' Baker complained, with an eye to his women readers. 'The feeling is not understood, nor does it exist in the shape in which we understand it. Everything is practical, without a particle of romance.' Bokke's appeal was not in her beauty (which the explorer found very apparent, despite the missing teeth) but in her physical strength. 'Women are so far appreciated as they are valuable animals. They grind the corn, fetch the wood, gather firewood, cement the floors, cook the food and propagate the race: but they are mere servants, and as such they are valuable.'

For as long as he had the health and strength to persevere with afternoons like this, Sam indulged the Africans he came across with the idea that they were meeting very much as men of affairs did in the unknowable country from which he came. He never accepted a gift – say a goat or two or three chickens – without reciprocating in kind. In the evenings he would put on a satin jacket in which to dine. Of course it was all a deception, one which he practised on himself as much as on those he met along the way. It had not taken long to realise that what the Latooka and the Obbo wanted was not a demonstration of table manners but everything that lay within his tent.

What he perceived as their greed maddened him. He was being unsystematically plucked. If he gave a man one shotgun, he wanted two. A handful of beads was accepted with a bad grace, for could not everyone see that there was a trunk stuffed full of such geegaws? As he went on, his possessions began to fall away, leaving only his indomitable will. When the last of the quinine went, he was in dire trouble. On Grant's sketchy map the Luta Nzige was no more than a few days' march away. It seemed to recede with every step Sam took. In one village the headman calmly announced that it was six months distant. The horses and donkeys died, the camels were lost or stolen.

The search for the second feeder lake of the Nile is an epic of adventure in which chiefs come and go, minor successes are followed by catastrophic setbacks and a sense of despair is held at bay only by British pluck and British grit. The landscape shifts, rivers run the wrong way. To go on is almost certainly to perish – but then to turn back is to die along the way. What gives the story its extra piquancy is the presence of a white woman. Florence did indeed very nearly die at the crossing of the Kafur river.

> The river was about eighty yards wide, and I had scarcely completed a fourth of the distance and looked back to see if my wife followed close to me when I was horrified to see her standing in one spot, and sinking gradually through the weeds, while her face was distorted and perfectly purple. Almost as soon as I perceived her, she fell, as though shot dead.

She had suffered what Baker took to be sunstroke. For several days she lay in a coma, breathing no more than four or five times a minute. Her lover, filled with bitter self-recriminations, sat by her side, waiting for her to die. But she revived, only to rave incomprehensibly, limbs twitching. The few Arabs left of those who had set out with the Bakers from Gondokoro fitted a new handle to the mattock and began digging Florence's grave. She used to claim in later life that it was the sound of this implement chopping the red earth that brought her back from the dead. At dawn on the morning of 12 March 1864 she opened her eyes. Baker, who had not slept for seven nights, burst into tears – 'The gratitude of that moment I will not attempt to describe.'

They staggered on for two more days and arrived at a village he took to be called Parkhani. It was the Unyoro word for 'very nearby'. On the 14th, staggering up the slope of yet another dry and bitter hill, the glory of our prize burst suddenly upon me! There, like a sea of quicksilver, lay far beneath the grand expanse of water – a boundless sea horizon on the south and south west, glittering in the noon-day sun: and on the west, at fifty or sixty miles distance, blue mountains rose from the bosom of the lake to a height of about 7,000 feet above its level.

It was a moment that transformed both their lives. Without a detailed map, without medicines or guides, using only his own money and the resources of an English country gentleman – though a decidedly eccentric one – Samuel Baker entered the annals of African exploration to stand on a par with Speke and Burton and those, like Stanley, who came after him. He immediately named the lake Albert Nyanza: in a wonderful and touching parallel gesture, Florence took from her hair a ribbon woven in the Hungarian national colours and tied it to a twig at the water's edge. Men had suffered similar privations without discovering a single thing that was new: and the littoral of Africa, especially in the west, was crowded with the graves of young brides who had come to the continent only to die: no couple had ever done so much and borne so much. Now, just like Gordon's, Samuel Baker's name was written in history. If he lived to tell the tale he would be famous for ever. But much more than that, he had brought with him into the light of the nineteenth century a girl who, but for the mere chance of a midwinter shipwreck on the Danube, would have lived and died a slave.

The Bakers staggered back into Khartoum on 5 May 1865. They had drifted north in a dhow filled with plague victims and then, when they met a headwind, made the last painful leg on camels. They were welcomed with incredulity by the entire European population of the city and lodged in the house of a M. Lombrosio. The Pethericks were not there – Speke had not waited to return to England to vilify the Cornishman, and he and his Kate had been summarily dismissed from the consular service. There was a French translation of Speke's book in Khartoum and only at the end, in a footnote, did Baker learn of his accidental death in England from gunshot wounds. No letters were waiting for them, for the world had given up the Bakers as lost. There was typhus in the city and a huge drought in the surrounding countryside. Now nothing mattered but to get home.

Sam could not face the overland route north to Wadi Halfa but elected instead to go by Berber to Suakin. There were two last small adventures. The Nile was extraordinarily low and as a consequence, wherever it met obstructions in the river bed, turbulent. Sailing north to Berber, the vessel was broached and very nearly capsized. Only Sam's presence of mind saved the boat, Florence (who could not swim) and his tin trunk of papers and observations. Then, on the road to Suakin, his party was threatened by some Hadendowa tribesmen. Sam parried a sword thrust with his umbrella and jammed the ferrule down the man's throat. Florence picked up the fallen sword and flourished it in the mêlée that followed. After a short and bloody fight the tribesmen were overcome and Sam broke up their lances to light a fire and boil coffee. He offered either to take them as captives to Suakin or to thrash them there and then. They chose the thrashing. At the last moment he remitted the punishment. The story is told to indicate how one resolute Englishman can conquer any odds. Baker, with his umbrella and his bellowing Arabic, had broken the will of men the British army – and Kipling – would come to immortalise for their hairdos as Fuzzy-Wuzzies.

The Bakers took ship in a troop transport to Suez. In the hotel he made straight for the bar and ordered an ice-cold Allsop's India Pale Ale. In Cairo he persuaded Shepheard's to take on his personal servant as an employee and opened his mail, which had been accumulating in the consulate. The Royal Geographical Society had awarded him the Victoria Gold Medal. As he could not help pointing out, the honour had been made to him when it was thought very likely to be a posthumous award. Instead, he was alive – and if he had greatly overestimated the size and significance of the Albert Nyanza, it did not matter. He was going home a hero.

SIX

On 18 October 1865 Lord Palmerston died at his wife's home at Brocket Hall in Hertfordshire. He was eighty-one years old. Next day the *Times* leader touched on the country's mood:

> He has left none like him – none who can rally round him so many followers of various opinions, none who can give us so happy a respite from the violence of party warfare, none who can bring to the work of statesmanship so precious a store of recollections. It is impossible not to feel that Lord Palmerston's death marks an epoch in English politics. 'The old order changeth, yielding place to new.'

Sam Baker and Florence arrived back in England three days before these gloomy reflections were printed. The Prime Minister died at a time when Parliament was dissolved for a general election and the subtext of the *Times* piece was clear: without Palmerston as counterweight, the next government – however it was formed – would surely be made to bend towards more reform. Moreover, the country at large was in one of its deepest anti-monarchical phases. This gave rise to a second consideration. If indeed an epoch had passed, where was the response from the queen? Victoria was not in London, nor had she been for four years. The lights burned bright at Marlborough House, the London address of the Prince of Wales, but at the other end of the Mall Buckingham Palace was unlit and untenanted. Sam learned from his clubs how, the previous Christmas, someone had hung a notice on the railings of

Buckingham Palace: THESE COMMANDING PREMISES TO BE
LET OR SOLD, IN CONSEQUENCE OF THE LATE OCCUPANT'S
DECLINING BUSINESS.

For someone who had not been in the country since 1860 and
who arrived home in that momentous week, two topics would have
been a commonplace of any conversation – the widowed queen's
continued reclusion at Osborne; and the corresponding situation
of the prince, hurried into an early marriage and now coping with
a painful sense of his own redundancy at Marlborough House. The
queen had not been seen anywhere in public since Albert's death
in 1861, refusing even her constitutional duty of coming to London
to open Parliament.

This void in the representation of royalty had to be filled somehow and the task fell almost by default to the Prince of Wales,
belittled by both his parents as a sulky and socially clumsy boy.
Bertie was now the rallying point for London society, a rich and
faintly bewildered young man of twenty-four. At the moment of
his father's death he had flung himself sobbing into Victoria's
arms, promising to do his duty by her in any way he could. Instead,
there was a determination on the part of both the queen and her
ministers to keep him away from state papers, while retaining him
as a figurehead. For example, he represented his mother at the
funeral of Lord Palmerston, who was buried, against his own wishes,
in Westminster Abbey.

The prince, such a grave disappointment to his parents, was
actually very protective of the idea of monarchy and – at this stage
of his life – by no means the unprincipled rake. What public duties
he was given he discharged with commendable gravity. At
Palmerston's funeral he carried himself with habitual calm, good
looking, immaculately dressed, in many ways a perfect European
prince. The trouble with Bertie was his tendency to an unbuttoned
cronyism among his private circle, where his combination of affability and indolence often led him astray. He liked to attend fires in
the city, keeping company with his friend George Leveson Gower,
third Duke of Sutherland, who was passionately interested in
fire engines. Distraught victims, watching their house or business

premises burn, would be astonished to see two of the richest men in England pelt up by cab from wherever they had been dining.

Marlborough House was at the centre of clubland. White's, Boodle's and Brooks's were in St James's Street. In the Mall there was Carlton and the Travellers'. The prince was an honorary member of all these, as well as the Reform and Athenaeum. In time he founded his own club, the Marlborough, opposite his house, irritated, it was said, at being reproached by a waiter at White's for smoking outside the Smoking Room. In fact, his behaviour in all these male preserves was like the rest of his life, unexceptional. Often his days were quite as dull as his mother's. Bertie was, as Albert had always suspected, stupid without the inclination to improve.

His 'newspaper' at Marlborough House was the ubiquitous Laurence Oliphant, who had at last fallen foul of the Foreign Office. Oliphant saw the prince almost daily, presenting himself to the lone kilted soldier guarding the entrance. Footmen came forward to relieve the visitor of his hat and coat and then a porter in a tunic with leather epaulettes asked him his name and sent in his card. After a few moments a young page led the way to the prince. Bertie was seldom too busy to see his friends – in some ways his friends were his only business. Oliphant brought him the political gossip, never forgetting to burnish the reputation of a man who had become one of Bertie's favourite soldiers.

That was one of the first surprises to greet Sam Baker on his return to London: his brother had become a loyal, if distant, member of the Marlborough House set.

Much more the obedient servant than his brother, Val made his way in life by being intelligent without being enthusiastic, reserved without being dull; above all, dependable. He came home from the Crimea a captain. In 1860 he was given command of the 10th Hussars, following the retirement of Colonel Wilkie. He set about making his regiment not only an expression of his reforming ideas on cavalry drill and tactics, which he had set out in a sober little book published in 1858, but also a socially impeccable elite comparable in standing to any in the army. Reformer though the new colonel might be, there was nothing of the crank about him. What brought gentlemen forward in the eyes of their new commander-in-chief, the Duke of Cambridge, was a certain amount of common sense and a solid regimental background. The first stone of a staff college was laid at Camberley in 1859. The royal duke had his doubts. 'I don't like Staff College officers,' he remarked to a district commander in his guttural German accent. 'My experience of Staff Officers is that they are conceited, and they are dirty. Brains! I don't believe in brains! You haven't any, I know sir, and as for my Military Secretary over there on the other side of the table, and a damned good Military Secretary, too, he's the very stupidest man I ever came across.'

It pointed which way Val should lead the 10th Hussars. His efforts were rewarded in a very pleasing way. In 1863, a few weeks before his wedding, the Prince of Wales accepted the colonelcy-in-chief of the regiment.

The two men hit it off at once. The prince had been burned by his earlier adolescent association with the army. A scheme of his father's was to send him, dressed as a colonel, to the Guards camp at the Curragh. He was to spend his time there at carefully managed mess dinners five nights a week, reserving the remaining two for improving reading. It was a plan that went disastrously wrong, for the younger Guards officers had a different idea of what he needed and found the prince a girl to debauch. Nellie Clifden was an actress, or said she was. When news of the affair reached Prince Albert, he was appalled. The queen never forgot or forgave this incident, holding that it was a contributory factor to her husband's death.

Val was a soothing counterweight to this troubled background. Though he was thirteen years older than his colonel-in-chief, he was not so ancient that he stood in the position of guardian or tutor. Perhaps his best asset was that he had no aristocratic connections and so no standing at court. In a word, he was safe. The queen's most minute examination of his background could find no fault in him. He was made an equerry to the prince and became a founder-member of the Marlborough Club. When Sam met his brother again in London, after a gap of seven years, Val was just about to marry. There, too, his native caution had shaped his choice. His fiancée was Fanny Wormald of Potterton Hall in Yorkshire. The family had a military background and kept up an unassuming house at the edge of the Vale of York. The Prince of Wales chose as wedding present a white Arab charger, a gift which became a trademark in Val's military life.

The prince was also colonel-in-chief of the Blues, the Royal Horse Guards. In its ranks could be found another founder-member of the Marlborough Club, Frederick Gustav Burnaby. If Colonel Baker was among the more assiduous cavalry officers in the army, Fred Burnaby was the kind of soldier the Prince of Wales knew rather better. He first endeared himself to the prince at a Blues guest night by tying a poker round the royal neck. Burnaby was six feet four and weighed seventeen stone. He boxed, he fenced, he played cricket, lifted impossible weights and tossed impudent members of the lower classes about like rag dolls. The most famous story about him concerned a period when the Blues were on duty at Windsor. The queen expressed a desire to buy two Icelandic ponies and when the dealer arrived with them some larky members of the Blues mess drove these animals up a flight of stairs into Burnaby's quarters. Once there, they would not leave. As the hour for the appointment with the queen drew near, the joke seemed to have misfired badly and the young officers grew nervous. Burnaby was summoned. He picked up a pony under each arm and staggered down the narrow staircase, dumping them in the courtyard like suitcases.

The louche side of the Marlborough House set has often been emphasised but in truth the prince's position had many delicate folds and layers to it. The official court was in disarray. The household was terrified of upsetting the queen any more than she already was. At the same time, the constitutional situation was coming close to crisis. Marlborough House was merely a private residence, yet the skeins of patronage and influence had to be gathered up somewhere in London. The prince, for all his lack of interest in intellectual matters, his apparently empty hours spent smoking in one of his clubs, his taste for gambling and pretty women, would one day succeed to the throne. Nobody in 1865 imagined that date was nearly forty years off.

It was clear to which star Sam Baker must hitch his wagon. Naming his principal discovery Lake Albert was a piece of flattery aimed at Osborne – perhaps too obvious to be useful. He was much more likely to be taken up and patronised in the London clubs the prince made fashionable. One of the first things he did on his return was to pay his subscription to Windham's and get himself put up for the Athenaeum. (He was elected from a shortlist of twelve, along with Millais and the mathematician Thomas Hirst.) He too was a member of the Marlborough. Though he affected to disdain society politics and its murky world, he knew the rules of the game. He took care to name the Murchison Falls for the president of the Royal Geographical Society. There were pursed lips from some of Murchison's enemies but a generally sympathetic reception for Sam, whose witty public lectures on life in the heart of Africa did a lot to soften the shock of Speke's mysterious death, and the total collapse of Livingstone's Zambezi expedition. His friend Wharncliffe helped too, by canvassing discreetly among government ministers. Surely a man who would risk his own money as well as his life in exploration was worth at least a knighthood to add to his RGS Gold Medal?

Before that could happen, there was an urgent matter to resolve. Sam married Florence by special licence at St James's, in the heart of Mayfair, a week after Palmerston's funeral. There were no guests and no music in the echoing Wren church. The ceremony was conducted in a side chapel and witnessed only by the groom's younger brother James and his wife Louisa. These two were to prove loyal friends to Florence. Min, who was looking after Sam's children, was harder to mollify. The youngest child was now ten and the oldest, Edith, eighteen. It was a difficult situation which for a time threatened to split the family. 'Indeed it *is* a romance,' the unmarried Min wrote to her sister Ann, adding, 'We must all receive her with kindness and affection, which will not be difficult after her marvellous devotion; but as to future arrangements, I feel there would be something to sadden all concerned.'

Though she could hardly bring herself to say so, Min wanted the children for herself. She had brought them up with an aunt's devotion, never for a moment attempting to replace the memory of her sister Henrietta. Now came this strange, beautiful, mysterious woman hardly older than Edith. Would the children be asked to call her Mother? Min did not think it right for Sam to demand that of them. 'He must make up his mind to have a separate establishment for her in London and be contented to divide himself between the two homes.'

Min realised that Florence was so much a part of the Samuel White Baker story, accompanying him on to public platforms and being admired for her youth and fortitude, that she had to be accepted by the rest of the Bakers. Quite apart from having lived in sin with Sam for so long, it was distressing to all the Bakers that her antecedents were so very vague. Though she could speak English – albeit with a marked accent – she was barely literate. Signing the wedding register she made three attempts to spell her own name. In time, her stepdaughters helped teach her copper-plate handwriting and the formal requirements of the social letter. Florence had seen more than any of the children could guess at, but she was a very unpolished Victorian. The problem with her was pointed up in 1866, when Sam was presented at court and invested with his knighthood. His wife was not included in the palace guest list. Val too had been presented and it was hurtful that Fanny Baker had no trouble in being invited along with *her* husband.

Val Baker was an example of a stone that shone because of its setting. The army had raised him up to a social eminence from which greater things were possible. He had only to serve to be advanced. Things were nothing like as clear cut for Sam Baker, for whom the term rough diamond might as well have been invented. Then his chance came. Two years later – ten years after the Danube expedition with Duleep Singh – the Prince of Wales invited Sir Samuel Baker to be part of his entourage on a visit to Egypt.

The appointment required the queen's approval, which she gave only grudgingly. 'The company of Sir S. Baker (and I am sorry to hear also the Duke of Sutherland, whose style is not a good one in any way) grieves me . . . Sir S. Baker's principles are not good, and I regret he should be associated with you and dear Alix.' The queen was indicating her displeasure at reports that had reached her concerning the background to Sam's marriage. These were abundant enough. Lady Login had already expressed her dark suspicions of the Danube trip. If the couple had an enemy in clubland it was certainly Speke's former companion, the unpleasant and vindictive Captain James Grant; but Murchison also knew the truth about Florence; and Colquhoun. Livingstone, who had never met either of the parties, confided his doubts to the intrepid world traveller and widow of the arctic explorer, Lady Jane Franklin, as far away as Bombay.

The queen's list of suitable companions for her son was always a short one, no matter what the occasion. One of her foibles was a prurient interest in other people's sex lives. When the painter Millais was knighted she had to have it explained to her that his wife, who had once been Mrs Ruskin, was virgo intacta when Millais married her. Sniffily, she counselled the poor woman to keep quiet about it. Although the prince would travel to Egypt with his wife, the queen knew about her son's capacity for getting into scrapes. Sam Baker, with his piratical beard and juvenile sense of humour, his love of killing things, was just about acceptable. But when it came to Florence, so much puffed as the heroine of the Nile, yet so obviously lacking any English aristocratic connection, the queen put her foot down. She refused to allow Florence to accompany her husband.

The Egypt trip was part of a larger eastern Mediterranean itinerary. The royal party was to sail in several steamers to Aswan and then return to Cairo for ten days of balls and receptions. On the trip down the Nile Baker was assiduous in showing the prince a good time, shooting whatever could be seen from the deck of the little luxury vessel, at other times lounging in one of the gilt armchairs provided by the khedive and beguiling his host with tales of the hinterland. In the evening, moored to the bank and attended by silent-footed servants, there were cigars and semi-official conversation. Said was no longer viceroy and his successor was Ismail. One of the prince's duties was to open a sluice gate on a stretch of the new canal: it was natural then that they should talk about de Lesseps and French influence on the new khedive.

Sam was looking for more adventure. He suggested to the prince that it would be prestigious to England and Christianity to persuade Ismail to allow him to retrace his steps in the Sudan with a military force at his command and so open up territories presently controlled by crooks and slave traders. He proposed himself as the governor of an entirely new province, to be opened up south of Gondokoro, that would extend as far south as Lake Victoria, or even beyond. The Prime Minister of Egypt was a Christian Armenian, Nubar Pasha, and Sam disclosed that he had already written letters in this vein to Nubar.

The prince liked Sam but had only a slight grasp of such possibilities. What political wisdom there was on board was proffered by 'Billy' Russell of *The Times*, who was invited in his private capacity as a wit and raconteur. The royal party was travelling in a bubble of privilege, sealed off from the real condition of the country, which appeared to the prince and most of his entourage as simply tableaux of the quaint and timeless. They were in a way on an extended picnic, punctuated by gunfire and a little modest temple-bashing. Sam Baker introduced some English furniture and carpets to the saloons – Ismail had otherwise fitted out the steamers like floating French boudoirs. It was clubland on the Nile.

However, even the dimmest mind could have pointed out the obvious – that Egypt's days were numbered. The country was bankrupt. Moreover, between the fellah and Ismail, between his stupendous personal wealth and the fate of the nation, there lay nothing but the kourbash, the hippo-hide whip that acted as tax-collector. Moberly Bell, Russell's colleague on *The Times* and the paper's Cairo correspondent, was fond of explaining that Egypt was not and never had been a nation in any sense understood by Europeans. As for the Sudan, what was that, apart from the Nile's fever-laden extension, governed for the khedive by a gang of outright ruffians? There – with a wave of his cigar south – you could buy a black girl for a clean shirt or half a dozen sewing needles. Moberly Bell omitted to add that about 4000 of the annual cull of such girls and their families did not disappear into Arabia across the Red Sea, but came direct to Cairo.

The prince and many of his entourage looked on to the banks of the Nile and saw without rancour what they called blacks. Some they found romantic, like the wandering bedouin. Some were practically invisible, beings without personality, human mud. There was no guilt in thinking like this, and for the majority of Englishmen it gave no cause for moral outrage, either. Racism was a thing apart from issues of slavery – indeed, some anti-slavery propaganda was itself profoundly racist, heaping contempt and hatred on Arabs in order to glorify 'aboriginal' tribes. As he had shown, Sam himself separated what he thought about slavery from what he thought about indigenous peoples. He hated slavers with a passion but his championing of the African was never more than lukewarm.

The prince may have been astute enough to see this. Sir Samuel was no tub-thumper, no Holy Joe. What this brusque and burly sportsman wanted was a stage on which to shine, a way of drawing down yet more fame for himself. Both Baker brothers, the explorer and the colonel of Hussars, were models of maleness the prince understood without wishing to emulate. The world was held up on their broad shoulders, and those of others like them. Sam and Val Baker were attractive to the prince because they were doers, not talkers or, that even worse category in Bertie's eyes, thinkers. When the royal party returned to Cairo, he spoke to the khedive. As Sam had guessed, he was pushing on an open door. As soon as he knew he was going to succeed, he sent for Florence.

The preamble to the commission Sam finally secured read like this:

We, Ismail, Khedive of Egypt, considering the savage condition of the tribes which inhabit the Nile Basin;

Considering that neither government, nor laws, nor security exists in those countries;

Considering that humanity enforces the suppression of the slave-hunters who occupy those countries in great numbers;

Considering that the establishment of legitimate commerce throughout those countries will be a great stride forward towards future civilization, and will result in the opening to steam navigation of the great equatorial lakes of Central Africa and in the establishment of a permanent government ... We have decreed and now decree as follows ...

The clauses that followed gave Sam absolute powers, tempered by an immediate caution from London that he and any other Briton who travelled with him would not be afforded Foreign Office protection. This disavowal applied in the end to fifteen people, headed by Sam, Florence and his nephew Julian Baker (John's son), who was a lieutenant RN. Four of the party were shipwrights and boilermakers, for the plan was to transport not one but four vessels to the Upper Nile, the queen of the fleet being a 250-ton paddle-steamer. Sam was to command two battalions of troops, one Nubian and another drawn from the jails and detention barracks of Egypt. A small cavalry force was being assembled in Khartoum. (However, as soon as he got there, Sam took one look at them on their broken-down mounts and sent them all home.)

Every aspect of the enterprise was overseen by him with the same enthusiasm and meticulousness he applied to all his ventures. To carry the engine parts and plating of his steamers across the desert from Wadi Halfa to Berber, he bought several hundred fir logs to make carrying cradles for the teams of camels. It was typical of him to specify these poles should come from Trieste. The inventory included shovels, but also spades and hoes, for it had been proved to Sam that nothing induced a sense of security and indeed locality more than a garden: he had enough lettuce seed for each man of his expedition to grow a row or two wherever the commander decided to plant his headquarters' flag. He included band instruments, in the belief that rousing music was as good as a sermon to a savage heart. In addition to several tons of trade goods (the invitation to 'legitimate commerce') the camel trains also hauled an ample supply of fine wines, dresses suitable to a governor's lady; and a concocted uniform in the military pattern fit for a pasha.

The expedition was as well prepared as any that had ever left Egypt under the Turkish flag. Sam himself was on a four-year contract at an annual salary of £10,000, at the end of which time, in theory, the Sudan would be rid of slavery and the White Nile laid open to civilisation and commerce, the one a consequence of the other. That this seemed even remotely feasible to anyone in England, even the most purblind abolitionist, is an indication of how wishful was the thinking surrounding African colonisation. The first thing Baker discovered when he got to Khartoum was that the whole of the ivory trade, so patently co-terminous with the slave trade, had already been licensed by the khedive, a fact he could have gleaned in any Cairo coffee-house. The country he came to create – Ismailia – had no maps or flags, and no boundaries. While there was no government and certainly no justice, as a commercial trading territory it was brutally efficient. To rid the Nile basin of slavery would be to fight the very people the khedive had licensed. Whether or not Ismail felt guilty about this in the confines of the Gabbari Palace, surrounded by his own slaves, was beside the point.

The trick of Sam's appointment was to suppose the khedive had been in earnest when granting him absolute powers. When he first came to the Sudan, he had been suspected of being a spy. There could be no mistaking in what guise he returned. The scale of his presence was an invitation to war. The licence-holders had done nothing to improve the country since Sam had last seen it. Khartoum was squalid beyond description. Almost all the Europeans had vanished and with them the last vestiges of any western sophistication. The town had reverted to its original condition as a slave and ivory entrepôt. It stank. Reports from the south were that the Nile was completely blocked by the Sudd, on the far side of which was civil war. Sam was going to need his two battalions of troops. With a characteristic touch he formed a personal guard from the best of the Nubians, armed with the most modern rifles he had in his armoury. If push came to shove, it was on these men – 'the forty thieves' – that his own life and that of Florence would depend.

That the Sudd had choked the Nile threw all his plans into turmoil. Slaves and ivory came to Khartoum by water and if a governor could control the river, he could control the trade. Khartoum was merely the shabby front door to the problem. The stretch of the river that really mattered was at Gondokoro on the other side of the Sudd. In the years covered by Sam's appointment, that country might as well have been on another planet. To breach the Sudd was his first soul-destroying task.

The Nile at Khartoum was 200 yards wide. At the northern edge of the Sudd the clear channel was no wider than a Gloucester stream. The guides hired to find a passage for the expedition's steamer and thirty-nine other vessels pronounced themselves utterly defeated by the problem. At first Sam took them to be incompetent and there was a great deal of shouting and cuffing of ears. Gradually the truth dawned on him.

> It is a curious but most painful fact that the entire White Nile has ceased to be a navigable river. The boundless plains of marsh are formed of floating rafts of vegetation compressed into firm masses by the pressure of water during floods. So serious is this obstacle to navigation that unless a new channel can be discovered, or the original Nile be reopened, the centre of Africa will be entirely shut out from communication, and all my projects for the improvement of the country will be ruined by this extraordinary impediment.

The Egyptian battalion was specially demoralised. The river, which was full of fish, never-failing and life-giving in exactly the same way it was at home, now assumed a terrible secondary personality. The crocodiles were voracious, hippos attacked the vessels, clouds of mosquitoes and poisonous watersnakes made work a nightmare. Bellowed at, browbeaten, these soldiers knew what had to be done but not why. Accustomed to being at the bottom of the pile in Egypt, the light-skinned fellahin who made up half of Sam's soldiery found themselves no better off on foreign service than they had been in jail. Baker Pasha openly favoured his Nubian troops – and perhaps the sharpest insult of all was that when they did arrive at dry land, the local girls would not sleep with the

The *Black Watch* cheering Lord Wolseley on his way up the Nile, 1884.

Great anti-slavery demonstration fervour at Exeter Hall: the Strand Palace Hotel stands on the site today.

Valentine Baker as a young man (*above*) and (*right*) as the army made him.

Samuel Baker in his Ceylon hunting clothes (*left*) and (*above*), as fame tricked him out.

Left Charles Gordon.

Below David Livingstone, 1870.

Laurence Oliphant as a young man, 1854.

Florence Baker
as a Victorian
lady.

Above Queen Victoria
with an Indian servant.

Right The Prince of
Wales as a sulky and
unhappy puppet soldier.

Above Frederick Burnaby.

Left Maharajah Duleep Singh.

Left HRH George, Duke of
Cambridge, Commander-in-
Chief 1856–95.

Below Baker Pasha by Ape
(Vanity Fair)

The slave market, Zanzibar, 1860.

Sam and Florence Baker on horseback in Cyprus, prior to their world tour.

Egyptians, though they rushed to the beds of the rival Nubian battalion.

It was all too much for Dr Gedge, the medical officer, who drank himself to death. The Bakers' two servants were more often caught in bed with each other than polishing the silverware: they were sent back almost before the expedition started out. Readers of *Ismailia* were startled by a coarsening of tone in Sam's description of his tour of duty. In one way he was a victim of his own narrative powers: the book is just as racy, just as exciting as its predecessor, *Albert Nyanza*. But this time the guns are out, not just for game, but for human beings. Where once he had made his way among the tribes with a mixture of bravery and bluff, now the business was uncomfortably punitive. Government of Ismailia was going to be by warfare.

He kept discipline among his own men by the application of the dreaded kourbash – a hundred strokes here, a hundred there. Malingerers or thieves were loaded with chains, deserters and renegades sentenced to death. Most shocking of all to the English liberal conscience: the people he came to liberate did not wish to be liberated and certainly not by his methods.

> The bugles and the drums sounded the advance and the troops, having fired several volleys, rushed on at the double and stormed the position. This was well executed, and the rush so unexpected by the Baris that the stockade was taken at the point of the bayonet ... This attack was something the Baris did not comprehend. They had only been accustomed to face the slave-hunter's irregular companies ... They now began to clamber up the rocks and ascend the mountain with the activity of baboons, while a sharp fire from the sniper rifles acted like a spur upon their movements. A shell from the gun now burst over a number of the enemy who had collected about 800 yards in our rear. This was an unmistakable notice to quit. We set fire to the stockades, and the Baris having disappeared, I selected a position for a night's bivouac.

Sam badly misjudged his English readership's capacity to feel fear. The events he dramatised were very often terrifying –

stragglers from the main party hunted down in the high grass and speared to death, women water-carriers stripped, raped and beaten. There are passages in the book where his force, constantly depleted by desertion, is faced by overwhelming odds, even, as it sometimes seemed, by the entire countryside. But the anti-slavery lobby did not wish to hear about terror by night unless it resulted in a compensating good elsewhere: it wanted its moral indignation stoked by a story that also had a happy ending.

The short and sweet Ashanti War of 1873–4 was an indication of what British public opinion would tolerate. Fought on a coast already known as 'the white man's grave', where many a missionary had left his bones, the Ashanti had crossed the Pra river into the British possession of the Gold Coast. Resistant to Christianity, sufficiently homogenous to be considered a nation in the European sense of the word – and an idolatrous one at that – the Ashanti were crushed by a force so superior to them in terms of men and *matériel* that what happened could hardly be considered warfare at all. In one incident a terrified Ashanti warrior captured by the British was tied to a steam roadroller and sent crashing through the banana plantations and mangrove swamps to deliver a final warning message to his own headquarters. The author of methods such as this was Garnet Wolseley, who commanded a force hugely top heavy with up-and-coming officers of the same cast of mind as his own. Wolseley did not exterminate the Ashanti, as he would have liked, but he did blow the capital of the country, Kumasi, into dust and rubble. His country loved him for it.

Sam's war against the slavers of the Upper Nile was never as clear cut. The story had a villain, the powerful and wily slaver Abu Saud, but more often than not he could not be brought to battle. He fought by proxy with tribes only too willing to enslave their own people. Cut off by the terrible Sudd from resupply, Sam's little forts and redoubts and their tiny garrisons were nothing more than fleabites.

We appeared to have forsaken the known world, and, having passed the River Styx, to have become secluded forever in a wild land of our own, where all were enemies, like evil spirits, and where it was necessary either to procure food at the point of a bayonet, or to lie down and die . . . If the White Nile had been the fine, navigable river that I had known in former years, I believe I should have had no difficulty, as I could have quickly overcome the scruples of my officers by direct reports of their conduct to the Khedive; but we were lost to the world almost as absolutely as though quartered on the moon.

He was very conscious of the fixed term of the contract he had been offered: he needed to come home with something to show for all the effort and frustrations. Instead the months and years slipped by in marching and counter-marching, ugly little skirmishes and the ever-present threat of an all-out attack, sufficient to annihilate the entire force. Baker's campaign for the hearts and minds of the new Ismailians was no more successful. He tells the story of a sheikh who came to watch his soldiers sowing corn. The sheikh turned to Baker and asked: 'How long are you going to remain here? You had better go back to Khartoum, and I will eat the corn you have planted when it has become ripe.'

I explained that Gondokoro would be headquarters, and that troops would always remain there, and we should cultivate a large extent for corn. He replied: 'Then who does this land belong to? – to you, or to me?' I explained that his people had been driven out by a superior force, and that we had found it abandoned; at the same time, neither he nor his people dare remain here without my protection, therefore the land belonged to the Khedive of Egypt; but if the natives wished to resettle, I would give them their original property.

The sheikh studied this answer and then pointed to the tree under which he and Sam stood. Looking him full in the face, he asked, 'Who does this tree belong to?' Sam controlled his irritation and said that the tree belonged to the khedive of Egypt, 'who is now protector of the whole country and I am his representative to establish his government'. The sheikh shrugged and murmured, 'Then you had better be off to Khartoum, for we don't want any government here.'

The imperturbable Bakers face down some excited natives.

Sam's reaction to this encounter is painfully honest.

> There can be no doubt [he wrote], that in the abstract of people's rights, any annexation of the territory of another is an infringement. Had this principle been adhered to throughout the history of the world, there would have been no progress. Savages of all countries are prone to strife; and a state of chronic warfare with neighbouring tribes is an example of African politics.

After a moment or two of reflection he added, 'A strong government is a necessity.'

In January 1873, five months from the conclusion of his term of office, he enjoyed a few days of relief from this prosecution of government by gunfire. At one of his most southerly forts, Fatiko, he received envoys from Mtesa, whom he styles king of Uganda. He was suddenly face to face with highly intelligent men, beautifully dressed in crisp Indian cottons, and enviably well-informed. They carried letters written in Arabic from the king.

A ghost was in the air, for it was eleven years almost to the day since Speke had first walked into Mtesa's camp with his companion Grant. The envoys told an interesting and touching story concerning him. Among the king's most treasured possessions was a memento of their encounter: to amuse him, Speke had made, on folding paper in the manner of seaside postcards, sketches of the uniforms of leading British regiments. Mtesa now wished to receive Sir Samuel Baker. It was an invitation to diplomacy on the equator that he was forced to turn down, pleading the end of his commission. Instead he wrote to the king, asking him to look out for Dr Livingstone. This message was duly carried back south and in time the king replied sympathetically. He had for many months past sent his men in every direction to look for this great man.

Livingstone's name drifts into the story of *Ismailia* with a ghostly chill almost as powerful as Speke's. As the Ugandan envoys and Sam sat in the round palaver hut at Fort Fatiko, all the great names of Nile exploration were convoked in a conversation that lasted several days. Sam had with him a soldier, Selim, who had gone with Speke all the way from Zanzibar to Cairo. He was summoned to contribute his own anecdotes to the long recital of courage and endurance. The Arabs who comprised Mtesa's delegation were gratifyingly well informed. First there had been Speke and Burton; then Speke and Grant; next, Sam and Florence; and now, finally, Baker and Livingstone. As the coffee was passed round and the compliments exchanged, they discussed sixteen years of European exploration, much as they would have had they been sitting in a committee room of the Royal Geographical Society.

Livingstone's part in the story was especially poignant. In 1864, after the collapse of the Zambezi expedition, the great missionary came home to England for what was to prove the last time. He was a beaten man. When he was greeted in the street nowadays – and it happened all too seldom – it was by what he called 'imbecile old ladies'. Palmerston received him, and Gladstone, but more as a matter of courtesy than for any other reason. The rocket fame of *Missionary Travels* that had lit up the sky so brilliantly in 1857 was gone and now all that remained was the stick. He had broken faith with the London Missionary Society and his stock among geographers was very low. The government held him at arm's length.

He found his patron Sir Roderick Murchison in agitated mood. Speke and Burton were to meet in public for the first time since that fateful conversation at Aden when Speke had promised they would go up to the RGS together. The venue was the British Association annual meeting, held that year in Bath. Anticipation of this confrontation was intense. It was common knowledge by now that Speke detested Burton. His publisher Blackwood had to excise a long final passage from Speke's *Journal of the Discovery of the Source of the Nile* for fear of a libel action. Speke insisted that it be printed and bound into the copies he wished to distribute to members of his family. In it, Burton is accused of malice, incompetence and, most damaging of all, cowardice. Speke shared publishers with Oliphant, who was capable of his own brand of malice. He gleefully reported to Burton that Speke had told him, 'If Burton appears on the platform at Bath, I shall kick him.'

Quite apart from the prospect of a bitter and recriminatory public quarrel, many scientists and explorers had come to question whether the modest outfall from Lake Victoria that Speke discovered could possibly be sufficient to animate the longest river in the world. In other words, when Speke cabled the triumphant message, 'The Nile is settled,' had he been right?

Burton did not think so and, to Murchison's alarm, neither did Livingstone. He arranged for the missionary to attend the British Association meeting. At the inaugural session on 13 September Burton and Speke sat on the same platform, studiously ignoring each other. Their debate was scheduled for the 16th. At the time appointed Burton sat alone, fingering his notes, watched by a full hall. Twenty-five minutes late, the organisers trooped gloomily on to the stage. They announced to the audience the shocking and dramatic news that, the day before, Speke had been killed in a gun accident on an estate in Somerset, quite close to Bath. Many immediately jumped to the conclusion that Speke, who was a dedicated trophy sportsman, had not suffered an accident, but shot himself. Burton wrote to a friend: 'Nothing is known of Speke's death. I saw him at 1.30 pm [that is, the previous day] and at 4 pm he was dead. The charitable say that he shot himself, the uncharitable that I shot him.'

Without Speke, the whole question of Central African geography was thrown wide open. Burton did not contribute – by the end of the year he was British consul in Santos. But Murchison saw a role for Livingstone. The tragedy came at the time when Sam Baker found, to his huge excitement, a waterfall over 120 feet high at the northern end of the Luta Nzige, pouring millions of gallons an hour into a pool infested with crocodiles. It was this discovery he had rushed to name the Murchison Falls. Though news of it was still unknown in England, it happened to coincide with some current geographical theory, including Livingstone's. Central Africa was as much about lakes as it was about rivers. The question being asked was this: who could say with absolute certainty that the Nile fell out of Lake Victoria?

It was Speke's case that the Nile started in Lake Victoria, fed the Luta Nzige in some fashion or another, and then, at the northern end of that lake, began its more stately progress as the Nile proper. As it happened, he was right, but it was merely an assertion. Livingstone had his own theory. Though he detested Burton, whom he described as 'a moral idiot', he was quick to pick up on one key feature of his objection to the Speke hypothesis. Burton, with his brutal candour, pointed out that no one had yet made a complete circumnavigation of Lake Victoria, and so it could not be proved that on its southern and western flanks there did not exist another river, either entering or leaving the lake. Nor could it even be shown for certain that the lake Burton and Speke saw in 1858 was the same one gazed on by Speke and Grant in 1863. Though Speke was dead, the controversy was not. Even the friends of Speke were forced to concede Burton's point.

If Speke *was* wrong, then the whole question remained wide open and it was this that Livingstone seized on. He had a proposal that was staggering in concept. In country nearly a thousand miles further south than Jinja Falls on Lake Victoria, *there*, if only they could be found, were the fabled Four Fountains of Herodotus! In

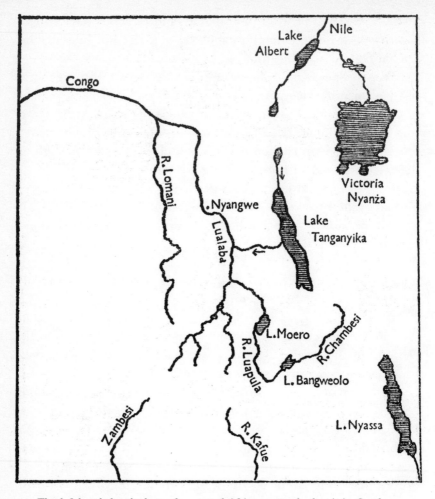

The left-hand sketch shows the central African watershed as it is. On the right is Livingstone's submission to Sir Roderick Murchison, which placed the rise of the Nile over 1000 miles to the south.

the area he indicated were the headwaters of the Zambezi and the Kafue, which flowed south; and the Lomani and Lualaba, which flowed north. Here was a chance to substantiate what people had supposed formerly to be a mere piece of poetry, a conceit. Yet what if it were true? Suppose, he suggested to Murchison, it was the Lualaba that rose from some ancient fountain and, perhaps assisted

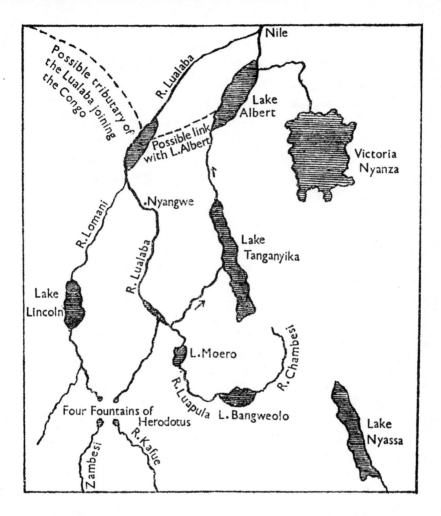

by the Lomani, ran its huge course northwards to become at last the Nile?

Whatever Murchison thought of the Four Fountains theory, which would have put the source in what we now call Zimbabwe, he already considered it possible that some chain of lakes and rivers running west out of Lake Victoria did indeed exist. Murchison was a very rich man who had also earned his huge share of public honours. He gave the matter some reflection and then decided: what could he lose? He prepared to make one more investment in David Livingstone. The terms were humiliatingly modest. Murchison regretted he could not send his man out to Africa a second time with anything more than a £500 grant. What's more, he was to go alone. He was to keep better scientific journals, make more accurate maps and turn everything over to the society on his return. Murchison was seventy-four when he struck this mean-spirited and self-serving deal. Offering so few resources, sending his man off without the least encouragement from the Foreign Office, was as good as consigning Livingstone to oblivion. In 1866, consumed with bitterness, the missionary set off in search of the Four Fountains of Herodotus.

When Sam met the envoys from King Mtesa, therefore, his interest in Livingstone's whereabouts was much more than philanthropic. Though he knew he could not get much further himself, the southerly limits of the province he had brought into being – Ismailia – might be, according to Livingstone, a quite enormous distance away. Fatiko was three degrees north of the equator. Livingstone was talking about somewhere as much as fifteen degrees of latitude further south. Perhaps Sam was a little dazed by the suavity of Mtesa's messengers. The conference at Fatiko was a change from arguing with some ragged sheikh about who owned the tree under which he stood.

There was a second and deeper motive in wanting to know more of Livingstone. Anything that disproved Speke only highlighted Sam's own discovery of the Luta Nzige. In Livingstone's fevered mind it was the Lualaba that came crashing into Baker's lake. At the end of the envoys' visit he sent Selim off with them, bearing a letter to Livingstone wishing him well and announcing his own presence. Watching the envoys depart, he concluded, with more hope than common sense, about the other matters they had discussed: 'The road was now declared to be practically open between Fatiko and Zanzibar by means of M'Tese's friendship.'

The long waterway (sometimes lake, sometimes river) that might just conceivably bypass Lake Victoria was a dream that cost Livingstone his life. The Lualaba river was the headwaters not of the Nile, but the Congo. At the very moment Sam sat swapping geographical theory with the envoys at Fatiko, the missionary lay a thousand miles away. Almost blind, horribly emaciated and bleeding to death from ulcerated intestines, Livingstone was too weak to leave the last miserable village he had come to. Those who lived there explained, with dreadful irony, that they were not people who travelled much. Outside his hut was a sluggish and shallow stream on which the mosquitoes danced. Livingstone died in the early hours of 1 May 1873. His faithful servant Susi embalmed the body, after removing the heart and viscera, and then set out on the epic journey to bring his master home to Westminster Abbey.

Sam met the Ugandan envoys after his greatest diplomatic failure. In the country of the Bunyoro he made an effort to pacify and flatter the young king, Kabarega, and so create an ally. All the trade goods they had lugged from the warehouses of Messrs Silber and Fleming of Cheapside with such colossal effort were laid out in an improvised exhibition, as an example of what might follow from peaceful commerce. It was a huge play for the trust and friendship of a powerful African tribe that hitherto had known only Arab slavers. The band instruments came out for the last time, and Florence's finest crinolines. Sam, in his official uniform, transformed himself into Sir Samuel Baker, the representative of two utterly unimaginable countries, Egypt and England. Kabarega's throne was stained with blood, but he was accorded the deference Exeter Hall desired when parleying with the intelligent and willing savage.

It soon became clear that, far from feeling any gratitude or interest, the Bunyoro intended to destroy the whole expedition. In the end, the trade fair exploded into a pitched battle. Only by burning and destroying everything they could not carry and fighting their way back to the Nile did the party survive. The Bunyoro treated the interlopers with the contempt of the victors over the vanquished. Neither the trade goods, nor the expedition rifles, nor Baker Pasha's undeniable power of personality deterred them. They simply slung the intruders out of their country, leaving them with little but the kit they could carry on their backs.

There was trouble of another kind. Sam at last managed to interview the powerful slave-trader Abu Saud, who professed his loyalty and promised an end to his depredations. The scoundrel then hotfooted it to Cairo, where he spread rumours of incompetence and cruelty on the part of Baker Pasha's expedition. Even more irritatingly, one of the shipwrights Sam had with him, a godly man called McWilliam, had taken against his leader and, as with Grant in the previous adventure, was planning to denounce him to the London papers. Baker had made a play for lasting fame without having the means at his disposal to bring about the one thing his English public demanded, an end to slavery in the Sudan. The reason was not hard to find.

> I was most thoroughly disgusted and sick at heart. After all the trouble and difficulties that we had gone through for the suppression of the slave trade, there could be no question of the fact that Abu Saood, the great slave-hunter of the White Nile was supported by some high authority behind the scenes, upon whom he could depend for protection ... His vessels were actually sailing in triumph and defiance before the wind, with flags flying the crescent and star, above a horrible cargo of pest-smitten humanity, in open contempt for my authority.

A reflective reader of *Ismailia* might have laid the blame and the shame at the khedive's own door and it was a mark against Baker's integrity that he went out of his way not to do that. Instead, he ended his tour of duty with six weeks of fêting and dining with the viceregal family before going home in the autumn of 1873. The khedive handed out medals for himself and Julian Baker, while the surviving Europeans, the shipwrights and artisans who had actually built the 250-ton paddle-steamer now at anchor in Khartoum, were rewarded with nothing more than an additional month's pay. As for the unlucky remnants of Baker's two battalions who garrisoned the four miserable forts or 'stations', they were rich in lettuce, but unlikely to be paid until the day the Nile froze over.

In 1875 Sam bought the estate of Sandford Orleigh, near Newton Abbot, the kind of property he might have bought thirty years earlier if he had not had the itch to travel. He was fifty-four years old and ready to settle down. The house was an expression of his tastes and prejudices, a sportsman's and a traveller's retreat, not impossibly far from London, but remote enough to feed that desire in him to be the man apart. He was not done with, not yet, but for as many who saw in him the romantic freebooter, there were others who found his brutal realism when it came to Africa shocking and distasteful. Shortly after his return to England he upset the anti-slavery lobby both by his lectures and by the publication of his book. Mr McWilliam and Julian Baker conducted an acrimonious correspondence in *The Times* about the expedition's methods. In the second edition of *Ismailia* Sam tackled the issue head on in a paragraph written with some asperity.

> Few persons have considered the position of the Egyptian ruler when attacking the institution most cherished by his people. The employment of a European to overthrow the slave trade in deference to the opinion of the civilized world was a direct challenge and attack upon the assumed rights and necessities of his own subjects. The magnitude of the operation cannot be understood by the general public in Europe. Every household in Upper Egypt and the Delta was dependant upon slave service; the fields in the Soudan were cultivated by slaves; the women in the harems of both rich and middle class were attended by slaves; the poorer Arab woman's ambition was to possess a slave; in fact, Egyptian society without slaves would be like a carriage devoid of wheels – it could not proceed.

In other words, the anti-slavery lobby asked too much of him, expressing, as he saw it, much of their anger from the cosy vantage of some club armchair. Sam Baker was never very concerned to defend himself from criticism made by people he openly despised. He was not a controversialist (although fond of writing to *The Times*) and the palaver hut he built at the end of one of his estate walks was put there to sit in and contemplate the view, certainly never as a place in which to engage in discussion of the moral worth of the African and the corresponding iniquities of the white man.

With this second expedition to the Upper Nile an age passed. The khedive had his canal. The largest concentration of steam machinery ever assembled in one spot had done the work, augmented by manual labour on the pharaonic scale. Nearly a hundred million cubic yards of earth had been moved. Beside this, what were a few hundred men hacking at waterweed with bayonets and billhooks? Ismail was still interested in what lay south of Khartoum but the canal was now indisputably the hinge of Asia. One of the blessings offered at the spectacular inauguration was given by Monsignor Bauer, the apostolic delegate and confessor to the Empress Eugenie. It included these words:

> There ride the vessels of all the nations, ready to cross for the first time this threshold which makes of the Orient and Occident a single world. The barrier is down. One of the most formidable enemies of mankind and of civilization, which is distance, loses in a moment two thousand leagues of his empire. The two sides of the world approach to greet one another, and in greeting recognise that all men, being children of one God, tremble with the wonder of their mutual fraternity.

Perhaps.

SEVEN

Gordon was on the Thames. Between 1865 and 1871 he commanded the Royal Engineers depot at Gravesend, where his
main responsibility was to supervise the building of defensive forts
up and down the river. He amused the staff by carrying out these
duties as though life itself depended on them. Rowed everywhere,
he doubled up his boat-crews and made them rush him up and
down the tideway like lifeboatmen on their way to a sinking ship.
Once ashore, he would dart off to chivvy the civilian contractors,
swishing impatiently at dandelions and thistles with the Wand of
Victory. It did not matter that he privately thought all the forts
under construction were badly sited and, in the event of an attack,
would be perfectly useless. In China he might have done something
about it. Here in Kent it gave him bitter pleasure to toe the line
and file another anodyne report. He found evangelical friends, Mr
and Mrs Freese. For some time he did not even tell them of the
Ever Victorious Army – so complete was his disguise that Mrs Freese
idly asked him one day whether he had ever come across the
Taiping Rebellion during his tour of duty.

At Fort House, his official residence, he gave the garden keys
to elderly paupers and encouraged them to dig up his lawns and
flowerbeds and turn them into vegetable allotments, refusing to
accept in return even the slightest gift of a bucket of potatoes or
a handful of string beans. Any gratitude they might have felt was
beside the point. Still seized with that same desire to belittle the

Gordon teaching his 'kings' geography in Chatham.

great fame to which he had returned from China, he succeeded only too well. The Horse Guards ignored him and professionally he felt himself sinking into the obscurity that engulfed most Royal Engineer officers.

His new passion was bringing young men to God. He had leaflets printed at his own expense that he would pin to trees or scatter in hedgerows. If he saw a destitute child in the streets, he would ask him home for a bath and breakfast, energetically scrubbing the boy with his own hands. He made it a point of duty to sit mending tattered clothes, asking sharp little questions of the bewildered owners. By these means he came to know and encourage first dozens, then hundreds of what he called his 'kings'. A second, even more evocative name for them was scuttlers.

The front of the house was all military spit and polish, from which Colonel Gordon would issue with all the dignity of a depot commander, his brisk manner defying criticism, his boots scattering the gravel. There was, as it were, a house within the house. In his study, as ever furnished with awesome simplicity, there was a map of the world strewn with pins showing where some of his kings had fetched up as merchant seaman – Surabaya, Valparaiso, Perth or New Orleans. Postcards from foreign parts, boys in his bath-tub, helpless old pensioners asleep in the comfort of the forsaken green-house – and as often as not, when friends called socially, Gordon himself was nowhere to be found. On one occasion he hid in the cellar rather than waste time on unimportant small-talk. If his fellow officers thought him odd there was nothing Gordon could do about that. He was going about God's business and waiting for His call.

In 1872, after six years in Kent, he was posted to Romania to take up the British seat on a boundary commission and also to act as vice-consul at Galatza. He was 150 miles north-west of the rail-head at Constanta, where Sam and Florence had first lived together, at a place where the Pratul river ran in from the north and joined the exhausted Danube as it spread into marshes and lakes. The post he had been given was an unimaginative use of his talents, for this was the third time he had served on such bodies, the first two when he was a young captain in the aftermath of the Crimean War. But now, as he approached forty, he was a brevet colonel with the added distinction of a CB to his name. The emperor of China had honoured him and filled his chest with decorations. He had only to take one look at the pompous yet broken man he was succeeding to see how deeply he was being buried. As to Galatza, it was a bitter disappointment.

> The place is a large, very ill-found, straggling town [he wrote]. You have mud ankle deep in all the streets, the population cosmopolitan, and numbering many Jews who are an evil look-ing lot and who are much disliked. There are lots of Greeks. If you saw the Jews you would certainly wonder that they should have been and are now the chosen people of God, and that our Saviour was of their nation. They are the leeches of the country. The Roumans are a thriftless race, and get into debt with them so that they squeeze the lives out of the people, and living on very little, never spending anything, they drain and exhaust the country.

Gordon sensed that he had been shunted out of the fast track. The commissioners were paid a salary of £2000, which was by no means unhandsome; much of it he remitted to Gravesend to help in the missionary work he had set in train there. Money and the good things in life were never of interest to him but he would hardly have been human if he had not felt a twinge of indignation, looking round his miserable and tedious existence. Whatever God wanted of him, it seemed clear that those lesser deities the commander-in-chief and the Secretary of State for War were quite happy to forget him. In September of his second year in Galatza Wolseley and 'the Wolseley Ring' (a handpicked group of officers who were his Crimea contemporaries) sailed to the Ashanti War without him. The *Daily News* mounted a campaign to have him recalled to active service. With his maddening sense of rectitude, Gordon wrote to the inspector-general disavowing this press clamour.

But God *was* guiding his steps. The previous summer he had taken leave to revisit the Crimean battlefields where, nearly twenty years on, the ground was still being raked over for loot. Even more disgracefully, the British cemeteries were being systematically vandalised by robbers looking for wedding rings. Gordon was accompanied by Colonel Adye, a gunner who had fought at Sebastopol and been wounded three times. Their duty was to write a report (for which, incidentally, Adye was promoted to major-general and given a Knight Commander of the Bath the following year; Gordon got nothing). He came down to Constantinople in sombre mood. At a reception in the British embassy he was introduced to a genial and friendly fellow Christian, Nubar Pasha. It was, of course, an engineered meeting. This was no accidental encounter – Nubar had found the man to succeed Samuel Baker.

It was an inspired piece of headhunting. Gordon spoke some Arabic, though not enough to make him a linguist. He knew nothing at all of Egypt or Central Africa. As Nubar studied him, he saw an Englishman cut from an entirely different cloth than Baker's – devout, apparently non-committal about the Arab world yet, when asked, capable of decided and abruptly expressed opinions. His military genius as a commander of irregular troops was a matter of record – indeed, there was no officer in the British army with a higher reputation in this area. The social naivety he might exhibit in such settings as Sir Henry Elliot's embassy, the unbending stiffness and almost contemptuous reserve, was neither here nor there. Nubar was looking for a commander, not a courtier. He played his hand cleverly. Did Gordon know of any RE officer who might accept a commission to serve the khedive? A little later on he allowed himself to wonder whether such a man might not be Gordon himself? Having planted the idea, he let it drop.

Gordon accepted the post in October 1874. He went home to arrange the details of his secondment and make arrangements for his Gravesend charities to continue. On his last day in London the morning papers reported the death of Livingstone. Before boarding the cross-Channel packet at Dover, he sent a plain postcard to his friend Mrs Freese. On the face he sketched a minute and solitary figure standing on a road that led away to the celestial city. A palm tree suggests the location. The message was contained in a scribbled inscription: 'Isaiah 35'. Turning to her Bible, Mrs Freese might read in the opening verse: 'The wilderness and the solitary place shall be glad for them; and the desert shall rejoice and blossom as the rose.' That was certainly a text appropriate to Livingstone. But she knew her man and as she read on she found a deeper meaning in verses seven and eight.

> And the parched ground shall become a pool, and the thirsty land springs of water: in the habitation of dragons, where each lay, shall be grass with reeds and rushes. And an highway shall be there, and a way, and it shall be called the way of holiness; the unclean shall not pass over it; but it shall be for those; the wayfaring men, though fools, shall not err therein.

If the Nile was the highway indicated in scripture, there remained much to be settled about it. Still no one had traced the river all the way to Lake Victoria. There were huge gaps in the map, about both the course of what Speke had called the Somerset Nile and the true extent of Lake Albert, the size of which Baker had gravely overestimated. Nor had anyone established the limits of the khe-dive's new province east and west of the river. Gordon could read a map. His initial studies of the Nile basin and its tributaries were depressing. Gondokoro was a thousand miles from Khartoum, two thousand from Cairo, and yet for the purposes of government, that was where he must begin. If the Sudd channel was open – and thanks to the efforts of Abd el Kader, one of the 'forty thieves' who had stayed behind when Baker left, it was – then to get to Gondokoro from Khartoum under steam, burning wood gathered from the banks as you went, was a passage of twenty-five days. One of Gordon's first appointments was a shipwright, William Kemp.

There were nine paddle-steamers already in the water at Khar-toum, of which Gordon had control of six. The queen of the fleet was the *Bordein*. These vessels were commonly referred to as Thames penny-steamers, which was in essence exactly what they were. The weakest point of their design was not, surprisingly, the boiler or engine, which were simple enough to repair on the spot. The problem was with the paddles themselves, housed amidships in huge casings. Such vessels were a common sight in the Thames estuary and Kemp and Gordon had recent memories of them thrashing along cheerfully, churning up the waters, turning grey into yellow on the way to Margate. Here it was a different story. Hippos and crocodiles easily broke the vanes and any inequality in thrust went on to make steering a nightmare. The best fitters in Khartoum were engaged solely on the maintenance of the governor-general's vanity project, the steam-yacht *Tewfikieh*, with which he amused himself and his entourage in short pleasure trips up and down the Nile.

Kemp snooped around Khartoum and found the unbuilt sec-tions of a Baker steamer, along with its 32 horsepower engine, languishing in some rat-infested warehouse. At Gondokoro he dis-covered, stacked neatly in the grass, the parts of the much smaller screw-engine steamer that Sam Baker had carried there under such appalling conditions. He easily persuaded his chief to order another four sectional steamers of the same pattern from the Yar-row yard.

Gordon, like Baker before him, accepted his commission on the understanding that he must stamp out the slave trade before he could advance to government of the region, however rudimentary that might be. He took up his appointment when the controversy over Sam Baker's way of going about things was being aired in *The Times* in the bad-tempered quarrel between McWilliam and Julian Baker. Even before leaving Cairo, he astounded his supporters by having the slave merchant Abu Saud released from house arrest and naming him deputy-governor. In London that looked like a calculated insult to the anti-slavery movement. Not disposed to like the khedive of Egypt any more than they did the worst Arab slave-trader, the abolitionists felt that Gordon had already been seduced by Africa.

It was encouraging to them that the incoming governor refused the £10,000 a year the khedive had paid Baker. However, the anti-slavery movement, which had no field agents and was maintained by the subscriptions of the geographically ignorant, still found much to criticise. Those words of Monsignor Bauer at the opening of the canal had begun to seem more than flowery rhetoric. The empire of distance *was* being destroyed. When a telegraph message could be passed in five hours from London to Bombay and a sea voyage now took only thirty days, then the laborious flog from Khartoum to Gondokoro seemed – or could to the uninitiated – like mere dilatoriness. Meanwhile, sending Abu Saud back to his old hunting grounds was surely to add fuel to the fire Sam Baker's book had described.

As it happened, the appointment of Saud *was* one of Gordon's quixotic gambles that did not pay off. After only three months the slaver was discovered in further treachery and double dealing and once again sent back to Cairo in disgrace. The mood in London was grimly triumphant. It always seemed so simple from there. If slavery existed then surely the job was to find the chief culprit, arrest him and (although there were few who were willing to specify how) destroy him. If Abu Saud himself was not the villain of the piece then it was Gordon's job to find that man. England was getting impatient with Africa, all the more so now that Livingstone was no more.

Gordon's time as governor of Ismailia was dictated by his military training. He came as a soldier and he expected discipline. For example, when the governor-general of the Sudan and his ministers said goodbye to him at Khartoum, they hardly expected to see him again for years, if at all. They were amazed to find him back among them after only a couple of months, bounding from the steamer and marching grimly towards the government offices. He had discovered how the existing garrisons were being paid – in girls and spirits. This would not do, would not do at all.

It almost passed belief that someone so august as the provincial governor should make a round trip of fifty days, driving his steamer crew like Gravesend boatmen, simply to upbraid his opposite number in Khartoum over a matter that a few kicks would have solved locally. Sam Baker in his day had such a tenuous hold on the territory that a journey of a hundred miles was a great adventure. Here was Gordon destroying distance to make himself understood: the job would be done his way, or not at all. If civilisation in this benighted country meant an infinite capacity for taking pains, then the khedive had appointed the right man.

It was an article of faith with Gordon that what caused sickness and death in the pestilential country he had been asked to govern was inaction. Never a man who kept horses, he had already mastered camel-riding sufficiently well to astonish his Arab colleagues. On his journey from Suakin to take up his appointment, he covered the 210 miles in record time, riding alone and subsisting on dates and his own specific against all common ailments, Warburg's Tincture. In England old ladies took a few drops of this in a glass before bedtime. Gordon swigged down a mouthful, shoved a handful of dates into his jaws and rode by compass-bearing across the sands, unstoppable and imperious. It was the beginning of a legend.

He was fanatically punctilious about stores and equipment. He liked counting things and labelling them. As his staff found out, he was the sort of man who never misplaced a spanner or left a box unfastened at the end of a day's work. Unable to delegate responsibility properly, he made a thing out of his contrariness. When it came to building forts up-river, for example, it happened on several occasions that his lieutenants, racked by fever, would erect a palisade and blockhouse with the last of their energy, only to have Gordon come along a week or so later and briskly move the whole thing a hundred yards this way or that.

Seven of his ten staff officers were dead or broken down within the first three months. Witt, a German botanist who offered to follow him as a supernumerary, died three days after he arrived in Khartoum. His interpreter, Auguste Linants de Bellefonds, died ten days later. Kemp the shipwright could just about tolerate life along the quays and slipways of the capital but when he went up to Gondokoro to supervise the construction of Baker's steamer, he was pole-axed by malaria and had to be invalided back downriver. Gordon's nephew, Willie Anson, a young man who had thrown up a secure job in the General Post Office to follow his uncle's flag, died of fever. William Russell's son Freddie was sent home to England. Major Campbell was put on the steamer down to Khartoum raving and delirious and died shortly after he arrived. Gordon was philosophical about all these disasters. 'No comfort is equal to that which he has who has God for his stay: who believes, not in words but in fact that all things are ordained to happen and must happen. He who has this, has already died, and is free from the annoyance of this life.'

Sam Baker wrote to express admiration for Gordon's patience, although long-suffering might have been a better description. Where Sam had stuck at the task with an explorer's semi-despair, wanting to chuck it all up and yet driven on by a kind of secret and guilty appetite, Gordon was far more the organiser, scheduler and map-maker. Sam might call on the last of his strength to make one more camp, in the morning one more march. Gordon, faced with the same difficulties, tried to plan his way. He had two enormous advantages over his predecessor – an open channel down the Nile and a brilliant quartermaster in Romolo Gessi, an Italian he had persuaded to join him from the Danubian commission.

In February 1875 Gessi brought a steamer up to one of the new forts at Lado carrying a visitor, Fred Burnaby of the Blues, on annual leave and curious enough to make the journey. He wrote two articles about his visit for *The Times*. On 6 February it was revealed that Gordon himself was on his way in the paddle-steamer *Khedive*, an announcement that caused great excitement. In front of an enthusiastic crowd of naked Shilluk the commander of Fort Lado led his pitiful little garrison out to do the honours. They numbered seventeen.

> Nearer and nearer came the steamer and, gracefully rounding the sharp curve where the White Nile is joined by the still whiter looking Sobat tributary, anchored within a few feet of the shore. The one bugler nearly burst his lungs in ringing out the clear strains of a general salute, the black captain lowered his sword and the seventeen men composing the garrison brought their arms to the 'Present', as a short thickset man, who appeared to be in the picture of health, and was attired in the undress uniform of a Colonel of Engineers, hastened down the ship's side and, approaching the officer and his small contingent, rapidly inspected the men and their accoutrements.

With Gordon were some of the famous 'forty thieves' that his predecessor had trained up as personal bodyguard. Burnaby watched in secret amusement as Gordon went back on board and, speaking in rapid French, had his wishes and judgements expressed in Arabic to the petitioners by an Egyptian interpreter. When it was time for him to interview the great man, Burnaby found him brusque and unhelpful. There was nothing surprising about this – it would have been hard to find two Victorian soldiers more widely divided by tastes and temperament. Gordon was very unwilling to let Burnaby go any further south and barely concealed his distaste for what he called journalists. This was hard on Burnaby, who was not about to endure an insult of any kind from a mere Royal Engineers officer. After a night-time dancing display by the tribesmen, which took place against a backdrop of many miles of burning scrub, the giant cavalryman sailed back to Khartoum. There, idling his time away in an office, his eye fell on a newspaper report that the Russians had forbidden an English officer permission to enter Khiva, in Uzbekistan. That was quite enough encouragement for Burnaby, sweating it out with nothing to do but look out of the window at the dust and dogs of Khartoum. He decided to have a look at Central Asia for himself. In this way Gordon was indirectly godfather to one of the great travel classics, *A Ride to Khiva.*

Burnaby was made much in the same mould as Sam Baker. What Gordon was trying to do with his palisaded forts and his flagpoles, his inventories and standing orders was hardly the adventure of a lifetime. It happened that Burnaby already had a yarn with which to entertain the Marlborough Club when he got home. Setting out for Khartoum from the coast he had blundered into a slave caravan on the road from Berber and tried to arrest the merchants with nothing but a revolver. (His companion in this escapade was Marcopolo, Sam's old storekeeper.) It was an unfortunate story to tell Gordon, for it demonstrated once again how the Sudanese government was privately colluding with the slavers. Whether or not Burnaby thought the khedive was exploiting his British appointees, it was an idea that had begun to lodge in Gordon's own mind.

Part of his assignment was to open the way to the Great Lakes, as they were now being called. Murchison was dead – in fact he had predeceased his protégé Livingstone by a year – but it was now the conventional wisdom among geographers in London that a vessel starting from Khartoum could sail, under proper direction, right up into Lake Victoria. The political implications were vast. For the time being such a vessel might fly the Turkish flag but if the route could be established, who knew what use might be made of it in the future? On 17 October 1875, after indefatigable mapping and surveying, Gordon came across the Nile's last secret at a place called Fola.

IT IS ALL OVER! I started from Dufilé this morning and keeping on the higher level to avoid the wet edges of the river, came on it about five miles from here. I fancied for some time I had heard a voice like thunder, which increased as we approached the river. At last we stood above it on a rocky bank covered with vegetation, which descended abruptly to the stream, and there it was, appalling to look at, far less to think of getting anything up and down, except in splinters. It was more a rush down a slope of one in six than a fall. Above it the water was smooth, and 80 to 150 yards wide; and here it was suddenly contracted to two passages of 15 and 20 yards ... It boiled down, twisting into all sorts of eddies, while the banks, steep and precipitous, prevented a great length of view. These shoots last for two miles.

No boat would ever sail from Khartoum to Lake Victoria. Gordon accepted this crushing realisation with an almost super-human calm. Everything was ordained and God had brought him here to show him something. A lesser man would have been broken completely. It hardly made a difference to his escort, who saw, if they saw anything, an end to weeks and months of backbreaking labour. Like Gordon, they believed that what was ordained would come to pass. It was painful; but it was written. For a true Briton, the pain was immeasurably sharpened.

He retreated with only two servants to a tiny settlement called Afuddo, where he commandeered a hut by a stream. All around was a sea of chest-high grass, whispering and chuckling. The horizons suddenly shrank to a few yards, with nothing but the sky and the night stars to contemplate. Placed in the same situation, Sam – and particularly Florence – would have made friends, traded beads for food, held interminable palaver, sketched. There would have been a search for the sporting shot somewhere in this surreal landscape, at the very least an exhibition of Baker's schoolboy heartiness, an attempt to drive away the blue devils. Gordon smoked, went early to bed. The few people who lived in Afuddo, whose world it was, knew all about him, though not in any detail – he was the white man whose troops made such a racket, whose dreams and plans were meaningless. The least of his possessions – a box or a glass bottle – was utterly foreign to them.

Gordon stayed in Afuddo a fortnight. Mortification was part of his nature and God had surely struck his pride a savage blow. For fourteen sunrises he woke under the rustling roof of his mud and wattle hut, watching the lozenge of light from the doorway creep along the wall. He had his Bible and some crusty ink, pens, a wallet of maps and notes. His journal made bitter reading. He almost

certainly spent some of the time in this cruel holiday from duty
pondering the central question of Africa. As Livingstone had come
to understand in his own much more prolonged isolation, and
Baker had always asserted, nobody could help the native without
first breaking him. It was said of the riverine tribe the Shilluk that
it had no words for north and south. The Shilluk camped by the
river when there was no rain and then in a better season moved
their cattle east into the hinterland. What else was Gordon trying
to do but teach them north and south? How could he do anything
without taking the further step of colonising them and in so doing
destroying what they already were?

Whether or not they wanted anything from the white man was
likewise uncomfortable to think about. It was true that when they
crowded round a boat or menaced a foot patrol they wanted *everything* – but what did that really mean? Certainly his neighbours in
Afuddo, moving about with that maddeningly laconic economy of
movement and gesture, would like to be free of the slavers, but
was it really freedom to be rid of one set of invaders only to be
asked to salute the flag of another? If Ismailia was a country, a
nation, in what way could these poor people be considered Ismailis,
compatriots of the Bari, the Dinka, the awesome Unyoro? The first
thing they would have to shed was everything that had previously
mattered to them.

Gordon's servants could have told them – maybe did tell them
– the sole benefit of civilisation. Where before they were unknown
and unknowable, in the future they could be taxed. They could
be raised in their hundreds to cut a boat free from the Sudd or
help build a stockade; or in some other way express a new loyalty
they would do well to find pleasing. For example, in the very short
term it would be good for the people of Afuddo to thank the white
pasha for eating their chickens and sleeping in a hut they had built
for someone else.

Gordon was no particular friend to the African. As in China,
everything would go well if the people only did as they were told.
As with his treatment of the Ever Victorious Army, what Africans
actually thought mattered very little to him. In the pages of Sam

Baker there is one example after another of his childlike sense of humour, his joshing familiarity. Some of the sketches from his notebooks, illustrating not so much African nudity as shameless and wanton nakedness, had to be reworked by his publisher before they could be printed. African girls were jolly and all the more so for being in their birthday suits. Gordon had none of Baker's crudity and certainly none of his clumping curiosity about other people. At the end of his brief period of isolation in this little huddle of huts, he wrote:

> If *we* conquered the country, we would at least in some measure
> benefit the conquered; but here I cannot say I see the least
> chance of the country being improved or the people benefitted;
> the civilisers are so backward themselves that they cannot be
> expected to civilise others.

He was thinking in one broad sweep of the sly men back in Khartoum, so deeply implicated in the slave trade; a further thousand miles distant, the ministerial carriages plying to and from the Abdin Palace; the polyglot cafés surrounding the Ezbekieh Gardens; all the luxuries and indulgences of a great city that was not European but was hardly African either. Between all that and himself, with his boxes of surveying equipment, his rotting clothes and ruined boots, there was the thinnest of connecting threads. For as long as the Nile needed exploration and mapping – as with the discovery of its ninth unsuspected cataract – there was a reason to go on. But after that, what? There were more and more explorers and adventurers coming south and a white face was no longer a complete novelty. The question was whether it was worth Gordon's time to insist on something he seemed to sense would dwindle to nothing after a few years, a political imposition backed by guns that would simply revert to nature in the same way as an untended garden.

There was one tribute Gordon could pay to his predecessor. With a thousand porters Romolo Gessi carried the sections of Sam's twin-screw steamer and two steel whalers up on to Lake Albert. By April 1876 Gessi had completed the circumnavigation of the lake.

There was no huge waterfall as imagined by Livingstone, the mighty Lualaba crashing into the lake. Gordon himself had approached to within sixty miles of Lake Victoria. But mere exploration was not enough to keep him interested. With the abruptness that characterised all his decisions he retraced his steps, went down to Khartoum, thence to Cairo. There he learned with amazement that Disraeli had made his swoop purchase of the khedive's shares in the canal only a month after the long night of the soul he himself had passed in Afuddo. Cairo disgusted him. On 29 November he wrote to his sister, 'I have (D.V.) made up my mind to serve his Highness no longer.'

He spent Christmas in England, busying himself with an alternative to service with the khedive. This was a scheme to mount an overland expedition from Zanzibar, to be led by Gessi and himself, and so strike into the Great Lakes territory from the south. Such a conquest would be purely British. Gordon would bring his organising genius and indomitable will to the same ground trod by Speke and Burton. He would outflank Egypt altogether – no more serving under a Turkish flag. But Ismail was not quite so stupid as all that. When he heard of these plans, he sent his man a long cable which contained this unanswerable sentence: 'I refuse to believe that, when Gordon has once given his word as a gentleman, anything will ever induce him to go back on it.' Gordon capitulated.

He had very quickly forgotten an incident that occurred at Korosko only a month earlier, when he was going down to Cairo. A mystery boat had come sailing south, its windows nailed up with planks, armed guards sitting on the roof of the saloon. Inside, it was said, lay the chained and starving Minister of Finance in Ismail's government, on his way to a shot in the head somewhere out in the desert. It was to this man's employer that Gordon had given his word. He agreed to go back to Cairo for consultations. The price he asked for a resumption of his duties was breathtakingly simple. 'I have promised,' he wrote to his sister, 'that if his Highness will not give me the province of Sudan, I will not go back to the

Lakes. I do not think he will give it; and I think you will see me back in six weeks.'

The khedive called his bluff. Gordon was sent south with full authority over a million square miles extending from the tropic of Cancer to the equator. All government already in place was superseded. Ismail Pasha Ayoub, the former governor-general, was stranded speechless and powerless in Cairo: his sister raged round the palace in Khartoum, breaking more than a hundred panes of window-glass and cutting up the furniture with a Turkish dagger.

Gordon now had seventeen separate provinces under his control. He had exchanged the frustrations of the Fola Falls for a different kind of impossibility – how to govern men he had never met in places he had never been. In the second term of his employment with the khedive, the camel ride replaced the Nile steamer as the expression of his indomitable will. The khedive had written: 'Use all the powers I have given you, take every step you think necessary; punish, change, dismiss all officials as you please.' The new governor-general took him at his word. The implacable side of his nature, which had been illustrated in China by his calmly shooting one of the rebel NCOs in front of his fellow conspirators, became the norm of expectation. Gordon was no longer the solitary white man camping in the sea of grass at Afuddo. He was the avenger.

One of the key provinces was Darfur in the east. In 1874 the sultan of Darfur had been turned out, along with his sons, and the slaver Zobeir declared himself ruler in his place. He was persuaded by a nervous Khartoum to accept a governorship and when he went down to Cairo to agree terms, he left in place his youngest son, Suleiman. The khedive was more than a match for Zobeir – instead of being handed the warrant for his appointment, he was dispatched to fight in the Turco-Russian War. It had the consequence of leaving his son Suleiman and a small army of about 4000 adherents masters of a huge tract of land that was nominally one of Gordon's new provinces. It was the sort of challenge the governor-general liked most in life.

They met on Friday 31 August 1877 in characteristic fashion.

Suleiman's army were amazed to see riding into their camp a man dressed in the full uniform of his rank, which included a coat garnished with gold lace, but apparently unarmed. The white-robed horde of warriors parted before him, making an avenue of spears. They were, Gordon observed, 'smart dapper troops, like antelopes, fierce, unsparing, the terror of Central Africa'. It would have been the easiest thing in the world for them to spear him to death there and then. Gordon rode quietly towards Suleiman's tent, dismounted, strolled up to him and, after a few curt exchanges of traditional greeting, accepted the offer of the greasy glass of water which the Koran indicated was the first duty of the host. Naturally enough, Suleiman, who was hardly in his twenties, asked him what he wanted. With the greatest nonchalance Gordon said he was there to command this young man to report to him next day at his own camp, a few miles distant. Then, with sublime condescension, he remounted and cantered away down the avenue of spears.

It was a classic piece of Victorian plot-making, worthy of the indefatigable children's writer, G. A. Henty. The German explorer Schweinfurth had recently visited Darfur and found a level of sophistication and wealth he had not suspected possible among such tribesmen. It was a warrior society founded on slaves – many of the 'antelopes' Gordon saw that day were slave-soldiers. But part of the reason for the success with which chiefs like Zobeir had built up their power was that they always treated strangers as enemies. Gordon especially was not welcome, not only because he was an infidel, but because he was that greatest of all interlopers, the tax-gatherer and tribute-seeker. The peremptory manner of his arrival among them stunned Suleiman and his army.

Darfur had enjoyed a proud and powerful independence long before the coming of the Turk. It had fifty years' experience of what was called the Turkiyya – the government imposed on it that Gordon now represented. It paid taxes or it did not, much as it pleased. As a province of the Sudan, it was in the position of a rich man haggling with his neighbour. All this was swept away now, for Gordon Pasha's powers were those of the destroyer. In Suleiman he saw only a sulky boy whose opinions and wishes counted for nothing. Civilisation had come to Darfur in the person of a British officer.

It was merely a matter of getting everyone to understand that. Once it had been grasped, things would go along just fine. In the hands of Henty (who was indeed to write a book set in the Sudan less than ten years later) Suleiman and his army might be picturesque, they might even be steeped in their own traditions, but they were in reality nothing but a backdrop to British courage. They were there to provide the necessary enemy. Gordon thought so too.

For the time being Suleiman came to heel. Gordon's ceaseless quartering of the Sudan, his sudden and dramatic appearances, coupled with the reputation he had for unsleeping vigilance, did bring about change. It was by his example and the truthfulness of his reporting that Egypt and Britain signed an Anti-Slavery Convention. Slave-hunting was now stigmatised as 'robbery and murder'. All slaves had to be registered forthwith and complete abolition was scheduled for 1885 in Egypt and 1892 in the Sudan. It was just another piece of paper but it restored Gordon's reputation in England.

The Victorian belief in progress furnished the necessary details by which this treaty could be carried out. The famous Nile steamers pointed the way. What exhortation had not achieved, technology would. A proper enforcement of the treaty would need roads and customs houses, the telegraph, policemen, jails. It would need piped water, kerosene depots, libraries of records, photographic evidence, a postal service – and guns. Well and good. A mere twenty years earlier this vast tract of land was as alien as the far side of the moon. Now, thanks to Baker and Charles Gordon, it could be named, chastened and tamed. If the moral imperative that was implicit in such a colonisation meant in the end the destruction of everything that was there before, the benefits clearly outweighed the losses.

There was another, far more brutal way of putting this. The European powers had finally begun the scramble for Africa. The need to find new markets and plunder the raw materials of the world shifted from Asia, and the industrial nations were contemplating, not the civilisation of the African continent but its exploitation on an epic scale. Perhaps only Bismarck, in his generation, saw so completely how the new order might work and his cynicism was perhaps too painful to contemplate. Manufacturers in England with goods to sell and concessions to buy were also God-fearing citizens, who at home endowed churches, added wings to hospitals or departments to university colleges. For them capitalism *was* civilisation and the benefits of a shirt on a black man while he worked for wages in a palm-oil mill, or laid track for a railway through some swamp, were self-evident. The explorers and men like Gordon had provided the maps. Men like William Lever would exploit the opportunity. At the end of the 1870s Lever had two wholesale grocers', one in his native Bolton and one in Wigan. His share of the capital was £800. He started to specialise in soap made from palm-oil and invented a name for it – Sunlight. In 1894 he floated a company called Lever Brothers with a capital of £1.5 million. Thirty years later it was worth £57 million and was the biggest industrial undertaking the world had ever seen.

Above Khartoum there was, in the middle of the stream, an island called Abba. Steamer captains would never land there for wood: when they were unaccompanied by government officials they blew their whistles four times and then prostrated themselves on the thrumming deck-plates. They were paying reverence to a holy man who spent his years in a cave hewn from the sand, studying the Koran. His name was Mohamed Ahmed, the son of a boat-builder from the northern reaches of the river round Dongola. He was not old, nor was he frail. He had no family and was without followers. But the captains sensed in him an exceptional piety and their obeisance came from a far deeper well than any provided by service to the Turkiyya. Mohamed Ahmed had been praying and fasting on Abba for as long as Gordon had been in the Sudan.

EIGHT

━━◦◦◦◦━━

The group of officers surrounding the Prince of Wales had as their informal house-organ *Vanity Fair,* edited by Thomas Gibson Bowles. This was a semi-satirical magazine of gossip, interspersed with pungent articles on contemporary politics, always from a Tory perspective. The point of connection between the magazine and the Marlborough House set was Fred Burnaby, who lent Bowles half the capital to found it – £100. The French artist James Tissot, who was hired originally to cartoon for the publication, painted Burnaby in 1870, capturing the essence of a polished, drawling languor. The subject reclines on a settee, a cigarette cocked in his left hand. He is wearing blue patrols, the trousers decorated by an immense and dramatic red stripe. A Life Guards helmet and cuirass are in the background of the picture, along with a map of most of the southern hemisphere and – a subtle touch – a burnous, suggesting travel and mystery. In this portrait are all the elements of a cultivated ennui. As it happened, Burnaby was almost childishly hyperactive, an adventurer and a brawler who had a particular passion for ballooning. During his long leaves from duty he was also a war-chaser of some courage. The Household Cavalry seldom served abroad and Burnaby, who was not a rich man, made his own mild explorations of foreign places while on leave, under the guise of being a special correspondent for *The Times.* In many ways his world-weary pose was a joke, but a carefully constructed one.

The army was dividing once again between the claims of aristo-

cratic officers, with their insolent adherence to the old ways; and
the beginning of a new-broom policy bringing a meritocratic service
in its wake. The Duke of Cambridge represented the first; the
politician Edward Cardwell (abetted by Wolseley) the second. Cardwell was educated at Winchester and Balliol, where he took a first,
and his gifts were the unpatrician ones of immense energy devoted
to public service for its own sake. Any ministerial brief put before
him was analysed with a lawyer's attention to evidence and then
acted upon with ruthless efficiency. There were plenty of ditherers
in Victorian cabinets over the years but Cardwell was never one
of them. As Gladstone's Secretary of State for War, he enacted
wide-ranging army reforms, but the chief of them, the one that
attracted most attention from serving officers, concerned the abolition of the purchase system. Until it went, the service could never
be made fully professional.

When Cardwell insisted that the commander-in-chief move his
desk to the newly created War Office, the royal duke went with a
bad grace but stubbornly continued to head his notepaper 'The
Horse Guards', out of sympathy for the old ways. The duke hated
Cardwell's aider and abettor Wolseley with a passion. He was a red
tunics and pipeclay kind of soldier: Wolseley was khaki. Tissot's
portrait placed Fred Burnaby squarely in the duke's camp: such a
man who was shown there was not very likely to know too much
about reform. Should he trouble himself to throw away his cigarette
and unwind those long limbs he would do his duty by his queen;
but this would come about by personal choice and not as a consequence of battalion reorganisation or any of the other nonsense
now being aired.

Colonel Baker of the 10th Hussars was of the same general party.
It was true that he had modernised cavalry drills – by drastically
simplifying them – and had experimented with moving troops and
squadrons of his regiment by rail. Nevertheless, the parade, the
ceremonials of the mess, the sporty side of regimental life were of
equal importance to him. Like their colleagues in the Household
Cavalry and the four Guards regiments, Val's officers were part of
a rich elite that chose to soldier and could as easily choose not to.

In London Guards officers could commonly be seen arriving by hansom cab to go on parade with their men at Hyde Park; by lunchtime they had disappeared back into the comfort of their clubs. As for the men they commanded, the disgusting condition of all London barracks had been exposed in 1859 by George Godwin, editor of the journal the *Builder*. They were, Godwin claimed, inferior to the poorest common lodging house. *The Times* agreed. Was this a matter of money, or a lack of leadership? When the abolition of purchase was finally enacted by Parliament in 1871, *Punch* published a swingeing mock advertisement, addressed to what it described as gallant but stupid young gentlemen: 'You may buy your commissions in the Army up to the thirty-first of October next. After that you will be driven to the cruel necessity of deserving them.'

There was a ready clue to where the colonel of the 10th Hussars stood in the war over reforms. On parade duties he never rode anything but the white charger given to him as a wedding present by the Prince of Wales. In 1872, after glittering success in the autumn manoeuvres – reintroduced after a break of nearly forty years – the 10th Hussars were ordered back to India. A farewell dinner was given to all the officers at Marlborough House. There it was learned with regret and some consternation that Val was relinquishing his command and would not be going with them. He had served twelve years in command of the regiment, his predecessor twenty-two.

His immediate intention was to make one of those semi-official, semi-secret expeditions undertaken by army officers that passed themselves off as leave of absence. He had done such a thing before, acting as an observer on the Prussian side in the Franco-Prussian War of 1870–71. (His friend Thomas Bowles of *Vanity Fair* was trapped inside Paris, eating rats like everyone else.) Val's new plan was to investigate the borders of Persia and Afghanistan with Captain Gill of the Royal Engineers and a Captain Clayton of the 19th Lancers. The itinerary he proposed identified him with the question that had engrossed military men for a generation: how far would Russia extend itself southwards and with what consequence to the borders of India? Fred Burnaby expressed the problem with his usual verve when he came to write the introduction to *A Ride to Khiva* (1876).

> According to some politicians Khiva was a long way from India, and it did not really signify to England whether Russia annexed it or not. Again, it was urged by others, if Russia does eventually reach our Indian border, so much the better for England. We shall have a civilized nation as a neighbour instead of the barbarous Afghans. A third argument brought forward to defend the action of the Liberal Government was, that India did not signify so much to us after all, that she was a very expensive possession, and one we should very likely have taken from us, but one certainly not worth fighting for.

It was a jibe aimed at Gladstone. Burnaby, like the overwhelming majority of the army, was a Tory of the deepest hue. It was true that Turcophilia had ebbed in Britain and nobody really believed Disraeli when he described the Turks as 'the gentlemen of the East', but it was just as hard to take Gladstone's point of view and assume that the Russians had nothing on their mind but the defence of Christianity in the collapsing Ottoman Empire. For soldiers, the future flashpoint lay beyond the Caspian Sea, in country very hostile to western scrutiny, already better known to Russia than it would allow. Burnaby made the point by quoting skilfully from a book recently published in St Petersburg by a 'Captain Terentyeff'.

> *The East India Company* is nothing less than a poisonous unnatural plant engrafted on the splendid soil of India – a parasite which saps away the life of the most fertile and wealthy country in the world. This plant can only be uprooted by forcible means; and such an attempt was made by the natives of the country in 1857, though it failed for want of sufficient skill. Sick to death, the natives are now waiting for a physician from the North.

Put like this, the threat could hardly be any clearer. Val Baker set off with his two companions and a ton of luggage in April 1873 and returned to England just before the year ended. Clayton did not last long and had to be invalided home. Captain Gill scrupulously mapped their journey, measuring the angle of every bend in the road while Val, as he explains without irony, occupied himself with the broader picture. They fished, they hunted, they faced down hostile tribesmen and fell ill from bad water, Gill nursing his companion through a five-week nightmare of dysentery. The results of the journey were a tribute to their pluck and determination but the political and military benefits were unexceptional. In much of the territory they passed through, the locals knew as little of the Russian threat as they did of Val himself. He came home, however, confirming what anyone with a good map could already see. Without an agreed boundary the north-west frontier of India was as open to invasion as it had been historically since the time of Alexander. Unsurprisingly, he recommended a forward policy. In May 1874 he gave a talk at the United Services Institute on 'The Military Geography of Central Asia', which ended with these words:

> We have only to look back to the events within the living memory of almost all in this room, to see how much there is to lament in the past. How many must there be present who served in the Crimean War? Do not those who then served look back with pardonable pride to all the deeds of gallantry and daring which were done in that hard and trying campaign and siege? And do not gentler thoughts come back of comrades gone from us, and what is more, lost to England for ever? But what should we have thought, that all for which they suffered and fought to conquer, be thrown to the winds by the actions of Diplomacy in a few short years?

It was a conventional ending but it made its point. Across the road in Whitehall was the Horse Guards, from which the army had been run in what now seemed the halcyon days of its political independence. For the word 'Diplomacy', few in Val's audience would have had any trouble mentally substituting the phrase 'gross political interference'. Like Burnaby, deep in their mind's eye they harboured the image of William Ewart Gladstone, if not the author of the Army Regulation Bill, the Prime Minister who had driven it into law by forcing a very unwilling Duke of Cambridge to speak in its favour in the House of Lords.

Later that year Val was appointed assistant quartermaster general. His base of operations was Aldershot and in the high summer of 1875 this was where fate found him out. Two months hence there was to be a grand review of the army, for which he was given overall responsibility. This was no small duty. In the previous year there had been a spectacular parade and march-past of 15,000 troops, at which Tsar Alexander II took the salute. The 1875 review was planned (significantly enough) for the pleasure and diplomatic seduction of the sultan of Zanzibar. These elaborate exhibitions of Britain's military might were close to the queen's heart as a remembrance of the Prince Consort, who had helped found what was then called 'The Camp' in the year preceding Crimea. Though she had not attended the Aldershot reviews since his death, she certainly interested herself in army affairs and was very well briefed. The Queen's Pavilion, a huge building with stabling for forty horses, was still kept up in all its splendour, waiting in vain for the sovereign to come and animate its many rooms.

Val had repositioned his career with great skill. For any ambitious officer, there was a line to be trod between adherence to the Windsor vision of an army that was an expression of Christian manliness and royal favour – 'the Queen's Army' – and the actual demands of the service, which the War Office was trying to make its own. The queen was hardly an uninterested spectator. She had a decidedly bellicose streak that sometimes surprised her ministers. At the outset of the Crimean War she had risen at six in the morning on a bitingly cold day to watch the Guards march out of Knightsbridge on their way to the docks. These were *her* soldiers. The Victoria Cross, which was in her personal gift, was very dear to her and the first 111 were awarded in that same war. Perhaps her nearest models of soldierly propriety were men like General Knollys, whom Albert had appointed first GOC Aldershot: and Henry Ponsonby, her private secretary, who was a Grenadier and a Crimean veteran.

Somewhere in the middle – somewhere between seeing the army either as the military wing of the court or the servant of Parliament – was the portly presence of the Prince of Wales, his

Two sentimental likenesses. Kate Dickinson is drawn as both innocent and wilful:
Valentine Baker as venal and stupid.

mother's deputy at Aldershot. Coached by Val, the prince had
commanded the Cavalry Brigade at the autumn manoeuvres of
1872. He was a valuable patron to have. In identifying himself with
the prince so closely, Val Baker trod dangerous ground but one
thing was clear – it was no time for an ambitious officer to be lost
to view in India. Giving up regimental soldiering with the 10th
Hussars had been a wise choice.

At three in the afternoon of 17 June 1875 Colonel Baker
boarded the train to Waterloo at Liphook station. He was on his
way to dine with the Duke of Cambridge. In the first-class carriage
he chose to enter was an unaccompanied young woman of good
appearance. She was also bound for London and so to Switzerland,
where she was to take a holiday with a relative. Her trunk was in
the luggage rack above her head. There was no connecting corridor
but in the compartment next door were two respectable young
men. An electric bellpush was located in the bulkhead of the compartment, the only means of communication with the guard.
Though there was no way of knowing this from its appearance, it
was broken. It was a warm day and the windows were open. Between

Liphook and Woking, where it joined the main line, the train made frequent stops at country halts. According to the timetable, Woking was fifty minutes distant. From there it was a thirty-minute non-stop run to Vauxhall before the train finally arrived at Waterloo.

Val asked the young woman whether she felt a draught and, when she said no, began a general and apparently amiable conversation. Her luggage was labelled 'c/o Dr Bagshawe, Dover', and though she did not give her name, any more than he offered his own, there was enough to talk about. She had boarded the train at Midhurst, which Val knew well. He explained that it was very convenient for Goodwood. The mysterious Dr Bagshawe, to whom her luggage was consigned, was her brother-in-law, who was meeting her at London. She had a brother in the Engineers who was stationed in Aldershot and Val volunteered that he himself was on the staff there. They talked about London theatre and Val – broaching a common topic – asked her whether she believed in mesmerism. After its many stops the train reached Woking, where it waited for signals.

At a quarter to five, as the train passed through Walton station at forty miles an hour, a bricklayer employed by the railway company saw a young woman half hanging from a first-class compartment, one foot on the step to the carriage and the other on the footboard. She held the outside doorhandle in her left hand and her right arm was being supported by a second passenger standing inside the compartment. The bricklayer, a man called William Burrowes, ran at once to the stationmaster's office. There someone signalled ahead and the train was brought to halt under emergency braking just before it reached Esher station. The driver, his guard and a number of passengers ran along the permanent way and helped the young woman down. Pointing to the man in the carriage, she said that he had 'insulted' her and 'would not leave her alone'.

Val Baker joined the group on the track and it was decided by the guard that he should travel locked into the compartment occupied by the two young men. A vicar, the Reverend Baldwin Brown, volunteered to chaperon the young woman for the rest of the journey and so they continued into Waterloo. Brown and the girl were escorted to the Inspector's Office, where after a few moments Val Baker joined them. A police sergeant called William Hatter was present and it was established that the complainant was a Miss Rebecca Kate Dickinson, who lived in Midhurst with her widowed mother and two sisters. Val gave his occupation and, as address, Aldershot and the Army and Navy Club. Miss Dickinson refused to enlarge upon the details that had led her to risk her life in this way. She had been 'insulted', a euphemism for sexual assault. Val was not arrested or even cautioned. The Reverend Mr Brown accompanied Miss Dickinson to her brother's house in Chesterfield Street, Mayfair.

That night Sam Baker was just taking guests into dinner at Sandford Orleigh when a telegram arrived from Val. He left at once for London. The following day Dr Dickinson, his sister and several of the railway employees who were witnesses travelled by early train to Guildford, where they went to the police station and applied for a warrant for the arrest of Colonel Baker. The charge was one of indecent assault. *The Times* already had the story and printed it with the cross-head EXTRAORDINARY CHARGE OF ASSAULT. The case was heard at Guildford Magistrates' Court, where it happened that the bench was chaired by another military man, the retired Colonel Marshall. Val engaged one of the fiercest cross-examining barristers in London, Henry Hawkins, later the learned judge Lord Bampton.

As to what had actually happened in the compartment, it was only Miss Dickinson's word against that of his client and Hawkins would have had no trouble contending that Val had actually saved the young woman's life. There were only two things to contradict a defence that Miss Dickinson had panicked in some way after a harmless gesture (such as the defendant moving to sit beside her). The first was the evidence of the guard and the two men Val later joined in the neighbouring carriage, who claimed that the defendant's clothing had been disarranged – put bluntly, that his flies were open. Sergeant Hatter also testified that Val had uttered these words to him at Waterloo: 'I am sorry I did it.' In the hands of a skilful lawyer even that could not be taken as a confession of sexual assault – it could mean anything. The real problem lay elsewhere. The defendant absolutely refused to testify in his own defence. He would not any further impugn the honour of a lady by calling her a liar.

Colonel Marshall and his colleagues on the bench were in something of a quandary. On the evidence they had heard the original charge of indecent assault was insufficient and Val was further charged with 'assault with attempt to ravish' – in other words, attempted rape. However, the case had already attracted enormous press attention and Marshall was unwilling for it to be heard by a common jury, for fear of prejudicing the trial.

> At the present time a very strong feeling exists against him in the county, more especially among the classes of society from which common juries are selected. I am convinced that under these circumstances, he is more likely to get a fair and impartial trial before a special jury than before a common jury at the Assizes. These reports are malicious and totally without foundation.

This final remark was extraordinary. Probably, Marshall intended only to draw attention to the press coverage, but to assert that reports of the case were without foundation was to discredit the complainant's evidence and may have raised hopes for a moment that he would throw the whole business out of court. He did not. He remanded the prisoner to the Croydon Assize Court, setting bail at £2000, which was paid in two equal sums by Samuel Baker and Lord Valentia of the 10th Hussars. Only now, at the very end of this first hearing did Val address the bench.

> I am placed here [he said], in the most delicate position. If any act of mine on the occasion referred to could have given any annoyance to the complainant, I beg to express to her my most unqualified regret. At the same time, I solemnly declare on my honour that the case was not as it has been presented today by her under the influence of exaggerated fear and unnecessary alarm. To the evidence of the police sergeant Hatter I give a most unqualified denial.

These were the only words, then or ever, that he spoke in his own defence. The code that made him a gentleman forbade anything more – Hawkins, his counsel, was to say that he would not have accepted the brief upon any other terms. The Dickinson family could have, if they chose, reciprocated in kind. Rebecca Dickinson's evidence had done nothing to suggest that Val intended rape. He had, she said, asked for a kiss and touched her on the leg above the ankle. The strongest clue to the Dickinsons' feelings about the matter is her brother's Mayfair address. In their view, Val had behaved towards a woman of quality as though she were nothing but a social inferior. This was what rankled. He had treated Rebecca no better than a wealthy and importunate man might treat a shop-girl. The newspapers agreed. As a consequence, even before the second trial came to court, Val had been ruined. A motion to have the case referred to the Queen's Bench Division was denied. Sam Baker wrote to his old Ceylon friend Lord Wharncliffe.

> With regard to Val's affair, I know more from him than I have a right to divulge. He has confided the *whole* to three friends, including myself, but you know in such a case a man is at the mercy of a lady, and his tongue must on point of honour be absolutely sealed . . . This places him at a ruinous disadvantage when it comes to *law*. At the same time Val must allow that his best friends cannot defend even as much as he confesses.

It was this last sentence that settled it. Though Val would not contest Rebecca Dickinson's evidence in court out of what might seem to us a misplaced gallantry, even his brother accepted that he had some sort of case to answer. Something had happened in the railway carriage either greater or less than her testimony. Whatever it was, Val had admitted some element of guilt. Though he was to plead not guilty in court, his admission to his brother and the other two men – Hawkins and (probably) Valentia – was unretractable. He was a gentleman for staying silent and a cad for having something to stay silent about.

The Croydon trial was held on 2 August, which was a Bank Holiday. This did nothing to diminish public interest but rather enhanced it. Val left Aldershot at 3 a.m. and travelled by the milk train in order to avoid being accosted on his way to the court. By eight in the morning the streets outside the Assize building were crowded and it was only with difficulty that the barristers engaged could fight their way in. The mob was kept up to fever pitch by the arrival of some very distinguished names – Lord Lucan and General Airey, Sir William Fraser MP, Viscount Halifax, the Marquis of Tavistock and Lord Valentia. Sir Thomas Steele, who had been Raglan's military secretary in the Crimea, and was now in command at Aldershot, was prepared to go into the witness box as a character reference. If his presence – and that of General Airey, who also gave witness to Val as a man of honour – was intended to be reassuring, it may also have been damaging. To the baying crowds outside it looked as if 'society' was closing ranks. Inside the courtroom every seat was taken. The heat was suffocating.

The case was heard by Mr Justice Brett, later Master of the Rolls and raised to the peerage as Viscount Esher. Brett was a notoriously severe and impatient judge, compensated for by a strong faith in the justice of the jury system. Though both sides had engaged the best and most fashionable barristers possible, there was really very little to be made of the case. Mr Hawkins, for Val, managed to get the complainant to admit that nothing in his client's behaviour had caused her the slightest alarm until the train left Woking, implying that a man set on debauching a young woman might have started his campaign earlier or given some immediate suspicion of his intentions. Mr Justice Brett seemed to agree with this, for in his summing up he so directed the jury that they found Colonel Baker not guilty of the graver charge of attempt to ravish. They found him guilty on charges of assault and indecent assault. In sentencing, the judge said to Val: 'Of all the people who travelled on the train that day you were the most bound to stand by and defend a helpless woman. There was nothing in her conduct to justify the course you took . . . Your crime is as bad as it could be.'

It was brutal but it was expected. The sentence of the court was a year's imprisonment and a £500 fine. The Dickinson family left the building to wild cheers from the highly partisan crowd. Most of them stayed on for another two hours to boo and jeer Val on his way to jail. In their opinion he had got off lightly.

He wrote immediately to the War Office offering to resign his commission. After a fortnight had passed a reply came that he was to be cashiered, 'the Queen having no further use for his services'. The brutality of this decision shocked the army. The Duke of Cambridge and the Prince of Wales pleaded with Victoria to let him resign but the case had touched a nerve in her that was very close to the surface. What had happened was an offence against the habits and manners of the Consort, never to be forgotten. Generally sentimental to a fault with her daughters, Victoria saw in her sons a constant reminder of that ideal of manhood she believed Albert to have been. They seldom came up to the mark.

It is in this context that the destruction of Val Baker has to be set. That notion of society that existed between inverted commas – the clubs, the salons, the Marlborough House banditti, even the army itself, were slow to judge Val Baker. There was a furious and unsympathetic press reaction to what he had done and the trial judge was criticised for not giving the convicted man the maximum sentence, which was two years' hard labour. But the real author of his woes was the queen.

It is hard not to see her intervention as a minor piece of spite directed against her son and his entourage. Although he was a married man in his thirties, Bertie was still treated as some sort of fractious child. He was in India when Disraeli persuaded his mother to accept the title empress and the first he knew about it was what he read in the papers. Victoria hardly bothered to inform him of any important development, so that for example when he sailed through the Suez Canal on his outward journey it was French and when he came back, it was British. The destruction of Colonel Baker was only one item in a long catalogue of 'Mother knows best'.

As far as England was concerned, Val was finished. Paris – the continent – was filled with men who had similarly disgraced their country and fled from debt or a grand adultery, homosexual scandal or some form of dishonest dealing. Val's tragedy was that he had never wanted anything more than to belong; when necessary, to trim. Men who were far more careless of life and reputation – men like Wolseley and Gordon; above all his own brother – had risked more and gained more as a consequence of it. The newspapers found Colonel Baker guilty of arrogance when his real social failing was trying too hard to oblige.

As a consequence of the trial there was an immediate modification of the carriage design on all railways. A triangular window – in effect a spyhole – was added to the bulkhead between compartments. Later on, connecting corridors were introduced, as well as 'Ladies Only' compartments, only discontinued in 1975, the centenary anniversary of the Woking incident. It is said by Giles Playfair that a spate of copycat crimes followed the Baker case: meanwhile, gentlemen were advised never to travel alone in a carriage with a woman, connecting corridor or not. If they had no choice in the matter, they should light a cigar and guard the length of the ash as a sign of their undisturbing presence. The British public was enjoying one of its periodic outbursts of moral hysteria.

The theme of *Clouds in the East*, the book he wrote of his Persian travels while he was in prison, more or less dictated what Val should do next. Turkey and Russia were very much in the news. An uprising in Herzegovina by Christian subjects of the Turkish Empire spread to Bosnia and, in trying to quell it, the Sublime Porte went through spasms and convulsions that alarmed European powers. The sultan was deposed and a new government proposed a partial repudiation of the national debt, arranging to repay half in an issue of bonds at five per cent. But existing bondholders had yet to be paid out on their latest coupon and the markets were further alarmed when Disraeli seized Britain's opportunity to pick the sick man's pocket, buying, on behalf of the nation, the khedive's shares in the Suez Canal. Disraeli distrusted the Russians: Gladstone, on the other hand, persuaded himself that they were standing up for Christianity in the foul nest of Muslim barbarity. Whether it was worth fighting another war about was questionable, until a hack called G. W. Hunt produced this:

> We don't want to fight but by Jingo if we do,
> We've got the ships, we've got the men, we've got the money
> too.
> We've fought the Bear before, and while Britons shall be true,
> The Russians shall not have Constantinople.

Before this was written, Val was already in the Turkish capital. It is possible that he was being used as an agent of the British government, through the urgings of the Duke of Cambridge. Disraeli's policy was not to go to war with Russia unless it was absolutely necessary – to keep Turkey alive, indirectly to thwart Bismarck's Prussia. Val wrote to the Prince of Wales to tell him that any chance of peace was futile. There would be war but it need not be disastrous. 'Since my arrival at Constantinople I have been minutely studying the probable strategic situation, and I am convinced that if England will act boldly and independently she wants no allies but can hold her own against any European combination.'

The results of these studies must have alarmed even the prince, for Val's recommendations called for a force of 100,000 men, disposed on ground he had discovered only twenty-five miles from Constantinople. It was a wildly unrealistic assessment of the situation, even more so when it concluded: 'Any difficulty in producing so large a force as 100,000 might be met by taking Turkish troops into British pay and giving them a proportion of British officers. There are no finer soldiers in the world than the men of the present Turkish Army . . .'

An Engineer officer was actually sent out to survey the strategic ground Val thought he had discovered – 'His view invariably coincides with mine,' Val reported gravely. But his letters to the prince described a pipe-dream, the most poignant part of which was the politically impossible suggestion of employing British officers with Turkish troops. There is no doubt that Val intended to propose himself in this special role, fighting alongside what would have been, had it come to it, the whole of the home army and a greater part of the troops held in India. Disgraced or not, he would with his proposals make himself of the army, if not in it. Whatever the prince thought of this plan, the politicians and the queen were in total agreement. Colonel Baker was out; and that was that. In the best circles etiquette demanded that he be spoken of henceforth as mere Mr Baker. In the very best, his name was not mentioned at all.

War was declared between Russia and Turkey on 24 April 1877. In August Val accepted an invitation from Mehemet Ali, the newly appointed commander-in-chief of the Turkish army, to join him at his headquarters. Mehemet Ali was a German, the son of a musician from Magdeburg. When he was fifteen he joined the merchant navy at Hamburg and left it at the first possible opportunity, which happened to be in the Bosphorus. The Turkish Foreign Minister of the day was, as the *Illustrated London News* delicately put it, 'attracted by his good looks' and, after converting to the Muslim faith, he was placed in the Turkish Military Academy. By the age of twenty-five he was on the general staff of the Turkish contingent in the Crimea. He was a major-general before he was forty and when Val met him he had just been made a field marshal.

Mehemet Ali believed that the key to the whole Russian invasion of what was then called European Turkey was at a place called Plevna, which commanded the only real pass though the mountains of Bulgaria to the ultimate strategic prizes, Adrianople and Constantinople. The *Daily Telegraph* sent its correspondent Drew Gay to inspect it. He was unimpressed.

> It is situated between a huge marsh and an odorous ditch, called by courtesy the River Vid. Its streets are paved on the principle of one huge boulder to three great holes. It boasts a mosque, a huge Christian church, a prison and a khan. In itself it is not of the slightest importance. Were Plevna, with the whole of its inhabitants, blotted out of existence, the world would run its round and nobody would say much about Plevna departed.

This is the necessarily world-weary language of a Victorian surveying life outside London. Gay missed the point. What made

Plevna remarkable to Val was not its unappealing civilian character but the use made of the surrounding terrain by the genius of its local commander, Osman Pasha. Plevna was a fortress-enclave of trenches and redoubts with a fourteen-mile front to the north, employing every scrap of useful defensive terrain. The Russians arrived before it in June 1877 and found to all intents and purposes an impregnable position. Nevertheless, it had to be taken. Two full-scale attempts at the divisional level were repulsed. Behind walls and in trenches, the principal weakness of the Turkish army – its craven and incompetent officer caste – was made tactically unimportant. The individual soldier came into his own in the rocky terrain round Plevna: what he had to do was obvious, and defence played to his strengths of extreme hardiness and excellent marksmanship. Nevertheless, the net tightened and soon enough Drew Gay found himself trapped inside the perimeter.

During the short-lived war there were correspondents and what were called 'special artists' on both sides of the conflict and the military details of the campaign were followed with intense interest in London. At Plevna, faced with the prospects of a long-drawn-out siege, the Russians called up their fortifications expert Todleben, whose presence at Sebastopol twenty-three years earlier had caused the allies such grief. The Imperial Guard was sent for, and the tsar himself crossed the flimsy boat-bridges across the Danube. The siege stirred memories of Sebastopol, with the difference that the Turks were now the besieged and the Russians in the position the allies had experienced.

Great interest was sparked by the unforgiving cruelty shown on both sides. This was, as well as a siege, an extraordinarily vicious conflict carried on between ethnic enemies. Centuries of hatred were unleashed and perhaps for the first time the damage war caused to civilian populations was given a modern slant in the press. The word 'atrocity' was suddenly a commonplace of press reporting. The Turks had shown a taste for torture that was exploited by Gladstone in an almost hysterical fashion: 'So far as it is in our power to determine, never again shall the hand of violence be raised by you, never again shall the floodgates of lust be open to you, never again shall the dire refinements of cruelty be devised by you for the sake of making mankind miserable.'

But then what were Gladstone's readers to make of the Russians who, as they liberated Orthodox Bulgarians, armed them and set them loose on their Turkish neighbours in a fashion that has not gone away to this day? The reporting of the war created a disturbing sexual frisson: stories of rape and hideous mutilation were quite as avidly studied as the siege of Plevna or the threat to Constantinople. Partisan feeling reached as high as the queen herself – her secretary, Ponsonby, who had strong Russian sympathies, outraged Victoria enough for her to summon the dean of Windsor to set him straight.

Drew Gay escaped from Plevna in September and his account of the terrible privations among the besieged helped stir the Duke of Sutherland to form at his home in London the Stafford House Committee, created to provide medical facilities for the Turks. (In St Petersburg society ladies from the tsarina downwards were providing the same charitable services for the Russian victims of war – going from house to house and even soliciting members of the general public. Colonel Colville of the British embassy staff described meeting one such aristocrat on a ferry steamer. She carried a brass box into which the passengers dropped their contributions.)

Fred Burnaby's *A Ride to Khiva* contained many barbed comments on the capacity of Russians for cruelty towards civilians. The sequel to the book was *On Horseback through Asia Minor*, the story of a journey he undertook from Constantinople along the southern shores of the Black Sea to Batum in 1877. (It is worth remembering that these epic jaunts were undertaken while their author remained a serving member of the Household Cavalry.) According to Burnaby, Russia considered him a desperate enemy of the state for the truth of his reporting: he found his photograph pinned up in every police station and border post. He worked up further indignation on this second trip, outlining Russian treatment of the Circassians.

Among other ways of compelling the Circassians to submit to their conquerors is one so fiendish, that if proof was not at hand to confirm the statement, I should hesitate to put it before the reader. In order to frighten the mountaineers and civilize them à la Russe, the Czar's soldiers cut off the heads and scooped out the eyes of several men, women and children; then nailing the eyeless heads on trees, they placed placards underneath them saying 'Go and complain to the Kralli of the English and ask her to send you an oculist.'

The queen received this interesting officer in private audience (though whether he told her this last anecdote is doubtful) and in the country at large his stock was high. It now occurred to him to volunteer his services to the Stafford House Committee to go to Plevna and see for himself what could be done. Drew Gay had managed to escape? Well then, he would do the opposite and break in. It was a characteristically hare-brained scheme which found him waiting on the up-line at Adrianople one morning in his bowler hat and an enormous overcoat, on his way to almost certain death. While he paced, smoking a cigar with appropriate sang-froid, he looked up and saw a familiar face staring at him from under a fez. When he squinted a little closer, he recognised his old friend Val Baker, attired in a Turkish general's uniform. As befitted two Englishmen, they shook hands with all the casualness of gentlemen waiting to board the train to Windsor.

They set off to Mehemet Ali's headquarters at Sofia. As Val explained, his friend had chosen a particularly inopportune time to visit. Mehemet Ali had written to Constantinople saying that he did not think he could hold the line. The army was crumbling and hundreds of deserters were being shot every day. Less than a week later Plevna fell, releasing 120,000 Russians for the thrust on the capital. The tsar bade his troops farewell and set off back to St Petersburg the day before it began to snow. He had seen enough. Victory was assured and the only question left was whether the Turkish army would be completely routed.

At the Orkrhanie Pass Archibald Forbes of the *Daily News* was in the Russian lines and asked Count Shuvalov if any British officers were to be found opposite them. He quotes Shuvalov in full:

> Yes indeed, quite a number! You can see them for yourself if you go up yonder. Two of them are old friends of mine and I ask for nothing better than to invite them to come over and dine with me. You are too young to have been in the Aldershot autumn manoeuvres of 1871, else you might remember the officer of the Russian Guards who rode with the Prince of Wales and Valentine Baker at the head of the 10th Hussars. I was that officer, and poor Baker was the finest light cavalry officer I ever saw.

Forbes asked the Russian if he knew what had befallen Val since. Shuvalov had, and obliged with a ringing endorsement.

> Had he belonged to us do you think we should have lost him to the service he adorned because of a wretched private folly? Pshaw! What a square-toed prudish lot you English are! If Valentine Baker could forsake those tatterdemalion Turks and come over the trenches to us, I'll engage the Tsar would make him a full general within a month!

Shuvalov was paying Forbes a compliment by suggesting he was too young to remember the review of 1871. The Scot was forty and had served as a trooper for ten years in the Household Cavalry before taking up journalism. As an old cavalryman he was disposed to write sympathetically of Val but it was not the first time the disgraced colonel had been praised in such fulsome terms. A little earlier in the campaign a correspondent on the Turkish side witnessed Val lead out eight squadrons of cavalry against the Russian lines.

> Some bodies of the Russian Cavalry came out to meet him and they came into contact in a large field of maize. But there was no holding back Baker and his Turks and the Russian Cavalry was soon tearing back as hard as they could go, to get under the shelter of their guns. The Turkish Cavalry followed them hard like tigers who had once tasted blood and longed for more.

Val's grey Arab stallion was shot from under him but he seized the reins of a loose horse and was up in a moment, 'hacking like a very Hercules'. As with the Shuvalov story, the report contained significant reference to the hero's background.

> An old Turkish artillery officer who was standing quite close to me laid down his field glasses and said: 'I swear by the Prophet that the infidel who commands our cavalry fights with the courage of ten thousand tigers.' 'And yet,' said another young artillery officer, 'Allah has smitten the English with such blindness that they allow a man like him to leave their Army.'

In these stories, which have the decided air of having been confected, both the Turks and the Russians were saying what many in the British military establishment believed: that Val Baker had been cruelly treated. Burnaby of course thought this, too – he was the other Briton pointed out by Shuvalov as an old friend. ('Quite mad, of course,' the Russian commented breezily. 'Always was.') Burnaby's Stafford House commission was now forgotten – the question was whether his friend Baker could do anything on the grand scale to snatch victory from the jaws of defeat. If he could, *Vanity Fair* was ready to puff it. On Christmas Day he threw a dinner for Val and the newspaper correspondents attached to the Turkish camp. They ate goose. The first one that Burnaby's servant fetched from Sofia would not do and his master sent him back for another, a total of 120 miles' hard riding. It was something of a funeral feast, for the Russians were massing for an all-out attack through the Orkrhanie Pass.

On New Year's Eve, at his headquarters in Tashkennan on the left flank of the Turkish position, Val was woken with the news that the Russian attack had commenced. He and his hastily assembled force of 3000 cavalry was all that could protect the retreat of the main Turkish army. The only newspaper correspondent on the spot was Francis Francis, reporting for *The Times*. Between dawn and dusk Baker fought an epic battle to prevent the main column of the Turkish army from being over-run. It raged on two fronts, the Bosnian and Albanian defenders stirred by blood-chilling bugle calls and pitiless hand-to-hand fighting. Afterwards the official War Office historian, Captain Hozier, wrote, 'It would be difficult to find, in all records of history, whether ancient or modern, a more brilliant act of military heroism.'

Burnaby thought so, and so did Francis Francis. But Edmund Ollier, who wrote the *Cassell's Illustrated History* of the war, a scissors-and-paste job compiled as the fighting went along, barely mentions Val or, come to that, Tashkennan. The omission is significant. Three months later *Vanity Fair* commented bitterly on a more serious suppression.

> Why is it that the *Times* still continues to believe in the stale old trick of suppressing every scrap of information it receives at all creditable to the Turks? The *Times* correspondent, Mr Francis Francis, was the one and only correspondent on the field of Tashkennan. He was naturally much elated at his exclusive situation and posted down to Constantinople in all haste to send off his letter to the *Times*. Yet that letter, which should have been one of the most interesting of all those published during the war, has been burked by the *Times* for no other reason that I can imagine than that it recorded a Turkish success.

The general retreat that followed Tashkennan was accomplished in appalling winter conditions, Burnaby nursing his exhausted friend through the mountains until at last they reached the Aegean. Putting up at the house of an Orthodox archbishop, they were poisoned with strychnine injected into their biscuits by an indignant acolyte. That, and the absence of a British fleet to honour the treaty obligations Britain had with Turkey, was the last straw. The beaten Turkish army was evacuated by sea to Gallipoli and, while it was there, peace was declared. Disgusted, Val took leave of absence in May and returned to London. The Duke of Sutherland gave a banquet in his honour at Stafford House, attended by Sam Baker, followed by a reception packed with peers and general officers. No ladies were invited.

NINE

The short war led to a disastrous peace. By the terms of the Treaty of Berlin the Ottoman Empire lost nearly half its territory and twenty per cent of its population. The sultan was not even a party to the negotiations and Disraeli, Bismarck and the Russian envoy carved the spoils as they wished. One side dish was the acquisition of Cyprus by the British. Under a further convention signed in 1878 Britain took over the administration of the island, paying the Turks what amounted to an annual rent of £92,800. In the following year Sir Samuel and Lady Baker paid Cyprus a visit, preparatory to making a round-the-world cruise.

Sam arrived with revolvers on his hip, expecting brigandage. He was quickly reassured. Though conditions were squalid, they were peaceful. He took one look at the accommodation on offer and with his usual practicality fitted out a cart to make a luxurious version of a Romany caravan. Drawn by an ox, it rumbled its way back and forth along the very few roads on the island wide enough to take it, while Sam and Florence rode ahead on horseback, ranging the stony hills with three dogs they had brought from Devon. Their plan was to escape the English winter and perhaps find enough materials to write a small book.

At night they slept among the olives. There were British soldiers on hand, surveying: when these came to visit they would find the explorer, who was two years off his sixtieth birthday, presiding over a camp organised by Amarn, a liberated slave and a particular favourite of Florence's who had come home with them to Sandford Orleigh and was by now their cherished major-domo. As to Aphrodite's Island, they found nothing in it to entrance them. Cyprus at that time was sunk in apathetic gloom. Four out of five of the population were Orthodox Greeks, the very people the Russians had vowed to protect in their two wars against Turkey. They seemed completely unaware of this good fortune, for in truth nothing had changed for them. Their landlords were still Turkish.

The celebrity-hunters who found their way to Sam's camp discovered he still had some of the *joie de vivre* exhibited in his books. A recent story was how he had ruined a fairground strong man's act at a Devon fair by winding a chain round his own biceps and snapping it, ping. Nevertheless, time was catching up with him. He had grown all too comfortably into his mature persona, Sir Samuel White Baker of Devon, the famed African explorer. If that was a title that borrowed from the past, the casual listener, offered a dozen anecdotes of life along the Upper Nile, found it none the worse for that. A more acute guest might have gone away thoughtful, treated to the open-handed liberality of a former Turkish pasha with his excellent wines and hampers of food from Fortnum and Mason, served in some buzzing Mediterranean grove. This was a great man tamed.

Sam had gained the honours and paid the price of being among the first in African exploration. Since 1843, the year of his marriage to Henrietta, he had lived only a handful of years in Britain, none of them in London. The self-congratulation of his life in Devon – the house 'somewhat in the Gothic style', the steam launch kept at anchor for the whim of sailing down to Teignmouth, the incognito visits of the Prince of Wales, shooting parties with his neighbour the Duke of Somerset – all these conspired to make him something of the old style of reclusive country gentleman, albeit one with an awesome pride of life. Another of his stories was how he had once bounded into the garden at Sandford Orleigh and thrashed the future George V for climbing into a specimen tree which he had been specifically warned not to touch.

He kept up a combative correspondence whenever his record

was threatened in the press. Such criticism usually came from members of the anti-slavery movement who found continual offence in his brisk opinion that in order to civilise a country you had first to annex it – what you gave to the cause of freedom with one hand, you necessarily took away with the other. (As we have seen, Gordon had come to the identical conclusion. Still busying himself in the Bahr el Ghazal, he had begun to think longingly of retiring from the army. He would have the courtesy rank of major-general and a pension of £450 a year. When his sister suggested he would find nothing to do with his time, he bridled. The Empire could go hang. He would have his Chatham boys.)

An era was passing. Just before Sam arrived in Cyprus, the island had briefly welcomed Wilfrid Scawen Blunt and his wife. They found it nothing very much, for they were on their way back to Arabia, and there, travelling by camel caravan, they would write poetry, make love and buy horses for their stud at Crabbet Park in Sussex. Their path would be smoothed not by guns or the exhibition of a superior way of life, but by willing submission to the desert. It was Blunt's fantasy that he could, if he chose, live like an Arab and be part of the country he passed through, without altering it. This, along with a hearty and deepening contempt for all things European, led him – his father was a Grenadier Guards officer, his mother a parson's daughter – to disdain 'civilisation'. More and more the noun had begun to attract such ironic quotation marks from literary figures, a point of view that gained enormous ground in the last quarter of the nineteenth century. Its most succinct expression was perhaps Conrad's *Heart of Darkness* (1902).

Blunt wrote in his memoirs:

> I found among the bedouin with their 'bird like minds', their happy nonchalance, their plain materialism, their facile consciences, their lack of spiritual fancies, a freedom from all bondage religious or political, above all their practical unbelief in any but the corporeal life . . . a solvent for the puzzles which had perplexed me . . .

It was not completely unusual for the European mind to find good in remote societies. It helped if the natives had something like the traveller's own skin colour and a similar skull shape, if they bore themselves with dignity and showed the common virtues of a white man. Martial courage was always praised, as was honest dealing and chastity in women. For poets and intellectuals, the cult of the noble savage stretched back a long way but in men like Blunt there was a new strain added. Among the Wahabi sect in the area of Baghdad he went through a ritual of brotherhood with his hosts. It made him, he hoped, not so much a traveller as a pilgrim, a petitioner from an old and exhausted culture.

Sam and Florence Baker were from a heartier tradition. They employed much of their time on Cyprus washing children vigorously in public fountains, teaching them the benefits of cleaning their teeth with wood ash and a bit of stick; and finding amusement in the clothes of their mothers, nominally western in dress but sadly lacking buttons where buttons ought to be. The Cypriots were a people who needed to brought up to scratch and these two were the people to do it. It was a completely unself-conscious attitude, such as managed many an imperial bungalow for another seventy or so years. The native had things to learn from the white man that he himself had learned from his parents and his nanny, the little things that mattered, like punctuality and cleanliness, the right dress for the right occasion and a tempered response to discomfort. The traffic in learning was all one way.

The great days of exploration as the highest form of adventure had begun to recede into the past. Quinine had first been extracted from cinchona bark in the 1820s and after various hesitations and false starts prophylactic daily doses of quinine became the norm. (The tree itself, which originated in Peru, was carried halfway across the world: cinchona was one of the crops John Baker was lately trying to raise at Newera Eliya.) Once the properties of quinine were understood, the old fear of miasma, curling out of the mangrove swamps in West Africa, or hanging like curtains in the Indian forests, was abated. It became an offence in the British army abroad not to take quinine when issued it, and though the dread of swamps and bad air took a very long time dying among the general public, one at least of the killer tropical diseases was tamed. It was true Sam had nearly lost his second wife to fever – and in 1855 had crawled back to Newera Eliya half-dead himself. But Livingstone took daily doses of quinine from the 1840s onwards and was sufficiently convinced of their prophylactic effect to make up his own compound, of which the alkaloid was the principal ingredient, admixed (characteristically) with rhubarb, little bombs he passed out to the Zambezi expedition as 'Livingstone Pills'. Now nobody who passed through Suez on their way to India and the far east was without their quinine. 'Keep hold of your mosquito net,' Gordon unromantically counselled his young staff in the Sudan; 'it is of more use to you than a revolver.'

Burnaby's ride to Khiva and its sequel along the Black Sea coast was one of the last expressions of the inspired gentleman amateur, riding eighteen stone, navigating by distant mountains, fishing for supper from some raging torrent. Alone under immense skies, such a traveller was no more than a little packet of civilisation misdelivered to the waste lands, the hero of a story that could only be told back in England. An important part of Burnaby's stores was his boxes of a patent medicine called Potter's Pills, which he swore by for all the minor ailments of an expedition. They connected him not to the landscape over which he travelled but to the chemist's shop in London where he had bought them.

Yet Burnaby had seen in Africa the future as it was soon to be in so many locations on earth – a river steamboat coming round the bend in the river, bringing with it mail and supplies but also the reaffirmation of what was sometimes a very distant authority. Standing at the rail might be a missionary or a district officer, a veterinarian or a headmaster; not world-weary like the dishevelled and sardonic traders who travelled with them, the beaten-up skipper or the drunken engineer, but men with the light of improvement burning in their eyes. Their expectation of their destination was equally high-minded. They came not to discover but to develop.

Within a generation, advances in general medicine, tinned

foods, specialised clothing, measuring equipment and the maps that resulted from them, telegraph stations and regular steam services by land and sea combined to change the picture of the world. Many of the old travellers' tales now found their refuge in children's books; for example, the remorseless enmity of the crocodile, which had hitherto been given a character more recently reserved by us for the Great White Shark. Deadly spiders, poisonous snakes, scorpions whose favourite hiding place was the boot under the bed now became plot devices for hacks. Generally speaking, if you could get there, you could live there. You might be the first, but soon enough others would follow. All over the globe were dockside wharves filled with British coal, serving British commercial vessels that plugged on through oceans. The very idea of a round-the-world cruise for pleasure such as the Bakers were planning was an indication of the changes that had been wrought.

One of the greatest of the new breed of imperialists was on Cyprus in imago form at the same time as Sam. Twenty years hence at Omdurman Herbert Kitchener would kill over 11,000 Arabs in a morning for the loss of just forty men from his own force. As the thunderstruck young war correspondent G. W. Steevens reported for the *Daily Mail*, 'It was not a battle but an execution.' When Kitchener found Sam Baker's camp on Cyprus and introduced himself, he was no more than a gangly and argumentative lieutenant of Engineers who had recently mapped Palestine and – the point of common interest – stood briefly alongside Val Baker in the Turkish trenches at Plevna. Sam would have found him strangely reminiscent of his brother, a young man with a full moustache and bulbous eyes, much given to staring the world down. He was twenty-eight years old, a fluent Arabist and already an unquestioning advocate of colonisation by conquest.

Kitchener was under secondment to the Foreign Office to make a full-scale survey of the island. He had already fallen foul of the high commissioner, who was an extremely ill-tempered Garnet Wolseley. Wolseley did not want a full-scale survey, he wanted enough information to make the island a jumping-off point for the war that might come in the near future, if (it was more commonly thought *when*) the remnants of the Turkish Empire collapsed. Moreover, he did not want a lieutenant of Engineers who was not under his direct command. However, when Sam met and commiserated with Lieutenant Kitchener, this particular thorn was no longer in his side. General Wolseley had been suddenly whisked away to the Cape.

At the beginning of 1879 one of the greatest reverses to British arms of the century took place in South Africa at a rocky outcrop called Isandhlwana. On 22 January 40,000 Zulus attacked Lord Chelmsford's column on its way to arrest their paramount chief, Cetewayo. By mismanagement and incompetence, but even more by overestimating the superiority of white men over black, Chelmsford managed to sacrifice an entire regiment of the British army. Every single officer and man of the 24th was slaughtered and his corpse disembowelled. In the whole battle only fifty-five white soldiers and 300 Natal kaffirs survived of the 1800 who took part. All the transport, guns and equipment, including 400,000 rounds of ammunition, fell into Zulu hands. It was the most stunning defeat imaginable.

Isandhlwana left British public opinion utterly bewildered. It was true that in the same week at Rorke's Drift some honour was salvaged and a hero found in the Devonian lieutenant of Engineers John Rouse Chard, who commanded the defence of the tiny kraal and hospital against overwhelming odds. Eleven VCs were awarded for this action, Chard receiving his from Wolseley in the field. But even this consolatory moment of glory was offset later that spring by the death of the Prince Imperial, the last of the Bonapartes, on the very first day of Chelmsford's avenging expedition.

The Empress Eugenie's son was a wilful and none too bright boy who had badgered his mother to let him go to South Africa to fight the Zulus. Though he had attended the Royal Military Academy, he held no rank in the British army and, it was agreed, could never be let anywhere near the front line. Attached to the headquarters staff with strict instructions not to get himself into trouble, he managed nevertheless to do just that. On Sunday 1

June 1879 the prince wheedled permission to go out on patrol to scout the ground over which the main column would pass later in the day. It seemed a safe enough request, for whatever he may have thought of its value, his patrol was really nothing more than a jaunt, a harmless exercise. Sent out with him was a minder, Lieutenant Carey, who was sufficiently overwhelmed by the dignity of his royal charge to let him assume command. They galloped around for an hour or so and dismounted in an apparently empty landscape. Carey was all the same anxious for them to return to base. In the act of remounting the patrol was ambushed by a small party of Zulus. There were a few seconds of blind panic and Carey, who had never been in battle, galloped off alone. When the prince's naked body was recovered, it was found pierced by eighteen assegai wounds. Carey's fate was sealed. He was at first sentenced to be shot for cowardice, commuted after further consideration to cashiering. The Empress Eugenie interceded on his behalf and he was restored to the army and sent out to Karachi. It is said that, for as long as he lived, no officer ever again addressed him directly.

What was an ambitious but unfocused young officer like Kitchener to make of this black year? In memoirs by B. de Sales la Terrière (*Days That Are Gone*, 1924) he was recalled as someone wanting above all else to be a great leader of cavalry. However, if that was his ambition, de Sales la Terrière found him curiously deficient in some important respects. He was not thinking of his lack of cavalry training. 'To explain what I mean. The ordinary topics of conversation of two youngish soldiers, living together as we were, would have been on such subjects as one's school or college friends, sport, shooting, hunting, fishing, life in London, the theatres, cricket, racing, country houses, etc.'

The Hatter, as he was nicknamed, could supply anecdotes on any of these topics. But whenever he attempted to do so, Kitchener simply fixed him with a wall-eyed stare. The son of a half-pay colonel who had taken land in Ireland after the Great Famine, never sent to school at all but educated by a succession of tutors; fluent in French, passionately religious in the mould of his fellow Engineer Gordon, Kitchener was out of a different box. The Hatter sensed this, commenting gravely in later years, 'I doubt if at that time he had ever owned a top hat, or knew his way to Piccadilly.'

Kitchener had the advantage of de Sales la Terriere in some other areas. The Hatter may have been at Madgalen College, Oxford, with Oscar Wilde, where he amused himself by pasting postage stamps over prints of nude young gods the Irishman had hanging on his walls; he may won the Royal Military Hunt Cup at Sandown. But while still a cadet at Woolwich Kitchener had seen war. Without bothering with leave of absence, he joined a French field-ambulance unit in the Franco-Prussian War of 1870–71. Attached to the Second Army of the Loire, he was present at the bloody three-day battle of Le Mans. He was invalided home after contracting pneumonia from a balloon ascent.

Kitchener was hauled before the awesomely choleric Duke of Cambridge and threatened with the loss of his commission. (The duke, after a huge and spluttering rant, dismissed him with these words: 'I am bound to say, boy, that in your place I should have done exactly the same.') Kitchener had a gift for joining wars that were not his own. He had wangled his way into Val's command in the Balkans while on his way home from surveying in Palestine. Once again he was on leave. Val took him up on a crag and showed him the Russian trenches below, every detail pin-sharp in the frosty air, before gently shooing him away the morning of the Christmas Day goose dinner organised by Fred Burnaby.

Kitchener was a Turcophile, a dreamer, an oddball; de Sales la Terriere was the epitome of a young cavalry captain. One of Kitchener's mild eccentricities was to persist in employing an Arab cook he had picked up in Palestine. The faithful Abu was more often than not drugged and insensible on hashish. It did not seem to bother Kitchener, who showed no more interest in what he ate or drank than he did in pretty girls. The Hatter, however, had his standards. One night he painted the stuporous Abu in red and white stripes and turned him out of the camp, where, wandering about in a haze of unbeing, he was nearly shot by a nervous sentry.

Too many Hatters and the army stultified. Too many Kitcheners and it became a circus of a different kind. The abolition of long service for the other ranks and commission by purchase for officers was intended to change the character of the army, and to this Wolseley was committed. If he had formed a bad first impression of Kitchener, much of it was exasperation at the misappropriation of even one army officer from general duties. For as the events of 1879 had demonstrated, modernised or not, the army was being stretched to breaking point. The Cape was for the moment pacified, but before Sam Baker was halfway round the world on his sporting tour, the British fleet had entered the Dardanelles and Indian troops were sent through the Suez Canal and garrisoned at Malta. In Egypt, Khedive Ismail had been deposed, not by the wish of the sultan but following demands made by the Commission de la Dette. The storm clouds were gathering once again.

In November 1879 *Punch* published a cartoon showing Henry Layard, the British ambassador to the Porte, addressing a cowering and timorous sultan. 'Your Majesty *must* reform,' Layard insists, with bristling beard. 'Must!!!' the sultan exclaims. 'Is there then a new Grand Vizier in England?' 'No, but there's going to be a General Election!'

It brought back Gladstone, who almost immediately recalled Layard. The outgoing ambassador believed that European powers – and particularly his own government – underestimated the ability Turkey had for muddling through. There were vast tracts of land that still belonged to the Ottoman Empire full of agricultural potential. There was a huge reserve of fanatically motivated soldiery in the asiatic provinces. The sultan, though he might be depicted in *Punch* as a mustachioed waiter, was the acknowledged leader of the Muslim faith, not just in the streets and alleys of Constantinople, nor even in his own domains, but world-wide.

Val Baker was back in post with a general's commission from the sultan to set about an urgent reorganisation of the Turkish army. To begin with he was snubbed by the new incumbent at the British embassy, until the Foreign Secretary cabled an interesting if enigmatic text: 'The Prince of Wales takes more interest in your receiving General Baker than he does in the Eastern Question.'

The ambassador's wife at once invited Val to dinner and he soon became a regular guest.

At home his name was being tirelessly aired in the pages of *Vanity Fair* as an example of a model British officer who had been left far too long outside the tent. This was Burnaby's work. It was the old question of reinstatement. Was an English gentleman distinguished by courage and initiative to be treated as some kind of leper for the rest of his life? This was the bluff and simple view of Val's predicament. But little by little it began to be accepted that exile to Turkey and the good work he was doing there – when he might, for example, have been spending his days playing baccarat at Monte Carlo – had made General Baker's name newly resonant. The question whether, in the event of new hostilities, Turkey would survive another savage blow, lay surely with its army. The man in charge of its reconstruction, who had been cut dead in some parts of London society, whose name was anathema to the queen, was now a key player in the Eastern Question.

In 1879 those European banks and bondholders who had been stung by Egypt's chronic insolvency seized their chance and the country was placed under French and British financial control. Egypt was in the unusual position of being treated as a province of the sultan's Empire and, at the same time, a company going through insolvency proceedings. The foreign powers had already shown their strength, first pressing Sam Baker's friend Ismail to abdicate and, when he would not, deposing him. The ex-khedive massed all his personal wealth and his harem on the luxury yacht *Mahroussa* and sailed to Naples and obscurity. In his place he left his pudgy son, Tewfik, and this too was not a decision of his own making but an imposition by the French and British. When Tewfik decided to rule without a ministry, he in turn was quickly made aware of his position: he was there to do as he was told. Such dramatic interventions in the sovereignty of another power could only be heading in one direction.

Between February and October of 1881 there was a series of nationalistic army mutinies in Egypt. The mantle of leadership fell upon a previously obscure colonel of infantry called Arabi, who

The disgraced Colonel Arabi, sketched from a photograph
taken in a Cairo prison.

levered his way from a jail sentence on a charge of sedition to an
appointment as Minister of War. Arabi insisted that the test of
Tewfik's sovereignty over his own affairs was military independence,
both from the foreign powers and from Turkey. In June 1882
things came to a head. For some days there had been rumours of
a civil uprising to be directed against Europeans in Alexandria. On
the 11th the mob came on to the streets and fifty white men
were murdered, the British consul narrowly escaping with his life.
Agitators ran through the port city calling for the death of all
Christians. Within a week 14,000 had fled the country and another

6000 had steamer tickets in their hands, waiting for the ships to recross the Mediterranean and take them away too.

The entire government of Egypt was suddenly in the hands of the army, led by their hero Arabi, a round-skulled, faintly brutal-looking man without a trace of European manners. At anchor off Alexandria was Admiral Sir Frederick Beauchamp Paget Seymour, commander-in-chief of the Mediterranean fleet and a Lord of the Admiralty, known to his cronies as 'the Ocean Swell'. He was every-thing Arabi was not – clear eyed, wavy haired, splendidly bearded; and impatient. Seymour had eight ironclads and six other vessels under his command and was itching for a fight. When he saw Arabi's soldiers improving the harbour fortifications he took this to be a belligerent act and gave the Egyptians an ultimatum. It was ignored. At 7 a.m. on 12 July 1882 there commenced a fleet action of ships from the most powerful navy in the world versus a line of sandy forts and embrasures. Seymour did not stint himself. The onshore breeze sent the smoke from the British guns billowing inland as they poured more than 3000 rounds towards the beach at ranges as low as 1000 yards. Gatling guns raked the forts, and mast-head marines tried to pick off individuals with Martini-Henry rifles. The ceasefire was called at 5.30 p.m. Next day Arabi gave his response. Alexandria went up in flames, starting with the European banking quarter of the Grande Place. The army fled, leaving a terrified European quarter crouching in cellars.

This was a situation the British could understand – a rebel leader who had to be hunted down and his power destroyed. The captain of the *Inflexible* was a Bible-quoting, hard-swearing eccentric called Jackie Fisher, whose fame was to spread well into the twen-tieth century. He came ashore with a Naval Brigade, fortified a train by cladding it with iron plates and set off down the tracks in pursuit of Arabi. Garnet Wolseley was summoned once again. It was the eventuality he had foreseen on Cyprus (where invasion troops were now quartered in the groves that Sam Baker had made his own). The House of Commons voted Wolseley £2,300,000 to put an end to Arabi and in September his troops attacked the Egyptians at Tel el Kebir. Much was made in the British press of the novelty of a night approach over the desert, and much more of how the Egyptian trenches were stormed at bayonet point; less was said about the indiscriminate slaughter of the routed army when Wolseley let loose his cavalry. It was 13 September. During the night a comet had appeared in the sky. Some said it was an evil sign.

On 29 June 1881 Mohamed Ahmed left his sanctuary on Abba Island, where the passing riverboats had paid him homage, and declared himself the Mahdi, the Expected One. He summoned every chief and notable to come to him and pay his allegiance, before joining him in the jihad that would cleanse the world of the infidel. There had been many before him who claimed to be the long-expected Messiah but none with such piety. There were certain other signs. It was said of Mohamed Ahmed that he could drink from a never-emptying cup and that he turned bullets into water. Some vengeful and jealous enemies – men from whom he exacted wealth or wives – tried to expose some of his miracles as party tricks, as, for example, when he struck the ground with his spear and fire and smoke arose from the sands. But the most telling anecdote of the early Mahdi uprising was this: armed government troops sent to arrest him, under the impression that he was merely a harmless fanatic, were beaten to death with sticks by his adherents. Whatever he was, Lord of Life or charlatan, he was held in complete awe by the tribesmen who flocked to him. When scholars complained that it was written of the Mahdi that his task was only to lead his people to Mecca and make them of the elect, his reply was smilingly simple. There were, he said, more ways than one to Paradise.

The *ansar* – the faithful – grew in number. They could be recognised by their deliberately patched gowns and, as the movement gained momentum, a ruthless fanaticism. Those unlucky Europeans they captured who refused to convert – like the Catholic priest Bonomi and his pitiful little party of Italian nuns – were stripped naked and led about in captivity like dogs. While he waited for the moment to raise the entire country in revolt, the Mahdi retreated south and west from Abba to the Nubian hills. It was the area where Gordon had so recently sat in his hut in the sea of grass, debating whether what he was doing was of any use to God. The comet that passed across the sky in September 1882, such an evil sign to Colonel Arabi, seemed to the Mahdi an omen and a blessing.

TEN

The Hatter took part in the battle of Tel el Kebir, commanding a squadron of the 19th Lancers. A few days earlier he had managed to knock down a pedestrian while attempting to gallop a mule-cart through the cavalry lines at Kassasin. The victim happened to be the French consul. To forestall any trouble he had 'the perfectly inoffensive old gentleman' locked up in the main guard room: the Lancers moved out into the desert the next morning and the Hatter was spared the trouble of apologising for a minor diplomatic incident. Herbert Kitchener, much to his chagrin, missed all this excitement. He had made a good start in July, watching the bombardment of Alexandria from the decks of Seymour's flagship. When he badgered the admiral for permission to storm ashore with the Naval Brigade, it was pointed out with some asperity that he was in mufti, on leave and not under naval discipline. He was sent back to Limassol to explain himself.

By ten in the morning of Tel el Kebir the Egyptian army had ceased to exist. Arabi himself left the battlefield by train and fled to Cairo. He was pursued by British cavalry, arrested and thrown into jail. Those of his soldiers who had not been killed (de Sales la Terrière includes the gruesome detail that after bayoneting the trenches, the British set fire to them, sending the scent of what he describes as 'roast mutton' over the sands) simply disappeared back to their villages. Further afield, garrisons were paraded and disarmed – the ultimate humiliation, joyously accepted by the fellahin conscripts as their order of release. The barracks emptied. Egypt staggered on without any means of defending herself while the victors galloped up and down the streets of Cairo, not sure what to do next.

In Constantinople Val Baker watched these events with a leaping heart. There were only two possibilities open to Gladstone's government – to occupy Egypt permanently with British troops, or to find some way of reconstituting the Egyptian army while retaining indirect control. Three weeks after Tel el Kebir the sultan gave Baker Pasha leave to go to Egypt and consider how to re-form the army, with himself as its commander. It was a magnificent opportunity, for it brought his name forward in a central role at a time of great crisis. He knew very well that it was Gladstone and not the sultan whose confidence he needed to win but he was sufficiently confident of that to uproot his wife and children from Constantinople and take them with him to Alexandria. He was moving out of the shadows and into the light. The hour had provided the man.

Val arrived in Cairo in October 1882, making his base of operations a suite of rooms in Shepheard's Hotel. There was a stream of sometimes jocular, sometimes deferential afternoon visits from young British officers anxious to serve under him. His temporary ADC was Eddie Stuart-Wortley, the son of Sam Baker's Ceylon friend, with whom the explorer had gone yomping in the greeny dark. There were also two young Arabic-speaking officers hanging around, in part for the pleasure of seeing Val's daughter Hermione. These mavericks were Herbert Kitchener, who had straightened things out with his chief on Cyprus; and Reginald Wingate, a twenty-one-year-old Scot with a commission in the Royal Artillery. (One of these two would go on to become a field marshal, the other governor-general of Sudan.) The mild-mannered Major Sartorius, who had been with Val in Turkey, was his informal chief of staff.

The allure of detached service in Egypt for those who petitioned Val was quite straightforward. His plan emphasised the need for cavalry and mounted infantry – as might be expected of its author – and this raised hopes of romantic border actions, far removed from routine garrison duties elsewhere. The situation in Egypt was so volatile – and the memory of Tel el Kebir so fresh – that it may have been hard for the young men who came to see Val to keep up the necessary display of nonchalance. Those who knew something about the list being formed, or were told by Val that they were on it, saw at once that, when it was complete, the reorganised Egyptian army would be staffed by junior British officers given a local jump in rank to captain or beyond. Nothing could be more exciting to contemplate. The prospect of imminent further action was very real – first reports of the Mahdi's revolt were filtering through and there was a demand for maps of southern Egypt and the Sudan. The most recent of these had been published by Blackwood in 1873. On it, the sheer scale of the Nile was made very apparent. Away from the course of the river there was hardly a place-name to be found, unless it was to indicate some wadi or oasis. The railway ended at Cairo in the west, and Port Suez in the east. There were no roads and the few caravan tracks identified were indicated by speculative straight lines. (The author of this particular map was Keith Johnston, who was a member of the Royal Geographical Society. He died of dysentery in 1879 while leading an expedition to Lake Nyassa.)

Cairo was a cosmopolitan centre of the kind India lacked, offering all the glamour of foreign service with the additional advantage of being well connected by sea to Europe and the home country. It had style. To this day the city cannot decide whether its roots are Mediterranean or more profoundly Arabic. The ancient Muslim university of the Al Azhar is cheek by jowl with a bazaar crammed with international luxury goods. In one alley there is a coffee-shop hung with huge mirrors. It is said that every time a regime changed in the nineteenth century a new mirror was added. The one from Napoleon's invasion is there. In 1882 a new one was hung to signify the triumph of the English at Tel el Kebir.

The anglicised luxury of Shepheard's was the common rendez-vous – there was first-class European food to be had and four-day-old London newspapers, ice-cold bottled ale, fine wines, excellent telegraphic communications. Any number of pretty young women passed through Shepheard's on their way to India with their parents. The hotel, though it was these days managed by an Italian, had a strong sense of the character and prejudices of its principal clientele – in a notorious story, the khedive's nephew attempted to entertain a white woman there and found his salad served in a waiter's fez.

Away from Shepheard's there was a thriving British colony established in the palm-strewn suburbs, where things were arranged in the high imperial style of handsome houses and extensive and watered gardens. While not all the guests who crowded the diplomatic parties could be received privately (too many fezzes, too many vulgar uniforms and doubtful decorations), practically every European country was represented in Cairo. There were about 9000 foreign nationals in Egypt at this time, few of them there strictly for their health. Greeks had a strong grip on the commercial sector – Wolseley confiding to his diary that he doubted whether these could be called European in any strict sense of the word, any more than the 'greasy Levantines' it amused him to see Kitchener and Wingate personate on their intelligence-gathering operations. The French watched moodily from the diplomatic side-lines, having seen the country – or their share in it – more or less snatched from their grasp.

The overclass was undoubtedly the British. They shot quail out in the desert, went racing, kept up magnificent yachts. The winters were agreeably mild and in summer the heat and dust could be avoided by residence on the Nile houseboats that lined the banks. Val himself lived on one of these with his wife and two daughters, the eldest of whom was Hermione, a palely attractive young woman who had delicate health. They looked out on a city that had been hauled back from the very edge of bankruptcy. Sterling bought a great deal in Cairo. It also conferred on its holders a powerful dignity. No officer worth his salt could live on army pay in Cairo if he entertained to the level expected of his station in life – he was after all one of the minor gods of creation. Wolseley calculated that it was costing him £20 a day to entertain in the proper fashion. Multiplying by the factor of fifty, this was the preposterous sum of

£1000 just to be seen in the street, or giving hospitality in the palace placed at his disposal.

Val Baker's plan called, after modifications, for an Egyptian army of 6000 men, or ten regiments, officered exclusively by the British. It would confine its activities in the first instance to internal defence, leaving the question of the Sudan to be decided by the politicians. However, few military men doubted that such an army would be engaged to the south sooner rather than later, for after all there were (though in what condition nobody knew for certain) survivors of the old army in the Sudan who might well have sympathised with the disgraced Colonel Arabi but had not thrown down their arms. Pregnantly, Khartoum was garrisoned with such men.

Val's submission, which took only a month to complete, was approved locally by Sir Edward Malet for the Foreign Office, Sir Archibald Alison, who commanded the army of occupation, and Garnet Wolseley. The agreement of the two generals was key, for Baker's proposal called for the transfer of eighty named serving British officers to his command. This was ambitious but neither Alison nor Wolseley demurred. The khedive was quite delighted. Val could afford to push his pen back from his desk with a small smile of triumph. He was back in the game at last.

In his own eyes he was entitled to some sympathy from his country. In the matter of Miss Dickinson and the railway-carriage incident he had served a term of imprisonment without writing a single letter protesting his innocence. Though he had many influential friends, reaching as high as the Prince of Wales, none of the help they gave him and his family while he was in jail was ever solicited by him. As soon as he was released he did the decent thing and left the country at once, taking his wife and children with him. He took service with a foreign power that was also an ally, with a higher rank than the one he held in the British army; and, in the Russian war that came soon after, he distinguished himself by conducting what was considered one of the finest cavalry actions of the epoch. Since when, he commanded the complete confidence of the sultan of Turkey.

Writing to the Prince of Wales in early December, the Foreign Secretary, Lord Granville, was perfectly frank about the government's response to the proposals. He drafted his letter after coming straight from a meeting with the Prime Minister, and the language was unequivocal. Granville wrote on behalf of Gladstone:

> We never invited Baker Pasha to go to Egypt – we did not commit ourselves to any appointment for him there. We constantly insisted and as often received the promise, that no plans should be discussed without our previous knowledge and sanction, and were surprised to find he had been appointed and had agreed to be Commander-in-Chief of the Army, without our having been informed of the fact.

Granville's political nickname was Puss and there is a story of how the Liberal Lord Goschen once wrote him an infuriated letter, detailing all his complaints and threatening that if he did not receive satisfaction he would be forced to resign. Puss replied in a single elegant sentence :'Thank you for sharing your thoughts so generously with old colleagues.' On this occasion, however, he had been brought up to the mark by Gladstone. He could hardly have expressed himself more bluntly to the prince: there could be no question of confirming Valentine Baker's appointment as sirdar of the Egyptian army.

The khedive made it a condition that the new army should be officered by the British. To this the Cabinet could agree – indeed, it was of the same mind. The sticking point was this: no serving British officer could be expected to take orders from a man who had been dismissed from the army. It was in vain for Val to point out that he had left Turkey for Egypt with the earlier tacit approval of both Granville and Gladstone and that thereafter the matter had been decided as it should be, by soldiers. This argument counted for nothing. England would not have him back at any price.

His hopes had been dashed by the sort of politics for which he – and the whole Victorian officer caste – had no real skill. Val had come overhastily from Constantinople on what turned out to be a highly deniable promise. The crushing of the Arabi revolt in such an emphatic manner with so little loss of life on the British side was, from the government's perspective, the triumph of that parliamentary session. Wolseley, who gave them their victory, was recalled to London at the end of the year to be given a peerage and a grant of £30,000. (Beauchamp Paget Seymour, who had ordered the fleet action against the dunes of Alexandria, accepted £20,000.) Gladstone and Granville heard the news of Tel el Kebir at the Garrick Club and then went on to a performance of *Patience* at the Savoy Theatre. The Prime Minister was greatly surprised to be cheered on entering and leaving the theatre. It was a novel experience and Gladstone reacted swiftly. He gave orders for gun salutes to take place in the parks that Saturday and for thanksgiving services to be held on the following day.

He had been given a bloodless Egyptian triumph to offset the fiasco of Isandhlwana at the other end of the continent. It secured for him not just popularity with the electorate but sudden possession of a whole country, one with a canal that ran through it connecting two seas. The burning question in London was whether or not Egypt should be permanently occupied. There were delicate diplomatic and political questions to be settled, in which context the claims of any individual soldier were a complete irrelevance. The queen had determined seven years ago, against the advice of the army, that she had no further use for Colonel Baker's services and the Prime Minister was not about to contradict her in the matter. He was no friend to the army but he knew enough to realise it was full of generals.

Friends like the Prince of Wales and the Duke of Cambridge pushed for Val's reinstatement. A formula was worked out: he could be restored to the Army List and at once resign, so removing the objection raised by Lord Granville. Wolseley's endorsement of Val's candidature was specially significant. The two men were poles apart temperamentally and the faint element of the courtier that clung to Val's reputation would usually have been given short shrift by Wolseley, who liked to represent himself as ostracised by society. (His virulent and long-running feud with the Duke of Cambridge over army reform had certainly damaged him at court. But in the army itself Wolseley was held to be both lucky and gifted with a wizard's skill – a negative word from him would have crushed Val's case completely.) In the event nothing made the slightest difference. There was only one opinion that really mattered. Nothing could shake the queen's implacable hostility to this officer.

The Prince of Wales continued to press. On 3 December he wrote direct to Gladstone about the way things had fallen out. 'It is not for me to comment on the decision of the Cabinet, but I must confess I think Baker Pasha has been very hardly and unfairly treated. To deprive him now of the important command, which the khedive conferred upon him, is simply to ruin him.'

The queen's third son, the Duke of Connaught, who fought at Tel el Kebir as a brigadier-general, wrote in similar terms to his mother. Both letters failed. Sir Evelyn Wood was appointed to be sirdar of the new Egyptian army that Val had devised. In a colossal blow to his self-esteem Val was offered, as a sop, command of the gendarmerie. It was a humiliation which in the circumstances he could do nothing but accept. He faced up to the near impossibility of creating something worthwhile from the dross he had at his disposal – the old and the blind, criminals released from jail and delivered to barracks in shackles; and a horde of illiterate fellahin conscripts. The story about the fez full of salad was now a bitter metaphor for how he too had been treated.

Evelyn Wood was careful to keep him at arm's length. He was the younger man, famously serving as a midshipman *and* a cornet of Dragoons in the Crimea, when he was only seventeen years old. He was awarded his VC in India when he was twenty-one. His more recent military career was bound up with Africa and he had caused wrath among the British public by following Gladstone's orders and concluding a peace with the Boers after the ignominy of Majuba (1881), where his commander General Colley was killed. It was only a temporary setback to his career. Wood was well connected at court, not least because of his friendship with the Empress Eugenie, who treated him very graciously in the aftermath of her son's death. The Prince Imperial had been under Wood's overall command when he was killed and he later escorted the empress to see the spot where her son had died. He came to Egypt covered in honours and with an unimpeachable social pedigree. The queen liked him.

For a different view of him we have to go to his supposed friend and sponsor Garnet Wolseley. In a campaign diary entry for 1884, not published until 1967, we find this:

> Wood's vanity and selfseeking and belittling of everyone but himself would be positively disgusting if one did not view it from the ridiculous side, and laugh at it & him instead of being angry over it . . . When I look back and remember my estimate of Wood's character as it was presented to me over ten years ago & for many years subsequently, I begin to think I can be no judge of character, for Wood's cunning completely took me in, & I must have more than once done men wrong in valuing them in accordance with Wood's reports to me.

Wolseley added this further pungent sentence: 'Everything with him is a personal matter: he is a good soldier but he has every bad quality that women have.' The remark throws a little extra light on Wolseley's preference for Val Baker, the man's man, a victim of a woman's spite. It may also explain why an endorsement from him was a double-edged weapon whenever Victoria turned her mind to military matters.

At the end of the year Arabi was tried, condemned, and had his sentence of death commuted to permanent exile. Wood paraded the whole of his new army at the railway station to see its fallen leader on his way. This elaborate humiliation smacks of India and the aftermath of the mutiny. By one of those strange quirks of history Arabi was bound for Ceylon. There Thomas Lipton the tea merchant befriended him and scandalised all Colombo by inviting him to a pot of the firm's premier blend on the veranda of the Grand Oriental Hotel. Nothing came free with Lipton, however – he managed to get Arabi to endorse his coffee and chicory essence, saying he had never tasted better. It was Lipton's friendship with the Prince of Wales that helped secure Arabi's freedom in 1903.

In late 1883 Egypt had a new consul-general, fresh from India, the implacable and fearsomely unromantic Evelyn Baring, whose hold on Egypt was to tighten over the years into a bear-like hug – French diplomats actually nicknamed him Le Grand Ours. (The Arabi-sympathiser, Wilfrid Blunt, always the wasp at Baring's picnic, thought he looked like the commoner form of grocer.) Baring maintained the fiction of an independent country while at the same time running it as a British possession, indeed, some said, as his private estate. 'The Egyptians,' he came to write, 'should be permitted to govern themselves after the fashion in which Europeans think they ought to be governed,' and by Europeans he of course meant himself and other Britons worthy of the task. It was a point of view that sat well with the army. The new consul-general had something of the know-all about him, something of the lofty and all-seeing Olympian (he was only forty-two years old), but he pleased men like Wolseley and seems to have struck terror into Granville at home. His appointment, as much as anything else, stabilised the country.

It also greatly enhanced the triumphalist mood. The French (or, in Wolseley's generic name for them, 'Johnny Crapaud') were outraged by the way in which the city had swiftly become Britain's most fashionable overseas posting, for civil servants as well as soldiers. Without directly governing the country, Baring intended to make it a model of imperialism – improving, scrupulously obedient to authority, and suffering the condescensions of the master race with a suitably fawning gratitude.

The Cabinet, meanwhile, had no intention of implicating itself in the fate of the Sudan, which it considered doomed. What Sam Baker (and after him Gordon) had done to suggest that a country called Sudan actually existed was a labour which many cold-hearted people took to be more fiction than fact. Gordon had been last seen in Cairo over the Christmas and New Year period of 1880, at the end of his tour of duty, when his weirdness seemed to almost everyone who met him excessive to the point of dementia. (At a dinner party, hearing Nubar Pasha say something disparaging about another Commander of the Bath, he immediately challenged him to a duel, or, as might have been described in the days of chivalry, mortal combat.)

As Baring drew together the skeins of power, he could be forgiven for supposing the Sudan existed only for so long as Gordon was making one of his interminable rides round it. As he passed across its desert wastes, so anarchy closed up behind him. Baring, who was from the banking family ('One would not have to go back to any remote period,' Gordon noted disgracefully, 'to find that their family mansions were near the Tower or the Minories, and that the head of the family knew the value of pretty worn apparel'), had seen the figures. The upkeep of the Sudan, even after taking into account the fact that the troops engaged there had not been paid for two years, exceeded the revenue by a factor of two to one. Khartoum alone was worth defending, as a bulwark against the Mahdi, but who was to say that there existed anywhere else in the Sudan any realistic model of civil administration? There were certainly soldiers scattered here and there in penny packets, their pay hopelessly in arrears, their nominal rolls eaten into by defection and desertion. As to their *matériel*, anyone who stuck their head round the door of a certain hut in the Suakin barracks could find as many as four different calibre rifle bullets, swept up into a single spider-infested heap. Baring had no great expectations of Sudan.

Gordon's career since leaving the governor-general's post had been chaotic. At first he bustled round London threatening to resign his commission and taking pleasure in watching the whole territory slide into chaos. It had nearly killed him with fever and fatigue and now he thought the Sudanese unworthy of his interest. They had not heeded his word and henceforth God would surely punish them – other people's ingratitude was always a great theme in Gordon's thought. At a dinner given by the Prince of Wales the Duke of Cambridge persuaded him to stay on in the army and, if he was exhausted, take extended leave. A long chapter of excursions began, culminating in a huffy round-the-world trip in 1882. His itinerary included a posting to be the viceroy of India's private secretary, which he resigned after one week in office. Later there was a brief interlude as governor-general of Mauritius, which he found quite as dull as had Sam Baker forty years earlier. He was not a man to take pleasure in lawn tennis and archery, small-talk and commercial gossip. He amused himself by trying to prove that the *coco de mer*, a palm which is only found in the Seychelles, was the forbidden fruit of Paradise, an opinion he tried to share with the consternated Anglican bishop of Mauritius and an equally sceptical T. H. Huxley. In Basutoland he met Cecil Rhodes, who was later to describe him as accurately as anyone in history. He was, said Rhodes, 'a fanatical enigma'.

If anyone was to speak up for the Sudan, it had to be its old governor-general, Sir Samuel Baker, and this he did. It was at his suggestion that his brother Val recommended to the khedive a totally undistinguished Indian army colonel, William Hicks, to go to Khartoum and command the remnants of the Egyptian troops left there. Hicks had the advantage of being a time-expired British officer and thus acceptable to both Cairo and Whitehall. He was dug out from India in the last days of his command and sent off at the age of fifty-three, bewildered and ignorant. One can only assume that money made him do it. The man who met him in Khartoum and gave him his commission was the genial Abd el Kader, formerly commander of Baker's famous 'forty thieves' and now governor-general.

Hicks had his own man scouting for him in Khartoum, Colonel J. D. H. Stewart of the 11th Hussars, whose dispatches could not have been more scathing. There was also a young Irish journalist and war-chaser wandering the city called Frank Le Poer Power. Power had been at Plevna in the Russo-Turkish Wars and was a monocled and sardonic observer of war and the profession of arms. He later characterised the Khartoum garrison in these terms:

> We have here 9000 infantry that fifty good men would rout in ten minutes, and a 1000 cavalry (Bashi-Bazouks) that have never learned even to ride, and these, with a few Nordonfelt guns, are to beat the 69,000 men whom the Mahdi has got together ... That Egyptian officers and men are not worth the ammunition they throw away, is well known.

These judgements are important because they help illuminate what Val Baker was up against with the formation of his gendarmerie. Like the army the unlucky Hicks inherited, many of the Baker force were conscripted Arabi sympathisers. Baker at least had the advantage of training his men under reasonable conditions and with an eye to the future – he could start from the parade ground up. In Khartoum, Stewart and Power – and soon enough Hicks – saw how impossible it was to change these hapless and disaffected Arab peasants, unpaid and far from home, into anything resembling European soldiers. They had all been dragged from the fields in their native Egypt and sent by their local sheikh to make up the army quota. They were villagers in uniform. The black Sudanese soldiers who shared their barracks despised them. They hated themselves and their officers treated them as hardly human. The moment Hicks Pasha set eyes on his command, he telegraphed Cairo for help. Though he was an honest man and not a complete fool, he was hopelessly out of his depth. Gordon's legacy to the country included 20,000 of such troops garrisoned in places that few in Cairo could find on a map.

The arising of a Mahdi and the declaration of holy war against the infidel, not just in Sudan but from one end of the earth to the other, was never envisaged in the glorious days of Ismailia, when by knocking heads together and flourishing a sporting gun under some tree or at the door to a palaver hut the 'fate' of vast tracts of otherwise unexplored territory had been decided. Readers of Sam Baker's *Ismailia* had been seduced by the raciness of its style into believing it to be not just a description of recognisably Victorian endeavours – a struggle for hearts and minds among wayward but biddable savages – but the foundation of something approximating a European nation state. It was this the anti-slavery movement in particular wanted to hear. Those who read their Baker in, say, Kent or Surrey, wanted to think of the Nile as a mighty but occasionally tiresome version of the Thames and the 'chiefs' or 'kings' in their 'villages' or 'cities' as comparable to stupid and recalcitrant aldermen whose knuckles needed a sharp rap. For Baker, with his easy mastery of a conversational prose style, the

The Mahdi (left) as seen by readers of the *Illustrated London News*.
He fares better than 'the worst slaver of them all' Zebehr (right).

task had apparently been that simple. He had imposed the Christian virtues, even when it involved a brisk clout or two, and so established the law.

Radical evangelicals were hot on God's purpose working its way out but weak on geography. Moreover, they made the perennial mistake of reformers by supposing that everyone in the world could be brought to the same understanding. The Anti-Slavery Society was quite sure about this. At only a little time in the future Gordon was to astound Baring by suggesting that he ride alone and unarmed into the Mahdi's camp and have it out with him, man to man. It was the old way, it had been Baker's way, and it held huge attractions for a significant section of the British public. Who were these people but vile slavers, never blessed by Christian understanding? Joviality and a barrel chest had done for them in Baker's day and a Bible under the arm and the famous Wand of Victory would do the same work for Gordon.

Hicks, whatever he thought about the Mahdi in the abstract, was very much nearer to the practicalities. In June 1883 he telegraphed

Malet at the Foreign Office that he had not enough troops to mount an offensive campaign and that if he tried it and anything went wrong, he could lose not just the provinces but also Khartoum. He ended with a Delphic touch worthy of Lord Granville himself: 'I think no risk should be run.' Did he really mean do nothing – was that the sentiment of a British officer faced with a declared foe to all things Christian and decent? After reflection, he sent another slightly more cheerful telegraph to his sponsor, Val Baker.

> In my telegram of 3rd of June to Malet, I pointed out what I thought was necessary to ensure success in Kordofan and guard against all possible eventualities. At the same time I am pre-pared to undertake the campaign with the force available; the risks are, as I said, in case of a mishap, but I think this not at all probable. Khartoum ought to be safe from outside under any circumstances.

This cable also offered problems of interpretation. Did Hicks mean that Khartoum should be protected as a first priority – was that 'ought' in the last sentence a normative? – or had he weighed the risks and concluded that even in case of a 'mishap' it was likely that Khartoum would survive? Nobody in Cairo could be sure and it is probable that Hicks himself had no idea. It was all very well for Thomas Lipton to be hobnobbing with Colonel Arabi over the teacups in Colombo. What Hicks had here was the poisoned chalice.

The expedition he was being asked to mount was to punish two quite disastrous setbacks at a place called El Obeid. Two hundred miles to the south-west of Khartoum, El Obeid was the capital of Kordofan. In 1882, during the days when Val Baker was drawing up his plans in Shepheard's, the Mahdi arrived before the gates of El Obeid and sent in his envoys calling on the military governor to surrender. Colonel Mohamed Sayed of the marooned Egyptian army had a garrison of 6000 men and a quantity of reasonably modern weapons. He felt lucky. He hanged the envoys from the walls of the town and scattered the Mahdi's letter in tiny scraps on to the sand below. After an initial attack failed, the Mahdi and his army sat down to starve the garrison out – a foreshadowing of the tactic they were to employ in Khartoum two years later. On 17 January 1883 El Obeid fell to an overwhelming night assault. There was a general massacre and Mohamed Sayed was singled out for torture and hideous mutilation. A relief column of 3000 men sent out from Khartoum to avenge him was likewise butchered.

We know something about the demonising of Islamic fundamentalism in our own age. Some of the shock and revulsion felt in Europe then was at what was seen as the inhuman cruelty of the Mahdi, his bewildering contempt for human life. Sam Baker's opinion, that he could never move far from his original powerbase and that the other tribes would not follow him, was clearly mistaken. Nor was this a case of pitting one tribe against another – the days of buying loyalty with an English decoration, some French furniture or a crate of guns – those days were over. What marked out the jihad and made it so inexplicable to the west was its ruthless simplicity. This was not a cunning and devious man working a political agendum that involved killing but following all the same a path that might lead perhaps to compromise. This was, for those who came up against him, a remorseless slaughterer: death to the last man, woman and child who stood in his way. The Mahdi, though held personally to be a coward, commanded an awesome killing machine. When he started out, it was with spears and shields and a few ancient old muskets. Now his camps were filled with fanatics armed with modern rifles and millions of rounds of ammunition. Their cold-bloodedness was a byword.

Hicks set out from Khartoum for El Obeid at the end of September. Led by apparently friendly guides, 10,000 men and 6000 camels blundered their way through days and weeks of acacia thickets, always short of water, constantly harassed by sniping and hit-and-run cavalry raids. The army marched as well as it could in the hollow square formation, which was really all that Hicks knew of tactics. The principle was simple enough: so long as the square held together, with its softest elements and staff in the centre, it could direct enfilading fire from its corners and so beat off an attack from any flank. But as had been shown at Waterloo, that required discipline and very cool nerves. On 5 November, maddened by thirst, dispirited by a hundred niggling casualties, Hicks was finally brought to a halt in country that could not have been more inimical to his formation. There was a sudden and calamitous all-out attack and the Egyptian troops allowed the three squares they had formed to collapse. Hicks and his officers watched in horror as the soldiers simply threw down their weapons and fell to their knees, submitting to death like sheep. He and his staff were among the few to resist. It was all over within the hour. The Hicks expedition and its leader were annihilated and their bodies were stripped and left to rot into the sand. Hicks himself was decapitated and his head sent in a sack to the Mahdi.

Almost at once the governor of Darfur, the German mercenary Rudolph Slatin, surrendered. Over on the coast a lieutenant of the Mahdi, the slave-trader Osman Digna, took his cue and raised the fearsome Hadendowa tribe to rebellion. On the very same day as El Obeid a much smaller Egyptian army was likewise annihilated outside the Red Sea port of Suakin, leaving no man standing. For some reason the British consul, a Captain Moncrieffe, RN, had elected to ride with the troops and he, like all the others, was hacked to death.

Baring now contemplated what was in effect a rising by the whole country. The easterly route from Berber to Suakin on the coast was threatened and the only way in and out was by the Nile. Khartoum stood, but it was surely only a matter of time before it too was attacked. Somewhere in the city was a greasy telegraph key. The journalist Frank Power had set out with Hicks for El Obeid but was (luckily for him) brought down by dysentery before the battle and sent back. He and an officer called Coetlogon were the only two British left in Khartoum. Power began sending vivid dispatches to *The Times,* the first announcing the defeat of Hicks. Nothing could have been more newsworthy – at the very moment the government was arranging for the withdrawal of British troops from Egypt, the bones of British officers in the Sudan were being picked over by vultures. *The Times* had a scoop on its hands.

The paper's high-profile Cairo correspondent, Moberly Bell, had already arranged with a member of Hicks's staff that he should send back suitably edifying reports of the routing of the Mahdi. Colonel Farquhar had died with Hicks in the last desperate charge. Bell, an old Cairo hand, with business interests in the city stretching back to 1865, saw at once what the destruction of Hicks meant and cabled London:

> The first responsibility, therefore, rests solely on the Egyptian Government, but, unfortunately, the results cannot end there. However emphatically the British Cabinet may repudiate its responsibility; however justly it may urge that no English [that is, serving] officers were employed in the expedition, it is hardly possible to suppose that such reasoning will influence the will of the Egyptian fellaheen, who are not habitual students of Hansard or the Army List. To them the Soudan is a province depending on the Government of Egypt, which is itself dependent on the English.

Bell also saw, and impressed upon Wood and Baring, that the Mahdi was not some nationalist upstart like Arabi but 'a pretender to the universal allegiance of Islam'. The Dutch explorer and political journalist Juan Maria Schuver had been killed by Dinka warriors in September 1883. In one of his last letters home he wrote: 'The war cry of the negroes is: Better all men die than live on as beasts of burden [Lieber alle Männer sterben als wie Lastesel fortleben].' That was the nub of it – all men, everybody. Such a virus would surely come to overwhelm Khartoum and was not likely to stop at the borders with Egypt, as Moberly Bell realised. The Mahdi was no flash in the pan – 'His military successes are producing a growing belief here in those pretensions, not confined to the least educated classes.'

Meanwhile Coetlogon cabled Wood from Khartoum with some idea of the urgency of the situation.

> Khartoum and Sennar cannot be held. In two months time there will be no food. All supplies are cut off ... The troops that are left are the refuse of the army, mostly old and blind. Again I say, the only way of saving what remains is to attempt a general retreat on Berber. This is the real state of affairs here, and I beg of you to impress it on His Highness the Khedive.

Cairo and London were completely at sixes and sevens over the issue. Gladstone had already announced in a speech at the Guildhall the withdrawal from Egypt of the British forces under General Stephenson. This he was now obliged to countermand. *The Times* showed no mercy. In its leader for 23 November it thundered:

> The policy, in which the evacuation of Cairo, recently announced but happily not yet accomplished ... has been adopted in defiance of the advice of every person of authority and experience in Egyptian affairs from Lord Dufferin downwards. It is time to put an end to this perverse pursuit of a doctrinaire's will-o'-the-wisp. The responsibilities of our position in Egypt are now fully understood by the country, and Ministers cannot afford to make any mistake about them.

Unable to budge the government on the sending of British troops to Khartoum and unwilling to commit the fledgling Egyptian army to the possibility of massacre, Wood permitted or encouraged what looks in hindsight like a crack-brained scheme. Valentine Baker and the gendarmerie were to go to Suakin and do what they could to secure the port and open the road to Berber. It was an alarming invitation that had its roots in purely local events. That summer there had been cholera in Cairo. The new gendarmerie had conducted itself extremely well and won the gratitude of all Cairenes. Wood's men stayed in their barracks while Baker Pasha's mounted patrols enforced the quarantine and maintained order. It was a striking example of what the fellahin could do when properly officered. Even so, it seems extraordinary that anyone should have contemplated sending the police, however semi-military its training and however distinguished its commander, to fight a campaign hundreds of miles from base in a country about which there was no up-to-date intelligence. It was also overlooked that the gendarmerie was specifically prohibited from leaving the national boundaries under its constitution and the terms of its employment, something the politicians might have forgotten but which every fellah pressed into service remembered only too well.

The khedive and his prime minister were in a quandary. The firman from the sultan of Turkey giving the Egyptian khedive his powers expressly commanded that he also defend the Sudan. Sending Baker to Suakin with the gendarmerie was not a stiffening of the defence but the obvious preamble to evacuation. Though Baring was the most imperturbable of men, he could not disguise from the khedive that the British Cabinet did not really know what to do. On the other hand, he himself had immediately grasped the essential logistics. To evacuate even Khartoum and its civilian population would require not hundreds but thousands of camels and months of planning. The shortest way out, if Berber remained friendly, was 250 miles east to Suakin. For such a huge caravan it was also the only way out. Over and over again it came down to this: the key was the road from Berber to Suakin. Who was to go and find out whether even that was any longer an option?

It went without saying that Val Baker jumped at the chance. It was an honourable way of undoing all the harm that had befallen him. His brother Sam wrote from England at the end of November, counselling prudence. 'Let nothing persuade you to attempt the passage of the Suakin desert with such troops,' he advised, 'otherwise you will share the fate of Hicks.' The letter contained a suggestion couched in the language of yesterday's men. 'Money and decorations will do more than fighting: but the force must be at hand. You can never catch Arabs in the desert; but they will flock towards dollars as sparrows fly to corn,' he advised, adding, in a curiously guileless and naive postscript, 'I have a great mind to come over to Berber to effect it: at this season the climate is charming.'

The remark struck exactly the wrong note. Back from his round-the-world voyage, Sam wrote these words in the study at Sandford Orleigh, surrounded by the mementoes of an exploring age that had passed into history – that of the gentleman amateur with a taste for faraway places, armed only with his sporting guns and materials for sketching, his bearers loyally following after with his supplies of brandy and potted meats, his books and the chair in which he was to take his ease when the day's march was done. In the house there were packing cases, as yet unopened, of items from his most recent jaunt – Japanese armour, buffalo rugs from

America, spears and arrows, curious swords and, of course, the trophy heads of animals. The indigenous people he had met on his cruise he treated in exactly the same way as he did the tribes he had met in Africa. They were children in some kind of nursery room, to be rewarded with little gifts of handkerchiefs or mirrors, coils of wire and Venetian glass beads from their kindly and mysterious uncle.

After a formal parade of his gendarmes at the Abdin Palace, in the presence of the khedive, Wood, Baring and all the foreign consuls, Baker's expedition entrained for Suez. The leave-taking was indescribably confused, with hysterical scenes when the rank and file said goodbye to their families. They knew far better than Sam Baker what they were letting themselves in for. According to one account, they had to be forced into their railway carriages by three squadrons of their own cavalry. By the time the train reached the port facilities at Suez, 280 of them, a quarter of the force, had deserted.

It had occurred to one person that a possible solution to the Sudan problem was to employ both Bakers, Sam to be governor-general and Val to command an army for him. The author of this mischievous idea was Gordon. It is even possible that, left to himself, Sam would have given it consideration. The stumbling block was Florence. She had made it plain she would never again go back – Cairo was possible, to give support to Fanny Baker and her children, but any further south was out of the question. Sam may have been secretly quite relieved. Life at Sandford Orleigh was to both their tastes, a luxurious and indolent existence in a house set in handsome grounds, the rooms crammed with furniture and books, Amarn gliding smilingly to answer their every wish. Florence had found her true heart's desire. There was a family story of the Prince of Wales calling on her when Sam was away. She was supervising the servants in the linen cupboards and sent word that he was to wait until she had finished. The royal visitor knew the Bakers well enough not to take offence. They were, both of them, charming innocents. Sam was known to the prince as a great patriot, an assiduous minor courtier and a dedicated clubman. What he was not any longer was a reliable witness.

Gordon himself was finishing up his year's wanderings with a visit to Jerusalem, where he supervised the making of models to demonstrate his own contentious theories about the site of the Sepulchre and Golgotha. When it was done, he took passage in an open boat to make his way to Acre, ran into a storm and came ashore at Haifa. Drenched to the skin yet straight backed as ever, he walked through the Arab town to visit a colony of German Jews who had built an ultra-neat village in the shadow of Mount Carmel. Gordon marched confidently through the garden to one of these houses and rapped on the door. It was opened by Laurence Oliphant.

The two men – who had only met twice, once at Sebastopol and again briefly in China – spent a few fevered days debating not world affairs, but religion. Much had happened to Oliphant since the days when he was the Prince of Wales's confidant. For a short while he was a member of Parliament, but in 1867 he was taken by the teachings of Thomas Lake Harris, an American self-styled prophet he had met in London as early as 1860. Harris completely subverted the courtier and man of the world in Oliphant. He resigned his parliamentary seat and went out to Brocton, Massachusetts, to place himself – and most of his property – utterly at the disposal of Harris's utopian community, the Brotherhood of the New Life. To purge him of his worldliness, he was given only the most menial tasks to perform, such as selling vegetables in the street. In 1872 he married and his wife Alice joined the sect. When Harris moved to Santa Rosa he took Alice Oliphant and Laurence's mother with him. Oliphant himself was sent away to earn money for the commune and for a time despaired of ever getting his wife back again. His mother died a pauper in California, not before seeing her late husband's watch in Harris's fob pocket. Once the scales had fallen from his eyes, Oliphant engaged in an exhausting struggle to recover his wife.

Gordon absorbed this tale without comment. As he could see, Alice *was* back and Oliphant, though he had grown dangerously cranky, had not lost his talent to intrigue. The reason that Gordon knew where to find him was that for three years the failed Brother of the New Life had found a better cause. Oliphant was not in a Jewish colony in Haifa by accident, for it was his work now to divert some of those Jews fleeing from persecution in Russia and its dependencies away from the boats to America and back into their ancestral homelands in Palestine. Incredibly, Oliphant was trying to set up, with British money, a proto-Israel. There was some urgency about the matter, for though he was convinced a Jewish homeland was a necessary historical outcome to their wanderings, he was also just as certain that the Day of Judgement was at hand.

Again, Gordon was unfazed, munching on dates and watching the afternoon shadow of Mount Carmel fall across Oliphant's face. For they were after all in the very place where, 2000 years earlier, the prophet Elijah had challenged the priests of Baal, as recorded in the Book of Kings. The Jews believed that Elijah would one day return, as the forerunner of God's vengeance on the wicked: Oliphant evidently believed the same. Gordon was hardly less devout than that, and while he could see that Laurence Oliphant was what we should today call disturbed – at one point in their discussions he jumped up and embraced his unexpected visitor with a sudden and embarrassing male passion – he was also utterly serious. With Gordon, that counted for everything.

As for Oliphant, he saw a man sitting in his garden who was almost at the end of his tether. He was astonished to learn that Gordon was about to resign his commission and take service with King Leopold of the Belgians, for where was the honour in that? What part of the coming Armageddon was to be played out there? Gordon was unmoved. It was in his nature to do the contrary thing. In the end it came down to this over the figs and wine, the chain-smoked cigarettes: Gordon was going to the Congo to spite the Sudan. And from that nothing would budge him. He would not even go to London to announce his decision. When he left Oliphant his destination was Brussels. The British army had declined to release him for service with King Leopold: he would go in any case. The brutal commercial company that Leopold was setting up in the Congo under the guise of bringing it civilisation would be his Calvary. He explained in his offhand way, a manner so painful to all those who had ever tried to befriend him: he was much more likely to meet a sudden death there than in the Sudan. After six days he marched away to catch the steamer at Acre, watched by a distraught Oliphant. As always with Gordon, once a farewell had been given there was no looking back. His figure disappeared into the dust and noise of the Arab quarter – and of course Oliphant never saw him again.

Val Baker arrived in Suakin with his expedition two days before Christmas 1883. There had been a terrible last-minute scene in Cairo when an unhappy officer had called on him to give the awful news that the Turkish contingent the sultan had provided would not go, standing on the terms of their engagement. It was a bitter blow. Val went down to the barracks and talked to the men. When every other exhortation failed, he said simply, 'I myself must go. Shall I go alone?' There was an uneasy silence before he was forced to add, 'I'll give you five minutes to think it over. The brave men will fall in on the right, the cowards on the left.' Understandably enough, about half the contingent fell in on the right – but none of them took the steamers south. There had been a second dramatic incident on the very night of his departure. A small family dinner had been interrupted by the arrival of Zobeir Pasha, one of the greatest of the Sudanese slave-traders. The histrionic Zobeir accompanied the Baker family to the train station, where he astonished Val by promising to join him in Suakin and 'watch over his safety'. That too was a pledge that had been broken. The press, however, had come – *The Times*, the *Standard*, *Daily News* and *Illustrated London News* all sent correspondents and sketch artists. There was an unshakeable sense of a disaster about to happen. The focus of interest was on Val himself.

His only friend at Suakin was the navy. Rear-Admiral Hewett commanded a Red Sea squadron that had helped secure the Suez Canal in 1882. Hewett joined the service when he was thirteen and won his VC with the Naval Brigade in the Crimea. Though he was not yet fifty, he was of delicate health, which he offset by resolution and a flair for improvisation. In the campaign to secure the canal he had his men build an armoured train, which steamed under naval orders and shelled wherever it could find targets. He was a much-needed reinforcement to the expedition. The gunship *Ranger* was practically the only serious means of defending the Suakin perimeter.

There were three further beleaguered garrisons at little ports down the coast and in the hinterland nothing but trouble. The Madhiyya controlled everything – wells, roads, the telegraph lines to Khartoum – and the Egyptians were hanging on to the littoral by their fingertips. Hewett was encouraging, but without communication with Cairo Val might as well have been a ship at sea. He had found the armoury building in the Suakin barracks and inspected its ludicrous stock of ammunition. The garrison bore muskets as old as Val himself, red with rust and half-filled with sand.

ELEVEN

⇒◦⇐

Sir Charles Rivers Wilson wrote to Lord Salisbury in 1880 concerning Gordon:

> I should never recommend your Lordship to send Gordon on a delicate diplomatic mission to Paris or Vienna or Berlin, but if you want some out of the way piece of work done in an unknown or barbarous country, Gordon would be your man. If you told him to capture Cetewayo, for instance, he would go to Africa, mount on a pony with a stick in his hand and ask the way to Cetewayo's Kraal, and when he got there, he would sit down and have a talk with him.

As it happened, Gordon met Cetewayo in Cape Town in 1882, after the great Zulu chief had been captured. He told him how, since Isandhlwana, he had prayed daily for his soul and then presented Cetewayo with an ivory-headed cane, man to man, soldier to soldier, exactly the sort of thing Rivers Wilson had in mind. He was voicing a general perception of Gordon and his strange powers. There could have been no one in Christendom less like Chinese Gordon than his commander-in-chief, the peppery and violently conservative Duke of Cambridge, but he too seemed mesmerised by those blazing blue eyes. The duke could hardly bring himself to be civil to Wolseley, his adjutant-general, but about Gordon he was adamant – the man had something. He repeatedly made it clear that the army did not wish to lose him. Almost everyone in England from the queen downwards believed he was a man who should be used in some way for the glory of Britain. For radicals inside and out of Parliament, the Mahdi, whom no European politician had seen, let alone interviewed, was a nationalist in the same way Arabi was. Very well – let Gordon go to see him, give him what he wanted, and allow Britain to disengage with honour.

The king of the Belgians took a more cynical view of Gordon's usefulness. The Congo land-grab that was now in full swing was being soldiered by the man who had found Livingstone, Henry Morton Stanley. What was needed was a respected figurehead, a man of quality – in the end a gentleman – which Stanley certainly was not. Gordon's flightiness, his bouts of mystical elevation, irritated the bourgeois in Leopold. Nevertheless, the Belgian king's African adventure was carefully designed to be wrapped in a cloak of philanthropy and presented to the world as a bid to bring peace and the blessings of trade to the moral dark that would otherwise persist in that region. Properly handled, there was no better man to foster this illusion than Gordon. Leopold correctly identified the streak of vanity that ran through him. Before Gordon arrived the king minuted Strauch, who was a staff officer of the Belgian Ministry of War and former chair of the so-called Comité d'Études:

> If Gordon says to you 'In England I shall be a general in three years' tell him 'With us you can be a Field-Marshal in the new State.' You know as well as I do that when such eccentrics are stiff-necked, one should run over the arguments again briefly and forcefully and then leave them to think it over.

In the end Leopold bagged his man all to easily. Gordon arrived in Brussels on New Year's Day 1884, just at the time that Val Baker was exploring Suakin with such a sinking heart. He met the king the following morning and, with his usual briskness, agreed to go to the Congo if Belgium would guarantee his pension from the British army. Leopold murmured his acceptance of these terms. Gordon asked no further questions, entered into no philosophic or philanthropic discussions and set out for London five days later to resign his commission. As a memento of the interview, he gave his new employer a model of the Rock of Jerusalem.

As ever with Gordon, things were not quite as straightforward as they seemed. The morning after his return, and while his letter of resignation from the army was on the way to Mount Pleasant to be sorted, he answered the door of his sister's house to W. T. Stead of the *Pall Mall Gazette*. Stead had heard rumours that Gordon was about to quit the army and saw it as his duty to fill in the recent political and diplomatic background as it affected Cairo and Khartoum. He specially wanted to make clear that Gladstone intended to abandon the Sudan altogether. Baker Pasha was in Suakin not to mount any offensive operation but simply to see whether it would be necessary to leave the unfortunate Sudan garrisons to their fate.

Stead, who was as evangelically devout as his interviewee, was then treated to a thrilling two-hour monologue stuffed with facts and figures, a dazzling *tour d'horizon* that few other men in England could have attempted. It included the suggestion that Sir Samuel Baker be sent out immediately to set things right. But Stead was a journalist before all else. He had come to the house for a scoop. He pressed Gordon – wasn't he already sitting knee to knee with the only possible saviour of the situation? Gordon seemed to brush that aside, but Stead, perched on a couch covered with leopard-skin from the Sudan, watched his interviewee attentively and knew he had his man. Before he left, Gordon pressed into his hands a copy of *The Imitation of Christ*.

The next day the *Pall Mall Gazette* published a front-page leading article headed CHINESE GORDON FOR KHARTOUM. It was a wish, almost a supplication, yet it rang bells all over London. On 9 January *The Times* reprinted much of the text and Gordon-mania began to sweep in like a monstrous tide, threatening to engulf the government. The queen wanted him, the country wanted him and it was only a matter of time before Gladstone would be forced to want him too. The only person who did not wish to be saved by Chinese Gordon was Baring in Cairo. Meanwhile, having stirred up the entire political establishment, Gordon fled. He went first by train to Exeter, and thence on to Newton Abbot, accompanied by a friend, the Reverend Barnes. Waiting for them on the platform was Sam Baker.

The three men set out for Sandford Orleigh in Sam's carriage. Mr Barnes was now treated to a classic vignette of Victorian history – the burly and bearded explorer with his loud manners and trademark jolliness, arguing the toss with the much more contained, slimmer and fitter Gordon. Both men had been governors-general of the Sudan: each urged the post on the other now. It may have struck Barnes that so wide was the difference between the two men, one of them must be deceived as to the suitability of the other: flesh was debating with spirit. Sam's candidacy was compromised by something of which Gordon did not yet know – Florence Baker's root-and-branch objection to the whole idea. At the same time, when Gordon himself was urged so forcefully to go, he may not have realised that his friend Baker had a score to settle with Baring and the Cairo crowd. Khartoum, Berber, Suakin – these were mere names to the bemused Reverend Barnes. They were any of three possible resting places for the bones of Val Baker.

Barnes saw Sandford Orleigh that winter night at its most imposing, handsomely lit and warmed by massive wood fires. It was more like a miniature palace than a domestic house. There was the library of travel and scientific books, the polished floors covered with the skins of tiger and bears: in pride of place a framed and glazed photograph of Gondokoro. The conversation begun in the coach continued over dinner, under the glass eyes of various trophy heads and whole walls of spears and swords. Family obligations to Val or not, Florence spelled it out to the bachelor Gordon. She did not wish her husband to go. Her brother-in-law's Nile houseboat overlooked one of the khedival palaces and had ten bedrooms. They might certainly go as far as there, by way of a holiday, but anything else was out of the question. The great adventures were over.

Gordon's defence against the Bakers' repeated assertions that *he* should go was simple. He had given his word to King Leopold and there was an end of it. After Barnes had gone to bed and the house was quiet there was a faint knock at the door. It was Gordon. 'You saw me today?' he whispered. 'You mean in the carriage?' Barnes asked. 'Yes!' Gordon said. 'You saw *me*, that was *myself*: the self I want to get rid of!' Barnes was not in the least confused by the remark. His good friend wished to abandon all earthly ambitions – in such a house, so richly appointed, it was an opportunity for prayerful congratulation. But he may have missed the subtext of this secret meeting, while Sir Samuel and Lady Florence lay sleeping at the other end of the corridor. Gordon had chosen. He left Sandford Orleigh after breakfast the next morning. Waiting for him in London was a three-day-old telegram asking him to present himself at the War Office.

It happened that Gladstone was out of town and the decision to send for Gordon was made by Lord Granville (Foreign Office), Lord Hartington (War Office) and Garnet Wolseley. Gordon reported himself at two in the afternoon and then waited placidly while a ministerial meeting took place behind closed doors. It lasted three hours. Finally Wolseley came out to explain the upshot. The War Office would not object to him serving in the Congo and thus he need not resign his commission; nor, as a consequence, injure his pension rights. However, there were tasks to be done for his own country that might take precedence over immediate service to a foreign king. The ministers wished to appeal to his patriotism as well as his sense of Christian duty. Would he be prepared 'to go to Suakin and enquire into the condition of affairs in the Sudan'?

The question was, of course, very badly framed. The Foreign Office already knew the condition of Khartoum from the urgent dispatches sent down by Coetlogon and Colonel Stewart. Elsewhere, El Obeid was destroyed, Darfur had surrendered, only the navy was keeping Suakin from being captured; and on the same coast, Sinkat and Tokat were under siege. It was true they had lost touch with Valentine Baker for want of a telegraph but they had all the same sent him to do much the same job as they now asked of Gordon. The difference was that Baker had a small army under his command. Gordon listened, he made notes, he wrote out an eight-point plan of action which began: 'To proceed to Suakin and report on military situation and return.' Under another head he proposed paying himself a per diem of £3.10.0. All present thought this excellent stuff.

Gordon further agreed to break his agreement with King Leopold, which he insisted on doing in person. After only a few hours' sleep he caught the boat train to Dover at six the next morning. He went to Brussels, had a brief and furious confrontation with the king and returned to London the same night. During his absence – and, as it was to prove, with fatal consequences – the terms of his commission had been dramatically altered. There was another meeting set for three o'clock. Gordon explained what happened in a letter to Mr Barnes.

> W. came for me and took me to the Ministers. He went in and talked to the Ministers and came back and said 'HMG want you to understand this government are determined to evacuate the Sudan. Will you go and do it?' I said yes. I went in and saw them. They said 'Did Wolseley tell you our idea?' I said 'Yes: he said you will not guarantee future government of Sudan and you wish me to go and evacuate it.' They said 'Yes' and it was over . . .

It was indeed. Death, with which Gordon had flirted all his life, was now about to take a hand. Standing in the breach at Quinsan, the gun had failed to go off. This time, it would. The ministers asked him when he would leave: he said by the evening train. When they turned up at Charing Cross, with the additional presence of the Duke of Cambridge, Gordon was entirely without luggage, save for a small satchel. Lord Granville purchased his ticket. At the last moment Gordon's nephew dashed on to the platform with a tin case containing a dress uniform. The Duke of Cambridge played the part of a footman by opening the carriage door. Only Wolseley had the presence of mind to ask the Saviour of the Sudan if he had any money. He didn't. Wolseley emptied his pocket book hastily and handed over his gold watch. The guard blew his whistle, the commander-in-chief of the British army slammed the door and the train steamed out.

Val's brief from the Cairo government was more precise and a great deal less ambitious. He was to study the situation and report, only resorting to force if it was absolutely necessary. He spent the

first few weeks of 1884 in cautious meetings with those he considered friendly sheikhs, trying to gauge just how tight a grip the
Mahdi's lieutenant, Osman Digna, had on the hinterland. The news
that the Gladstone government had finally come to the decision to
evacuate was a terrible shock, for whatever comfort that might have
been given to the expedition locally disappeared overnight. From
now on, any Arab on a camel could be considered hostile. As one
of the sheikhs explained: 'We must serve one master. If it is not
to be your government, it must be the Mahdi. Otherwise what will
happen to us? Our flocks and herds will be taken away, our wives
and children sold into slavery, and we shall have our throats cut.'
It was an unanswerable point of view.

The only good news was the arrival of Fred Burnaby, who
strolled into Val's HQ one day in civilian dress, an umbrella tucked
under his arm. His mission was entirely personal – the huge Life
Guard was using his leave to join the fight. In his own mind, the
Mahdi should be allowed to have the damn country if he wanted
it so badly. If, however, he was going to get shirty about it, then
Burnaby would like to be on hand to help administer the reproof.

Val decided to move his entire force fifty miles south to the
little port of Trinkitat. At Tokar, a few miles inland, there was a
besieged Turkish garrison that must somehow be extricated.
Smuggled reports to the coast told how the troops had been
reduced to eating dogs and were far too weak (and disinclined)
to make a sally against the tribesmen who surrounded them. For
the Mahdiyya, the prize was the Tokar guns which, once captured,
could be turned against any or all of the ports along that stretch
of the coast.

As a jumping-off point Trinkitat was unpromising. There was
no harbour to speak of and the bulk of the army had to be landed
by raft. Immediately behind the shoreline were salt marshes, in
places chest deep. After some energetic reconnoitring by Burnaby
a way through was found and Baker ordered earthworks to be
thrown up on the land side to make a defensive fort. He gradually
pulled his entire force through and set out on the road to Tokar
at seven in the morning of 3 February 1884. The terrain was in

his favour now – open, with only a few scattered trees and offering good ground for marching. They advanced in three squares with a cavalry screen of the mounted gendarmes. The first objective was some wells at a place called El Teb.

Almost at once they met Mahdist skirmishers. Burnaby wrote a lively and sardonic account of what followed. When a troop of cavalry was ordered to attack a few Arabs on dromedaries, not just the troop but the entire regiment charged. It seemed like good odds. But then, to the European officers' amazement, the rebels – there were only three of them – turned and charged in their turn. The result was spectacular.

> Our cavalry, instead of opposing their foes, broke off into a gallop, in spite of all Major Harvey could do. One of their Arab opponents rode deliberately into a squadron and I saw him cut down the officer in command, who made no attempt to defend himself, though his sword was drawn. The Arab cut down two more men, who equally did not protect themselves and would doubtless have demolished the whole of the Egyptian cavalry if a pistol bullet had not stopped his work of destruction.

The bullet came from Burnaby, wearing a Norfolk jacket and twill trousers and still sporting his umbrella. He and Harvey tried to rally the men but a moment or so later a massive crackling broke out as the troopers were put under panic fire from their own men. They began to fall from their saddles. Despite Burnaby's urgings they kicked up their horses and headed back to the fort, screaming in terror. Burnaby rode slowly back to the infantry squares, through bullets flying in every direction. To his horror, he found they had already broken. 'The sight was one never to be forgotten, some four thousand men running for their lives with a few hundred Arabs behind them spearing everyone within reach.'

Many of the troops tore off their uniforms as they ran. Some sank to their knees and waited fatalistically for the spear thrust between the shoulder blades. Wherever Europeans could be found – for example, around Val Baker and those protecting the field guns – there was organised resistance, but the truth was that an entire army had bolted. Burnaby's soldier-servant was a man called Storey.

He was on a horse without a saddle or a bridle and had only a collar chain with which to guide the animal. He was surrounded by Arabs and camels. Fortunately his horse was a kicker, and becoming alarmed, kicked the camels on one side and burst through the Arabs, my unfortunate domestic hanging onto his neck. A few hundred yards from the square the horse jumped a bush, when my man was precipitated from its back.

Storey clung on to the collar chain and was dragged away through the carnage by his heels. Burnaby caught up with him three miles away at the far end of a trail of naked and bleeding bodies over which the vultures were already beginning to circle. Val Baker was the last man back through the salt marshes, and when he came on to the beach he was treated to the sight of Egyptian sailors firing blindly on Egyptian gendarmes, the whole force reduced to a rabble. When a roll-call was taken, 112 officers and 2250 men had been killed. Almost all the expedition's equipment had been abandoned and was being picked over by the jubilant Mahdiyya. Only the marshes had stopped the attackers from chasing the Egyptians down to the water's edge and slaughtering every last man.

No one in the long history of the British army had ever seen or experienced such a complete rout: in purely European terms it was unbelievably shocking that a complete army, the equivalent to six or seven European battalions, could disintegrate before an order had been given.

Gordon had originally intended to go direct to Suakin via the canal. He was persuaded by an urgent telegram waiting for him at Port Said to visit Baring in Cairo first. To make sure he complied, the consul-general sent Sir Evelyn Wood to meet him on the quay like a baggage porter. After Gordon's death all the principal players in the tragedy were at pains to exculpate themselves but one has some slight sympathy for Baring, who could see that what Gordon was being asked to do was virtually impossible. This was a point of view the new arrival could not and would not accept. When he got to Cairo, Gordon was at his most objectionable, having arrived with sheaves of instructions he had written out on the steamer from Marseilles. Before he left, in a gesture not calculated to calm Baring's nerves, he tore the coat from his back in the consul-general's office and requested that it be given to the poor.

And then he was gone. His old Crimean colleague and fellow Engineer General Gerald Graham accompanied him by Nile steamer as far as Korosko, below the second cataract. So powerful was the mystique surrounding Gordon, they spoke only infrequently of the military situation. Graham, who held the Victoria Cross for feats of outstanding bravery at the second battle of the Redan, where he and Charlie Gordon had slithered about together in trenches ankle deep with blood, simply assumed his friend knew what he was doing. He was among the last Britons to see Gordon alive, watching his tiny camel train dwindle into the empty horizon, passing with an eerie silence across stony ravines blackened by the sun. Though he stood out in the open for an hour or more, Gordon did not once look back.

On the same day as Val Baker's disaster at El Teb Gordon rejoined the Nile at Abu Hamed, having crossed the pitiless desert the Arabs call the Belly of Stones. Three days later he rode into Berber. The inhabitants there recognised him and it seemed to them he had somehow appeared in their midst by a miracle. A Council of Notables was summoned and in all apprehension asked the white pasha to confirm that the government intended to stay and fight. Anyone other than Gordon would have lied. In his own mind, he was simply being realistic by telling them the truth. The Franks were going to evacuate the country.

The consequences of this admission were enormous. Like the sheikhs of the eastern seaboard at the other end of his escape route, the Notables of Berber were being given an invitation to abandon their previous loyalties – ordinary common sense dictated they changed sides at once. Gordon was no Arabist and it was in his nature to utter and not to listen. He revealed his plan to soften the blow: he would meet the Mahdi alone under a tree somewhere and thrash the matter out. This was received in polite silence. The normal rules of desert courtesy were strained to the limit at the idea.

The Sudan had changed, but Gordon had not. At Abu Hamed he sent a letter to his sister which included this sentence: 'I hope D.V. to get all settled in a few weeks.' Such optimism took a profound knock at Berber. Though he felt he had done the honourable thing by telling the truth he had in fact made a fatal error of judgement. Next day, erect and unbending, with only the cloak of righteousness to protect him, he boarded the decrepit Nile steamer *Tewfikieh* and set off upstream to Khartoum. There was irony in this: the vessel was that same symbol of power in which the governor of Khartoum had been wont to make his little river trips, the saloon full of harem ladies and jugs of iced sherbet. Now its plates were pockmarked everywhere by bullets and the crew had more eyes on the bank than on the stream up ahead. A day or so later there was a wild rumour circulating Cairo that the steamer had indeed been ambushed and Gordon butchered. There was huge relief when it was announced that he had arrived at his destination unharmed.

The same day that Gordon walked up the steps to the Governor's Palace in Khartoum, the headquarters of a relief column under General Graham arrived by sea at Suakin. They brought the worst news. Val Baker had been relieved of his command and Graham sent to supersede him with a purely British force. The troops under Val had already been disarmed and were no more than a truculent rabble – the port was being defended by 500 of Hewett's marines. Things had moved on with frightening rapidity – Tokar, the object of the original expedition, had capitulated and the garrison of Sinkat had been massacred, with only five men left standing. Added to the sense of panic was the presence of a half-maddened Austrian running around Suakin and trying to get someone in authority to listen to him.

He was a commercial agent named Levy who had lived in the town for many years and spoke excellent Arabic. Like Gordon, he believed the revolt was more political than religious and took it upon himself to ride out and visit Osman Digna – just as Gordon wanted to do with the Mahdi. It turned out disastrously. Levy was astounded to find an armed camp in the ultimate raptures of

fanaticism. The least of Osman's followers supposed the jihad destined them to over-run both the Sudan and Egypt, before setting
out to Mecca, thence to Constantinople and onwards to every
nation in Europe. Levy was forcibly circumcised and made to adopt
the Muslim faith – in fact he narrowly escaped with his life. After
a fortnight of captivity he managed to escape and crawled and
staggered back through the desert to Suakin. His experience was
a direct contradiction of the Gordon philosophy, that common
sense and rational argument would always prevail over excitable
local circumstances. Levy had seen the truth.

Gerald Graham tried to impress on a shattered Val that the
mood in Cairo was sympathetic towards him – that is, everywhere
but in Baring's office. Some of the British gendarmerie officers
who had already been recalled found themselves placed on half-pay
or diminished in rank. Sartorius, Val's second-in-command, whom
the khedive had made a pasha in his own right, was so badly treated
by Cairo that he cut his losses, resigned his commission from the
sultan and was preparing to rejoin his regiment in India. Without
any consultation with their commander the rank and file gendarmerie was being hastily reorganised by civilians – civilians! – sitting
in airy offices, scratching out all Val's work with their busy pens.

The Egyptian rabble ranging round Suakin and getting in everybody's way wanted to go home. When they first got back from
Trinkitat, Val had only kept them from mutiny by mustering the
Nubian battalions and threatening to fire into their ranks. Now
they were packed off by the first available transport. Suakin swiftly
became a town with more British in it than Arabs. Graham's punitive expedition comprised the Black Watch, the Gordon Highland-
ers and the 6oth Rifles. A battalion of the York and Lancaster
Regiment was summoned from Aden. When they were all
assembled, the entire force moved back down to Trinkitat.

It happened that Val's old command, the 10th Hussars, was on
its way home to England and was diverted to join Graham. If it
was ever possible to assemble a task force of crack troops in the
nineteenth century, then this was it. With it, Graham could have
recovered the whole country. His orders were simply to demon-

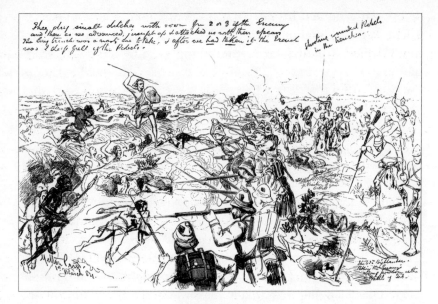

The uncorrected sketch by Melton Prior that led to questions in the House. The caption to the left reads: 'Shooting wounded Rebels in the trenches'.

strate sufficient force. He managed to preserve Val his last shred of dignity, appointing him chief intelligence officer. Burnaby was given a similar role. Once again the beach was piled high with equipment and an advance party was sent to occupy Baker Fort on the far side of the marshes. When the wind was in a certain quarter there was a sickeningly sweet stench coming from the sands over the horizon.

The second battle of El Teb took place on the last day of February, 1884. Baker's honour was avenged in a textbook action that claimed 825 followers of the Mahdi. Only thirty-five were killed on the British side. Among the 155 wounded that day were Baker himself and Fred Burnaby. The giant Life Guard went into action with a double-barrelled shotgun loaned to him by a naval officer and after a good deal of heroics was hit in the arm, the bullet skimming the bone and exiting without breaking anything. Val was struck by a three-inch shell fragment that entered his neck and lodged in the roof of his mouth immediately below the eye. He wrapped his face in a towel and continued fighting.

The British battalions were astonished at the courage of their enemy, which Kipling later memorialised in some famous lines:

We've fought with many men across the seas,
An' some of 'em was brave an' some was not:
The Paythan an' the Zulu an' Burmese;
But the Fuzzy was the finest o' the lot . . .
So here's *to* you, Fuzzy-Wuzzy, at your 'ome in the Soudan;
You're a pore benighted 'eathen but a first-class fightin' man.

There were two tiny tinklings from the Baker past. The final Hadendowa stand had taken place in a ruined sugar factory; and Val's wound had been inflicted not by the Mahdiyya but by renegade Turks from the Tokar garrison. When he deemed honour had been satisfied, Graham called off the carnage and the troops trudged back singing to Trinkitat, passing on their way the rotting corpses of Val's Egyptians, a swathe of horror three miles long and a hundred yards wide, the bodies as plentiful as in a crowded thoroughfare, say from Oxford Circus right through the West End to Notting Hill Gate.

The *Illustrated London News* man out there was the war correspondent and special artist Melton Prior. Prior sketched a moment before the battle when Val Baker boarded the troopship *Jumnah* to be received by Colonel Woods and the men of the 10th Hussars, who gave him 'ten or twelve rousing cheers'. This was exactly the sort of sentiment the Duke of Cambridge could understand – it was the essence of the old army, the one enshrined in the Horse Guards of beloved memory. Ten days after the battle he spoke to the queen's secretary, General Ponsonby, suggesting that in view of his valour and the warmth of Graham's dispatches, Colonel Valentine Baker might now be restored to the army on the retired list. The fellow was after all shockingly wounded and would hardly fight another day, if he lived at all. The queen refused. A further representation from General Stephenson made a fortnight later was also turned down.

Punch published an astonishing piece of doggerel about a

certain Trooper Hayes of the 10th who, seeing a comrade had fallen, dismounted and pummelled his way to the rescue with his bare fists, for which daring action he was awarded the Distinguished Service Medal. In the poem, Graham parades the regiment and asks the hero if he has anything to say. He has.

> 'I'll ask one single favour from my Queen and my native land
> There sits by your side on the Staff, sir, a man we are proud to own.
> He was struck down first in the battle, but never was heard to groan,
> If I've done aught to deserve it' – then the General smiled 'of course'
> 'Give back to the Tenth their Colonel, the man on the old white horse.'

This did nothing to soften the queen's heart either. Another sketch sent home by Melton Prior had unexpectedly removed some of the honour from the second battle of El Teb. It was customary for special artists to have their battlefield sketches worked up into the highly romanticised steel engravings that made the *Illustrated London News* so famous. Prior habitually left pencilled notes on his roughs to aid the engravers to add in stock figures and background details. On 22 March 1884 his paper published just such a draft, the better to capture the scoop. The sketch included the words: 'Shooting wounded rebels in the trenches.' Copies of that edition were brandished on the floor of the House: Britain wanted heroes, not killers. Everyone in the army knew that Graham had come ashore with naval detachments of Gatling gunners that he employed a week or so after El Teb at the follow-up action at Tamanieb. It was then that the Hadendowa had caused such incredulity among the British tommies by charging the guns with nothing in their hands but a leaf-shaped spear.

TWELVE

—⊃o⊂—

Val retraced his steps with a heavy heart. He was carried by
ship to Suez and thence by train to Cairo. He survived his
wound but the shame of having failed in his mission with such
abject consequences was a far more painful blow. It was inevitable
that Cairo society, even its most sympathetic elements, should look
at him askance. He was utterly and completely broken as a commander; there could be no stonier circumstance than the one
he found himself in now. His soldiering days were over. By the
gentlemanly code he had adopted when he joined the army he
could never, with honour, go home to live in England and it seemed
there was nothing for him any longer in the service of the sultan.
Fate had washed him on to a cruel beach.

He left behind him an impasse at Suakin. Militarily, Gerald
Graham could have forced his way inland to Berber, occupied the
all-important wells along the Berber–Suakin road and restored the
telegraph link to the coast. The distance involved was not much
greater than that from London to York. He made repeated requests
to be allowed to push on. Yet within a few more weeks the force
which had been so efficiently and swiftly assembled was dispersed,
without having brought Osman Digna's warriors to complete submission. Graham, who was a giant of a man with an unsurpassed
record of personal bravery, knew very well where the problem lay.
For five years, until pulled out by Wolseley for the Egyptian campaign in 1882, he had sat behind a desk in the War Office. He

knew that Cairo and common sense was for him. The problem lay
in London.

In the old days of Empire a local commander did what he
deemed fit, knowing that praise or criticism was months away by
sea and that what political advice he was offered would be hopelessly out of date by the time it arrived. That was how Victoria had
been given Sind. The telegraph changed all that. Though only a
handful of men in the War Office could have any sensible idea of
where Graham was, or what he could see when he looked out of
his tent, he was controlled by London as easily as if he had been
reporting from Salisbury Plain. The graves of the British fallen
soon enough merged with the sand from which they were scooped,
the maps flapping on the staff officers' tables blew away into the
desert or were stuffed in wallets to be forgotten. If for the common
soldier the whole experience was anyway not much more than dust
and flies, there was nothing new in that either. What made the
situation so novel was the speed with which a political response
could come down the wires and over-ride the commander on the
ground.

While Graham paced up and down, banging the sand from his
breeches with a swagger stick and imploring London to let him at
least secure the road to Berber, the Cabinet dithered. At the War
Office, where he might have expected more support, he was just
a pin on the map. Graham had his own way of gauging the mood
in London. Although another four Victoria Crosses were struck for
the two battles he had fought, the total decorations and rewards
list was niggardly. He had just fought a campaign the government
preferred to forget.

Gordon was – or should have been – as much the slave of the
telegraph key. He had two advantages, both of which he was swift
to exploit. In the first place, whereas his friend Graham was a
distinguished and fearless soldier, Gordon had been placed where
he was something even greater, a demiurge with exceptional and
apparently unlimited powers. Secondly, he was always very careful
to appear to speak – with elaborate courtesy – only to Cairo. He
began playing Baring like a fish. Without consulting anyone he

abolished the tax system. To the amazement of those within Khartoum, he carried out the festering boxes of existing tax records, along with a pile of rhino whips and other instruments of torture which had helped exact the payments – and burned them in the public square. He emptied the jails and forced the authorities to open the city gates, so permitting freedom of trade.

Everyone who had a right to be evacuated wanted to know when they would be allowed to leave. It was taken for granted in the miserable and unhappy Egyptian barracks that they would be the last out. Gordon had different ideas. He retained the Nubian troops but, against all local advice, evacuated the Egyptian contingent along with the sick and some women and children. To call this sending them home was something of an euphemism: they left for a very uncertain and dangerous journey with nothing but forty-five days' worth of biscuit rations. Gordon laconically ordered Korosko to send up camels for them, if Baring thought that a good idea.

This ironic air of deference became something of a theme within the stream of cables he sent, sometimes as many as a dozen a day. There was a particular problem about his remit that nobody seemed to have considered very much. Once the military garrisons had been evacuated, there would need to be some form of civil authority to replace them. Gordon did not intend to stay in Khartoum for ever but neither did he interpret his orders as instigating a general *sauve qui peut*. Colonel Stewart, who was still in the city and who placed himself at Gordon's disposal, was baffled. His chief was playing a dangerous game of some kind. The realisation dawned on him only gradually: despite evacuating the majority of the Khartoum garrison, Gordon thought the Sudan as a whole would weather the storm.

In conversation he consistently misjudged the power of the Mahdi. In his view, here was another local rabble-rouser who had managed to get hold of the wrong end of the stick. He was no more threatening than, say, Suleiman, the governor of Darfur in the days when Gordon had been the governor-general. It was hard for Stewart to contest this opinion, for while he was as much of an expert on Mahdism as anyone alive, Gordon had ridden right through the Sudan, to places Stewart himself had not been and no man in his senses would contemplate visiting now. Gordon's was the voice and conscience of the white man among every tribe. The fact that Khartoum was frightened out of its skin by the Mahdi only encouraged Gordon's habitual loftiness – for example, he gave it as his airy opinion that a mere two squadrons of cavalry could secure the Berber–Suakin road.

The question of who would follow him swiftly became the dominant theme of the exchange of cables with Cairo. It was clear to everybody who lived in Khartoum that the Englishman had been sent on a fool's errand. After the garrisons and those foreign nationals who wished to leave had been sent downriver, there would still remain the consular staff and the export-import agents on whom legitimate trade depended. It was also clear – though nobody had thought it through completely – that while Britain might want nothing more to do with the Sudan, to make the Mahdi a free gift of an entire country was not just to threaten Egypt but to send a message to every British possession with a Muslim majority.

Gordon agreed. He considered he could withdraw the military garrisons without bloodshed and so depart in honour. To do so would be the greatest demonstration of moral superiority possible. The question was, who would he leave in his place? The answer stunned Cairo. The man he nominated was his sworn personal enemy, an Arab whose name was anathema to liberal and radical opinion all over Europe. He wanted Zobeir, the most notorious slaver of them all.

It was Zobeir who had incited his son Suleiman to rebellion in Darfur, for which he was sentenced to death in 1879. He was still stooging around unhung in Cairo five years later and had even been given a khedive's commission to raise 6000 troops to accompany Val to Suakin. Gordon himself squashed that idea while he was still on the way out by boat from Marseilles. Fresh to the fight and scribbling directives as fast as his mind could conceive them in the steamer's saloon, he demanded as a precondition of his service that the slaver be re-arrested and removed to Cyprus. However, when Gordon was intercepted en route and fetched to Cairo by Baring, he met Zobeir quite by accident in the street. He could have accepted the slaver's vivid curses and passed on. Instead, he insisted upon a formal confrontation. The place they chose was Baring's house.

At the meeting Zobeir refused to shake hands and started out on a long list of injustices perpetrated by Gordon when he was governor-general, citing in his own case missing papers and false affidavits. In the middle of this tirade Gordon astonished Baring by taking him to one side and whispering that he had a 'mystical feeling' about the man. He reminded the consul-general that once before he had had this inner conviction. Sam Baker had denounced Abu Saud as a traitor and Gordon had taken *him* back to the Sudan. Why not Zobeir now? Baring was thunderstruck. After taking hurried advice, all of it violently opposed to the idea, he refused.

It did not do to cross Gordon's will. Now safely out of reach, he insisted on his choice. Zobeir, whom he had cheerfully characterised as 'the greatest slave trader that ever existed', was the only figure with enough clout among the tribes to have a chance of stabilising the country. It was in reality a sublime piece of petulance, for it led to this formulation: to thwart the Mahdi, Britain must restore the slave trade. If she had no further interest in the Sudan, then let it all revert to what it had been for some centuries and let the Anti-Slavery Society and the International Convention go hang. Very reluctantly, Baring cabled the suggestion to London. It left the Cabinet aghast.

Travis Crosby has written one of the most interesting recent books on Gladstone (*The Two Mr Gladstones*, 1997) in which he draws attention to the politician's lifelong habit of retreating from difficult or dangerous decisions on a plea of bad health. In 1884 Gladstone was beginning his seventy-fifth year and was genuinely out of sorts; it is all the same astonishing the number of cabinet meetings to do with the Sudan that he seemed to miss. Left to thrash out the Zobeir question without their chief, there grew in the mind of the Cabinet the alarming idea that Gordon was spinning out of control.

Sir Charles Dilke was the first to suggest that he was actually mad. They were, he suggested to his colleagues, dealing 'with a wild man under the influence of Central Africa, which acts upon the sanest man like strong drink'. The distraught ministers could agree about only one thing: popular opinion in Britain would not possibly stomach the appointment of Zobeir. Even to let his name be linked with Gordon's was to court political disaster. On 1 March 1884 Gordon cabled Baring from Khartoum with his reaction, couched in his usual faintly mocking style.

> I maintain firmly policy of eventual evacuation but I tell you plainly it is impossible to get Cairo employees out of Khartoum unless the Government helps in the way I have told you. You refuse Zebehr, and are quite right (maybe) to do so, but it is the only chance. It is scarcely worthwhile saying more on the subject. I will do my best to carry out my instructions, but I feel a conviction I shall be caught in Khartoum.

Gordon was exploiting an almost complete failure of under-standing. There was vanity in his stance, even arrogance. He was the man on the ground, the expert, while his masters were mere featherbedded politicians and penpushers. It came down to a question of who had the power and how it was to be used. Having got their man to the Sudan, neither London nor Cairo had the faintest idea what to do with him. It was a policy vacuum that would have been just as fatal if Sam Baker had gone in his place; or anyone else. But by now the Cabinet was wrestling with a new factor. Gordon had the queen and her entire country hanging on his every movement – for the first time in empire history, one man and his dilemma was the focus of all attention. Only if Gladstone had fallen down a well on his Cheshire estate could there have been a better running news story. In the race against time, would the great man escape with his life?

It is hard to avoid the feeling that Gordon actually relished the possibility of being trapped. Stuart Rendel, a crony of Gladstone's, once said that long association with savages in their own lands rendered Gordon, in a sublime phrase, 'useless for civilized work'. Here was the supreme irony. Civilisation had now sent him to do a job in the name of Gladstone himself. Baring had been fetched from India to be governor-general in Cairo because he was a gifted administrator and a safe pair of hands. With every day that passed, Gordon became more and more the embodiment of a spirit, a totem. He was like the Union Jack itself.

For Gordon, as for Wilfrid Scawen Blunt, there began to be, creeping round that word civilisation and its highflown cousins, derisive inverted commas. The phlegmatic Colonel Stewart considered it sufficient to do as he was told and leave it at that. There were others in Khartoum, like the Austrian consul Hansal, who held the view that they were the last bastions of a European order that must be defended. For Hansal, civilisation was a desperately practical question. Somewhere out there in Kordofan he had Austrian missionaries captured by the Mahdi whose lives hung on his efforts. It was surely no more difficult to understand than that. Hansal could reflect in all bitterness that a couple of dozen British missionaries led about in chains might have made the situation very different.

In the Governor's Palace, Stewart watched Gordon bound about the secretariat with his springy step, fixing, cajoling, always making a virtue of contrariness. He knew his chief had a reputation for quixotic behaviour but here it was reaching new heights. To Stewart's disgust, whenever Gordon ventured out into the streets, tribal women held up their babies to be touched as he passed, or knelt in the dust to kiss the hem of his jacket. Gordon made no effort to stop this sort of thing. He spoke Arabic with hardly any fluency and could not see that very often his interpreters were giving back answers they thought he might like to hear, rather than the truth. In the end none of it mattered. This was at long last Gordon versus the world. The man civilisation had in Khartoum as its supreme representative was not the soldier, but the agitated saint.

A few days after the telegraph of 1 March Gordon discussed with Colonel Stewart whether it would be appropriate to give an interview to the press, in the shape of Frank Power. The three men were the only Britons left in the city. True to type, Stewart thought that to speak to the press was out of the question, for it would break one of the strongest conventions in the army, namely that an officer was responsible only to his superior, to whom he owed all his loyalty. In the end that meant the queen. No soldier should feel the need to explain himself if he was doing his duty, least of all in the editorial pages of *The Times*. Gordon of course gave Power the interview. He cabled Baring: 'Times correspondent interviewed me tonight. I gave him my opinion. I asked Moberly Bell to show you telegram. If you disapprove of publication, then make Stewart my successor and ask Moberly Bell to cancel telegram.'

Baring ground his teeth and said nothing. The interview appeared in full in *The Times* for Monday 10 March. In it, Gordon again pressed for Zobeir to be sent up as the new governor-general. A small force should be dispatched to open the Berber–Suakin road. Its only other purpose was to give moral support to his evacuation plans. These were entirely predicated on a peaceful withdrawal. If this was baffling to those who had read of the destruction of the Baker force, at the end of his interview Gordon spelt it all out one last time. Just as the anguished Stewart had warned, he was talking not to his superiors but to the nation at large.

> I am dead against the sending of any British expedition to reconquer the Sudan. It is unnecessary. I would not have a single life lost. It is my firm conviction that none would be lost by the plan I propose and our honour would be saved. I like the people who are in rebellion as well as those who are not, and I thank God that, so far as I am concerned, no man has gone before his Maker prematurely through me.

Two days later the sand, which at the Nile's edge is as fine as talcum powder, was kicked up by 4000 mounted Arabs at a place called Halfaya, nine miles north of Khartoum. Someone shinned up a pole and cut the telegraph wire to Berber and then the force occupied both banks of the river and set up their tents, a huge arc of them, before which fires were lit and sheep and goats slaughtered. All roads to freedom were blocked. Gordon had spoken; and now silence descended on him.

In the state room of the Governor's Palace he had ordered an inscription in Arabic to be set above his chair. It read GOD RULES THE HEARTS OF MEN. A week after the occupation of Halfaya the first rebel bullet shattered a window and thudded into the plaster. Then came the long-expected news: the Mahdi himself, with all his adherents, was coming north to twitch this gadfly from the back of the jihad. Some 200,000 of the *ansar* – the faithful – together with their wives, families and slaves, swarmed down the White Nile in a huge rolling cloud of dust. Father Orhwalder, one of Hansal's Austrian missionaries captured by the Mahdi in 1882, described how the dust concealed everything but the tallest pennants and the army announced itself under its shadow by a massive eerie buzzing. Even to tribesmen willing to join in, it was a terrifying spectacle. The whole country seemed to be on the move. This was a journey that went far beyond questions of loot or any other short-term advantage. It was a march on the infidel. It was the beginning of the end and the fulfilment of prophecy. Those who left El Obeid and set out for Khartoum destroyed their property and burnt their houses behind them.

Sam Baker was in Cairo, helping his brother convalesce from his wound. He wrote Gordon several letters in the days before Khartoum was surrounded. He had in return a letter asking him to find some means of help, the substance of which Gordon copied to Baring. Dated 8 April, and smuggled out of Khartoum, it makes remarkable reading.

> I have telegraphed to Baker to make an appeal to British and American millionaires to give me £300,000 to engage 3000 Turkish troops from Sultan and send them here. This would settle the Sudan and Mahdi forever: for my part, I think you would agree with me. I do not see the force of being caught here to walk about the streets for years as a dervish, with sandalled feet; not that, D.V., I will ever be taken alive. It would be the climax of meanness, after I had borrowed money from the people here, had called on them to sell their grain at a low price, etc, to go and abandon them without making any effort to relieve them, whether those efforts are diplomatically correct

or not; and I feel sure, whatever you may think diplomatically, I have your support – and that of any man professing himself a gentleman – in private.

Baring's book, *Modern Egypt*, which he published in 1907 as Lord Cromer, came twenty-two years after the débâcle of Gordon's death at a time when the legend was so firmly established he had to tread very carefully. The proposition contained in this particular message must have sent him into paroxysms of anger. Baring might have been an imperious consul-general, even something of a cold fish; certainly a man as temperamentally different from Gordon as it was possible to imagine, but he was all the same a servant of the Gladstone government, as was Gordon himself. A man employed by government did not go about raising a private army by subscription. Gordon *was* out of control. On 18 April Baring received this follow-up.

> As far I can understand, the situation is this: you state your intention of not sending any relief force up here or to Berber and you refuse me Zebehr. I consider myself free to act according to circumstances. I shall hold on here as long as I can, and, if I can suppress the rebellion, I shall do so. If I cannot, I shall retire to the Equator and leave you the indelible disgrace of abandoning the garrisons of Sennar, Kassala, Berber and Dongola, with the certainty that you will eventually be forced to smash up the Mahdi under great difficulties if you would retain peace in Egypt.

Gordon had mentioned in private letters that once he got to the upper headwaters of the Nile he intended to resign the queen's commission and declare the country to the west a province of the Belgian Congo. Perhaps this was too much for even Sam Baker to stomach. The appeal to patriotic millionaires never came to anything and another fund that was set up in London also fizzled out. Nor was there success with the even more hare-brained scheme of raising a volunteer force of big-game hunters to sail down the Red Sea and turn their elephant guns on the problem.

Sam Baker – though his contempt for Gladstone's inactivity was enormous – had other things on his mind. The wound Val received at El Teb was serious but not life-threatening and the fallen commander was recovering slowly on his houseboat. It hardly mattered any longer what London thought of him – he knew he had been thrown away by his country and faced nothing but ignominious exile in some foreign hotel, or a hillside villa which no one would ever visit. All the same, the government was obliged to administer him the *coup de grâce*. As early as 12 February Lord Derby had hurried to put the official point of view:

> We may have known – we did know – that the composition of General Baker's force was not very good, but I venture to affirm that nobody supposed that a body of men calling itself a regular army would run away, almost without a shot fired, from half its own number, or less than half, of savages under no discipline whatsoever. It is a thing, I should imagine, new in war. It is a misfortune, but it is a misfortune for which we, sitting in London, can hardly hold ourselves responsible.

That is, if they truly believed the force that was routed was equivalent to 'a regular army'. Lord Derby knew very well that it was not – the story was being spun. In a speech to an uncomfortable House of Commons, Gladstone was at his most glacial. 'Baker Pasha was under no military necessity to undertake this expedition. He was not enlisted for that purpose, and was under no honourable or military obligation to undertake it, unless he thought it hopeful.'

Taken together, the two statements suggested error of judgement and failure of command. When Val was finally well enough to travel, he made a last journey back to England. In July the prince received the 10th Hussars in review. With a last poignant expression of the old relationship, Val rode a borrowed white charger, sad emblem of those better times when he had accompanied the colonel-in-chief on to the parade ground as colonel of the regiment. Now he was a mere spectator and took no part in the ceremonials of the day. He had with him at his side Fred Burnaby, whose standing with the prince was similarly strained.

Burnaby had come home in March to find himself enormously popular in the press but the subject of stiff official censure. He

Burnaby at the second battle of El Teb wielding a borrowed shotgun,
to the dismay of men like Wilfred Scawen Blunt, who considered it the
greatest savagery.

had after all been expressly forbidden to go to Suakin by the Duke of Cambridge, and his death-dealing shotgun, so enthusiastically reported by Melton Prior, was also much reprehended, as being contrary to the Geneva Convention. Wilfrid Blunt could hardly bring himself to shake the hero's hand when they met by chance in the Carlton Club. In a breezy article in the *World* H. M. Broadley accidentally did Val further harm while attempting to boost Burnaby's role at El Teb:

> Being on the spot when every good man was wanted, he was posted *pro forma* to the Intelligence Department – on such occasions a machine for giving a nominal *locus standi* to loafers who want a turn of fighting. I don't believe he ever got a scrap of intelligence, but perhaps it will be admitted that he made himself reasonably useful in other ways.

Val had been chief intelligence officer to the expedition. Both men must have reflected, as they sat on the sidelines of the 10th Hussars review, how much they were now compromised figures in Marlborough House circles. Burnaby had infuriated the prince in an affair concerning one of the royal cronies, General Owen Williams. It was alleged that Burnaby had sent an unsigned piece of gossip to the papers indicating that Williams had been turned down for the post of brigadier of the Household Cavalry. Williams wrote to the adjutant-general and when he heard that, Burnaby at once threatened to sue for libel. In the opinion of *The Times*, if the action had come to court it would have threatened the very existence of the Blues, of which the Prince of Wales was colonel-in-chief.

The clown in Burnaby, the over-eager jester, had grown stout and middle-aged. He shared with Val the experience of being cut dead in the clubs by fellow officers from time to time. Like Sam Baker, they were trading on times past and simplicities that had fallen out of fashion. Wolseley, who adjudicated in the Williams affair and who was himself from a modest background, was already mulling Burnaby's epitaph. 'His high military spirit, energy, zeal, & remarkable personal courage were not sufficient in the eyes of those Royal tailors [the Prince of Wales and the Duke of

Cambridge] to cover up the fact that socially Burnaby was distasteful to them and to their set.'

From the end of April 1884 Baring was also in London attending an International Conference on Egyptian Finance. He was away until June and the whole problem of what Gordon was doing and how to restore communications with him was left to a man who had only just arrived from a consular post in Athens. Mr Egerton had none of Baring's capacity for taking pains and had never met Gordon. The loss of the telegraph also meant that Frank Power was finding it harder and harder to get news out for *The Times.* As a consequence interest in the Sudan had begun to flag a little. There was a telling club anecdote that made men like Sam Baker purse their lips. Burnaby had put forward the idea of a volunteer force of 2000 men driving another 3000 camels to make a lightning dash to Khartoum along the Suakin–Berber road to rescue Gordon. Redvers Buller, a devoted crony of Wolseley's as well as a veteran of the second battle of El Teb, was quite blunt. 'The man is not worth the camels,' he drawled.

However, by the end of May the mood had changed. A clergyman proposed saying prayers for 'General Gordon in imminent peril at Khartoum' in every church in the land; anguished and agitated public meetings were held in London and the queen was known to be uneasy. The slow swell of indignation that finally produced the relief expedition began to mount. Gladstone, who had been cheered when the news of Tel el Kebir reached London in 1882, was hissed in public (in the unlikely setting of the Earls Court Exhibition Hall).

On 27 June the news was published in London that Berber had fallen and the garrison and most of the inhabitants massacred. It was information already a month old. There was only one conclusion to be drawn from any further government prevarication and delay – they actually intended to abandon Gordon to his fate. Immediately the clamour for his rescue became a national crusade. At the War Office Lord Hartington, who had sent him there in the first place, threatened to resign unless something was done.

Gladstone had always been in a minority among his own Cabinet about the need to extricate Gordon. Lord Granville's first biographer, Lord Fitzmaurice, who was his under-secretary at the Foreign Office during this period, suggests of what this minority view consisted.

> Others [he wrote], took the view that General Gordon had so entirely departed from his original orders and instructions that the Government were thereby relieved of responsibility. General Gordon, according to this view, had started in all gallantry on a mission to extricate the garrisons. He had chosen to remain to carry out a policy of his own, and British blood and treasure were not to be poured out like water to rescue a soldier, however distinguished, from the consequences of deliberate disobedience to the orders he had received.

This was not good enough for Hartington, whose resignation would have brought down the government. On 5 August Gladstone gave way. That night he moved in the House of Commons 'That a sum not exceeding £300,000 be granted to Her Majesty beyond the ordinary grants of Parliament of 1884–5, to enable Her Majesty to undertake operations for the relief of General Gordon, should they become necessary, and to make certain preparations in respect thereof.'

Even while he was speaking, the lights were burning in the War Office and Wolseley and his planners were working out how to spend the parliamentary grant they had been given for the rescue of just one man.

It is only now that the two Baker brothers begin to drift from the story, their voices lost in the hubbub of what soon became a national hysteria. Val was back in Cairo. He had been offered and accepted command of the new Egyptian gendarmerie, a greatly emasculated version of the force he had taken to Suakin. When the relief expedition was being set up, the Prince of Wales attempted to join it. Wolseley regretted he could not accommodate him but as a sop he included on his staff one of the prince's cronies, Sir Charles Beresford, and – a delicate touch – Colonel Valentine Baker. This last name was struck out by Wolseley's political masters in the War

Office. It was the final snub, but for Val there was even worse in store.

At the beginning of 1885 his eldest daughter Hermione, the one that Kitchener was said to love so dearly, grew very sick: she died in Cairo. Her mother followed only a month later. Affliction was being heaped on Val in biblical measure. As the preparations for the Queen's Jubilee celebrations went slowly ahead at Windsor, her private secretary General Ponsonby made one last effort on Val's behalf, motivated as much out of compassion as a sense of justice. Right at the end, Victoria relented. She gave her approval to have Colonel Baker restored to the Army List as a retired officer, provided it was done in a quiet and unobtrusive way. She stipulated it should never be seen as an act of clemency.

Val died of a heart attack on board a steamer travelling along the Sweet Water Canal in November 1887. His surviving daughter Sybil and two of Sam's children were with him when it happened; there was nothing to be done and it was all over in a few minutes. He was sixty years old. *The Dictionary of National Biography* was kind to him and gave as his place of death Tel el Kebir, so connecting him to a great British victory. When the news was received in London, the Duke of Cambridge at once cabled Cairo with orders for a funeral with full military honours. Seven serving generals acted as Val's pall-bearers, even though the queen's command to have him restored to the army had not yet been promulgated. At the very last, when it was too late, the man who had destroyed himself by refusing to speak in his own defence was vindicated by his kind. A new prime minister, Lord Salisbury, wrote to Baring:

> It is a satisfaction to me to be able to place on record my entire concurrence in the opinions you express . . . as to the importance and difficulties of the task that was entrusted to Baker Pasha, the high qualities he showed in surmounting those difficulties, and the devotion and fidelity with which the duties of his office were performed.

Sam Baker survived his brother by another six years. In many ways his views about the fate of the Sudan simply brought home a sense of his own redundancy. Nobody hated Gladstone with a greater passion, but Sam had chosen to live his life outside politics and he paid the price. His reputation dwindled, except among big-game hunters and a few Devon cronies. In his last years he dragged Florence off for several luxuriously fitted-out tiger-hunting expeditions to India, but in the end Devon claimed him with nothing but a rabbit gun in his hand. Out walking the ploughed fields round Sandford Orleigh the week after Christmas 1893, he came home complaining of an attack of gout. He died in his bed of a heart attack the next morning. While the house was still in mourning, a fifty-gallon butt of claret was delivered from Sam's wine merchants in London. Florence gave it to the butler and told him to entertain his friends.

It is an idle question, but if Sir Samuel Baker had gone in Gordon's place to Khartoum things might have been very different. Likewise, if Colonel Valentine Baker had gone to Suakin with wholly British troops, an immediate and decisive defeat of Osman Digna might have swung the balance of opportunity. Within the family, this was like saying that if the cards had fallen only slightly differently, there would have been glory. But glory is not a quantity, like money or rolling acres. About this at least Gordon was right. 'Better a ball in the brain than to flicker out unheeded,' he wrote in his journal. Glory was a form of disease, an aberration. It took a vainer man than either of the Baker brothers to say so.

In the siege of El Obeid, when the comet had appeared in the sky presaging either doom or victory for the Madhi, the garrison held out to the very last by boiling leather, digging up the bones of the dead and picking through camel droppings to extract an undigested morsel or so of food. When it was all over and the city had fallen, the children and women slaves of the rich were tied to posts and beaten with the kourbash until their bowels dropped out, in an attempt to discover where the wealth had been buried. To be a victim of the Mahdi was to sink to an animal level such that to be saved to slavery was a step up in existence. The fanatical element in Mahdism made war – made life itself – a shapeless, seemingly pointless bag of horrors.

This was the fate that now, in 1884, awaited Khartoum. The huge encampments on every side were a brawling mass of people, filthy with flies, their senses deadened by brass drums that beat incessantly, the noise rising above the huge surflike roar of hundreds of thousands of voices, human and animal. One way or another, the faithful believed they were on their way to Paradise, each warrior that fell in battle ushered in by forty lovely houris.

Behind the battlements of Khartoum and manning the redoubts Gordon threw up to the south of the city were soldiers and citizens whose allegiance had been decided for them. Unwillingly or not, they stood for the same sort of civilisation that had founded islands like Jamaica and spread inexorably across half the globe. They were the grubby and exhausted students of a moral superiority that flew in the face of facts and was forced on them by processes they could not completely understand. In their pockets was paper money issued by Gordon, to be redeemed in full for cash when proper government was restored. They might be starving but they were on the side of right – up on the roof of the Governor's Palace was a tripod telescope trained always to the north, to the bend in the river round which salvation would come. If the Mahdi had his mysteries, then so did Gordon Pasha. There was something so intrinsically absurd in the idea that a few thousand men could withstand what amounted to an entire country in arms, that only magic could save them. It was a matter of complete indifference to the defenders that Gordon was a better man than the Mahdi, or represented a better cause: he had only to be the more powerful conjuror.

In September, after refusing an invitation to surrender, Gordon decided to send Stewart and Power downriver along with a party of foreign nationals – Greeks and Syrians – in three steamers. One of these was the *Abbas*, brought out in sections by Gordon in 1877 and now peppered with a thousand bullet holes. The purpose of the journey was to get to Dongola and tell the world what would befall if Khartoum was taken. Gordon prepared the expedition with some of his old attention to detail. The little paddle-steamer was fitted out with wooden buffers below the waterline, the better to shoot the cataracts; and Stewart was firmly instructed to stay on board, come what may. With him went Gordon's journals and the now useless telegraph cipher keys.

In addition to the steamers, Gordon provided a small flotilla of nuggars, the same sailing boats that Sam had donated to Speke over thirty years ago. He repeated his stern warning: Stewart was to stay on the water and if the *Abbas* foundered for any reason, he was to continue by sail. He was not to land at any point, however safe it might appear. Stewart must press on until he found the support Gordon felt sure was on its way. Though they did not know it, they had just one friend along the route. Dressed as a bedouin, Herbert Kitchener had penetrated as far as Dongola, sent to gather intelligence for the cumbersome relief expedition finally being mounted. Under his jellaba, hidden from prying eyes, Kitchener wore a locket containing a curl of Hermione Baker's hair.

Stewart made it clear that he had understood his orders and set off, running the gauntlet of rifle fire from wherever Arabs had gathered. They got past Halfaya and then Berber and then, only a hundred miles from Dongola, the little paddle-steamer chose the wrong channel and ran up on to some rocks. The *Abbas* had somehow been separated from the rest of the flotilla and now, unable to extricate itself from the rocks which held it fast, was now just another Nile navigation disaster, of which over the millennia there have been thousands. Just as Gordon had dreaded, the guileless Stewart accepted an invitation to go ashore and accept the help of a sheikh who appeared bearing a white flag. He and Power left for this man's house unarmed. Only a short while after sitting down and accepting the traditional hospitality which the Koran enforces on hosts, the two men were butchered. All the papers on board were sent to the Mahdi, together with Stewart's severed head.

Meanwhile, the relief expedition was coming, but it was a long time coming. Wolseley had taken command over the head of Sir Evelyn Wood and chosen the Nile route in preference to Suakin–Berber. In 1870 he had made a name for himself with the Red River campaign south of Winnipeg, Manitoba. It was a footling affair but Wolseley had skilfully exploited the terrain by moving 1400 men in boats, all of them crewed by voyageurs, specialist French-Canadian watermen. As for one river, so with another. He ordered 800 steel boats from nearly fifty shipyards and had them sent out in nineteen commercial vessels. Thomas Cook was given the contract to move the entire army by tourist boats as far as the second cataract at Wadi Halfa, the steel whalers, as Wolseley liked them to be called, bobbing along in their wake.

His decision to take the Nile route was made in the teeth of strenuous opposition from all his colleagues, on the grounds of both speed and practicality. The official historian of the expedition says tersely that from the moment the decision was made to go by the Nile, Gordon was doomed.

Reclining with a fly whisk in the saloon of a Thomas Cook pleasure cruiser gave Wolseley a completely false sense of being in the right. It was at Wadi Halfa that the problems began. There were 120 miles of broken water to be negotiated in all and they were conquered at the rate of a mile a day. Along with the men, 1,500,000 tins of bully beef, as many ship's biscuits and all other stores and ammunition had to be loaded and unloaded, day after day, week after week. Wolseley was buoyed up by the thought that this was the biggest military expedition of its kind ever mounted. As to the urgency of his mission, it is hard to find in his campaign journal much evidence that he saw speed as a priority. Kitchener was all for pressing on with a small force, but then Kitchener was the young popinjay he had tried to crush in Cyprus. His tone in the journals is unutterably languid.

The English post of the 19th December arrived in the afternoon: it was due here last Sunday evening. It brought us a letter from the Queen written in the nastiest tone. I have written to Her because She desired me do so, and I have endeavoured to make my letters as interesting as I could and was even mean enough to spice them with hits at Mr Gladstone as I knew She hates him. But it is all to no purpose. I have an unhappy knack of freely expressing my opinions upon the one subject I feel justified in speaking on with some authority, namely war and our army as created for war. She, poor good woman, knowing nothing of the subject and taking her news from the Duke of Cambridge who is certainly as ignorant as the Queen is on war & its art and science, won't have my views at any price ... I have done my best and have failed. I even shook hands with John Brown and grinned at him as if I did not know how drunk he was, but all to no purpose, so as the children say 'I won't play any more.'

The queen's nastiness had to do with an anxiety shared by the whole country. Once mounted, however late, it was imperative for the expedition to succeed. Fred Burnaby had managed to get himself on to the rations list although directly ordered not to join the force by the Duke of Cambridge. He found a job as inspecting staff officer, which he quickly found out was a euphemism for bullying the boats over his designated stretch of the river. He wrote to his wife:

> The Nile here is like a small pond in many places and when the wind is not favourable the boats have to be carried over two and half miles across the desert on men's shoulders. Each boat weighs eleven hundredweight and her stores three and a half tons, so this will give you an idea of the labour ... There is a strange mixture of people here – Arab camel-drivers, black Dongolese porters, still blacker Kroomen, Red Indians, Canadian boatmen, Greek interpreters, men from Aden, Egyptian soldiery, Scotch, Irish and English Tommy Atkins – a very babel of tongues and accents.

Wolseley's plan was to assemble his main force at Korti, near where Stewart and Power had been murdered. On 17 January, one of the few officers Wolseley *did* trust unequivocally, Sir Herbert Stewart, led a massive party out towards the wells at Abu Klea. It moved in a square that was menaced and then finally attacked by 15,000 of the faithful, each of them with a prayer tied to his arm furnished by the Mahdi, promising to turn infidel bullets into water. Burnaby was outside the square and was the first to face the charge. He drew his sabre and began laying about him. Dismounted, he continued fighting though it could be seen that his life's blood

An artist's impression of Fred Burnaby's death at Abu Klea, 1885.

was spurting from a spear wound to his jugular. And at last he fell. It was said that men who were themselves fighting for their lives wept as he went down.

After the battle, which was very nearly a disaster on the Hicks scale, a huge beehive-shaped cairn of stones was raised over Burnaby's body. Like the Bakers, he had become a man out of his time. He was in his way a monstrously childish figure, erratic yet good natured, reckless of his own life and trapped by a reputation for tomfoolery. There were no depths to Burnaby, none of the demons that drove other commanders of this ill-fated expedition – no qualms, no fears and not much power of reflection. It was said that the enemy had only got into the square at Abu Klea because he had ordered a unit of cavalry to wheel and let the stragglers in. Too late, he had compromised the whole formation, like opening a gate in a sheepfold.

None of that was remembered and no blame was ever attached to him. Though he was young – he was thirteen at the time of the Crimea, when so many of the senior officers who regretted his death were already bloodied by war; and only forty-three when he died – he was a throwback to an even earlier age. Wellington would have had a use for his massive simplicity and imperturbable courage. An officer of the Rifle Brigade sketched the site of Burnaby's improvised grave, indicating with ant-like forms the unburied enemy dead: 1100 of them were counted, mostly in the vicinity of the square.

Twelve days later the steamer *Bordein* nosed upstream, its plates pocked by bullets, the paddles thrashing up the water. This was the vessel Gordon had used during his tour of duty as governor-general of the Sudan. Sitting in red tunics specially provided for them by Wolseley were a mere twenty soldiers, who by the colour of their uniform were meant to signify the world's most powerful empire. Under a hail of fire from both banks and steering between spouts of water thrown up by shells, the *Bordein*'s hull thrummed with the strike of bullets fired from Remington rifles captured from Hicks. Crouched with their heads between their shoulders, the sweating redcoats waited for what seemed the inevitable *coup de grâce*.

They did not land at the confluence of the two Niles for they could tell at a glance that Khartoum had fallen. Gordon was dead and his head was jammed into the fork of a tree on the right bank of the river, where thousands took turns at pelting it with stones. In a phrase that rang right round the Empire, they were too late.

*   *   *

The queen was at Osborne when she received the news. It was morning and she walked unaccompanied to the cottage occupied by the family of her private secretary. Lady Mary Ponsonby was still at breakfast with her two daughters when Victoria walked in and stood at the doorway, a short stout woman in her sixties whose expression had grown more sour with every year of her reign. Lady Ponsonby scraped back her chair, terrified. The queen stared at her for a few moments and then said, without preamble, 'Khartoum has fallen. Gordon is dead.' A few hundred yards away across lawns glistening with raindrops was the miniature fort Albert and the children had constructed as a surprise birthday present for the queen in 1856. Then, war was glorious and a man's honour could be measured against the pattern of a noble prince. The queen inclined her head to Lady Ponsonby's few semi-coherent remarks and then left, trudging back to the house, where the tall windows reflected an image of herself, a little black-clad old lady barely taller than a child, Queen of England and Empress of India. Though the attempt to relieve Gordon was the story of a monumental débâcle, it was also the apogee of Empire. Those red coats in the *Bordein* were the last ever worn by British troops in battle. From now on the way was down, always down, gently at first but then, well within the memory of those alive today, steeper and steeper until the end.

BOOKS CONSULTED

Books Consulted

Alexander, M. *The True Blue* (St Martin's Press, 1957)

Allen, B. A. *Gordon and the Sudan* (Constable, 1931)

Anderson, D. *Baker Pasha, Misconduct and Mischance* (Michael Russell, 1999)

Arrowsmith-Brown, J. H. *Prutky's Travels in Ethiopia and Other Lands* (Hakluyt Society, 1991)

Ascherson, N. *The King Incorporated* (Allen and Unwin, 1963)

Baker, A. *A Question of Honour* (Leo Cooper, 1996)

Beatty, C. *Ferdinand de Lesseps* (Eyre and Spottiswoode, 1956)

Bird, M. *Samuel Shepheard of Cairo* (Michael Joseph, 1957)

Burn, W. L. *The Age of Equipoise* (Allen and Unwin, 1964)

Burnaby, Fred *A Ride to Khiva* (Century paperback, 1983)

Carver, M. (ed.) *Letters of a Victorian Army Officer: Edward Wellesley, 1840–54* (Army Records Society, Sutton, 1995)

Carver, M. *Colouring the Rainbow, Mauritian Society in the Making* (Alfran Press, 1998)

Carver, M., and Ng, J. *Forging the Rainbow* (Alfran Press, 1997)

Coupland, R. *The British Anti-Slavery Movement* (Thornton Butterworth, 1933)

Cromer, Lord *Modern Egypt* (Macmillan, 1908)

Crosby, T. L. *The Two Mr Gladstones* (Yale, 1997)

Cunningham, A. *Eastern Questions in the 19th Century* (Cass, 1993)

Dangerfield, G. *Victoria's Heir: the Education of a Prince* (Constable, 1941)

de Sales la Terrière *Days That Are Gone* (Hutchinson, 1924)

Dietz, P. *The Last of the Regiments* (Brassey's, 1989)

Elton, Lord *General Gordon* (Collins, 1954)

Ewald, J. J. *Soldiers, Traders and Slaves* (University of Wisconsin, 1990)

Farwell, B. *Queen Victoria's Little Wars* (Allen Lane, 1973)

— *Burton* (Viking, 1988)

Forbes, A. *Memories and Studies of War and Peace* (Cassell, 1895)

Gatrell, S. (ed.) *The Ends of the Earth* (Ashfield Press, 1992)

Godwin, G. *Town Swamps and Social Bridges* (London, 1859)

Goodwin, J. *Lords of the Horizons* (Chatto and Windus, 1998)

Haafner, J. *Travels on Foot Through the Island of Ceylon* (London, 1821)

Hall, R. *Lovers on the Nile* (Collins, 1980)

— *Empires of the Monsoon* (HarperCollins paperback, 1998)

Hamshere, C. *The British in the Caribbean* (Weidenfeld and Nicolson, 1972)

Haythornthwaite, P. J. *The Colonial Wars Source Book* (Arms and Armour, 1997)

Headrick, D. R. *The Tools of Empire* (Oxford University Press, 1951)

Herold, J. C. *Napoleon in Egypt* (Hamish Hamilton, 1964)

Hobsbaum, E. J. *The Age of Empire, 1875–1914* (Weidenfeld and Nicolson, 1986)

Hodgson, P. *The War Illustrators* (Macmillan, 1977)

Homans, M. *Royal Representations* (Chicago, 1998)

Howse, E. *Saints in Politics* (Allen and Unwin, 1953)

Hurwitz, E. F. *Politics and the Public Conscience* (Allen and Unwin, 1973)

Jeal, T. *Livingstone* (Heinemann, 1972)

Johnson, P. *Front Line Artists* (Cassell, 1978)

Jones, Bauman and Johnson (eds.) *Juan Maria Schuver's Travels in North East Africa, 1880–83* (Hakluyt Society, 1996)

Judd, D. *Empire: The British Imperial Experience from 1795 to the Present* (HarperCollins, 1996)

Jullian, P. *Edward and the Edwardians* (Sidgwick and Jackson, 1967)

Kiernan, V. *The Lords of Humankind* (Cressett paperback, 1988)

— *Colonial Empires and Armies, 1815–1900* (Sutton paperback, 1998)

Livingstone, D. *Missionary Travels* (Ward Lock, 1857)

Login, E. Dalhousie *Lady Login's Recollections* (London, 1916)

Longford, E. *A Pilgrimage of Passion* (Weidenfeld and Nicolson, 1979)

Magnus, P. *Kitchener: Portrait of an Imperialist* (John Murray, 1958)

Manning, P. *Slavery and African Life* (Cambridge University Press, 1990)

Middleton, D. *Baker of the Nile* (Falcon Press, 1949)

Milner, A. *England in Egypt* (Arnold, 1892)

Naylor, L. E. *The Irrepressible Victorian* (MacDonald, 1965)

Neillands, R. *The Dervish Wars* (John Murray, 1996)

Nutting, A. *Gordon, Martyr and Misfit* (Constable, 1966)

Oliphant, L. *The Russian Shores of the Black Sea* (Koenemann editions, 1998)

Ollier, E. *Cassell's Illustrated History of the Russo-Turkish War* (London, n.d.)

Orwhalder, J. *Ten Year's Captivity in the Mahdi's Camp* (Sampson Low, n.d.)

Ponsonby, A. *Henry Ponsonby: His Life from His Letters* (Macmillan, 1942)

Playfair, G. *Six Studies in Hypocrisy* (Secker and Warburg, 1969)

Preston, A. (ed.) *In Relief of Gordon: Lord Wolseley's Campaign Journal of the Relief Expedition, 1884–85* (Hutchinson, 1967)

St Aubyn, G. *The Royal Duke* (Constable, 1963)

Skinner, T. *Fifty Years in Ceylon* (W. W. Allen, 1891)

Symonds, R. *Oxford and Empire* (Oxford University Press, 1986)

Taylor, A. *Laurence Oliphant* (Oxford University Press, 1982)

Walters, J. *Aldershot Review* (Jarrolds, 1970)

Waterfield, J. *Layard of Nineveh* (Praeger, 1968)

Weintraub, S. *Victoria* (John Murray, 1987)

Wilson, A. *The Ever Victorious Army* (Greenhill Books, 1991)

Woodham Smith, C. *The Reason Why* (Constable, 1953)

Woolf, L. *Imperialism and Civilization* (Hogarth Press, 1928)

INDEX

Index

263